AN
OLIVE SCHREINER
READER

■ **Carol Barash** graduated from Yale University in 1981 and then took a master's degree in English literature at the University of Virginia. She teaches English and Women's Studies at Princeton University, where she is completing a Ph.D. thesis on 'Augustan Women's Mythmaking: Gender, Language and Authority, 1660–1730'. She is the author of several articles on Olive Schreiner and feminist literary theory.

AN
OLIVE SCHREINER
READER

Writings on Women and South Africa

Edited and introduced by Carol Barash
Afterword by Nadine Gordimer

PANDORA
London and New York

For Winnie Mandela

First published in 1987 by
Pandora Press
Routledge & Kegan Paul Ltd
11 New Fetter Lane, London, EC4P 4EE

Published in the USA by
Routledge & Kegan Paul Inc.
in association with Methuen Inc.
29 West 35th Street, New York, NY 10001

Set in Baskerville, 10 on 12 pt
by Columns of Reading
and printed in Great Britain
by The Guernsey Press Co. Ltd
Guernsey, Channel Islands

Copyright © Carol Barash 1987
Afterword copyright © Nadine Gordimer 1980

Library of Congress Cataloging in Publication Data

Schreiner, Olive, 1855–1920
Olive Schreiner reader.
(Pandora Press readers)
Bibliography: p.
Includes index.
I. Barash, Carol. II. Title. III. Title:
Women and South Africa.
PR9369.2.S3704   1987   824   86–30608

ISBN 0–86358–180–3 (c)
ISBN 0–86358–118–8 (pbk.)

British Library CIP Data also available

Contents

Illustrations

Acknowledgments

The publisher and I would like to thank the following for permission to reproduce material in this volume:

Nadine Gordimer for permission to reprint 'The Prison House of Colonialism', first published in *The Times Literary Supplement*, 15 August, 1980, and Russell & Volkening, Inc. as agents for the author in the USA.

The Schreiner family and Cherry Clayton (ed.) *Olive Schreiner*, McGraw-Hill, Johannesburg 1983, South African Literature Series no. 4 (for Fig. 1 on p. 3 of this volume); The University of Witwatersrand Library, Johannesburg (Fig. 2, p. 4); Ruth First and Anne Scott, *Olive Schreiner*, André Deutsch Ltd, 1980 (Fig. 3, p. 7); the Director of Libraries and Information Services, the City of Sheffield (Fig. 4, p. 12), Carpenter Collection Photographs 8/81; University College London Library (Fig. 5, p. 12), Pearson Papers, Box 1; Africana Museum (Fig. 6, p. 15); University of Durham Library, Palace Green Section (Fig. 7, p. 64), William Plomer Collection; The National English Literary Museum, Grahamstown, South Africa (Fig. 8, p. 64); Patrick Brantlinger, *Victorian Studies*, Indiana University (Fig. 10, p. 189).

Many people helped to make this *Reader* possible. I wish to thank Elaine Showalter for seeing the potential shape of an unwieldy seminar paper and for her sound advice and criticism. Judith Walkowitz and Philippa Brewster also provided suggestions in the early stages. My research in England was funded by the Donald and Mary Hyde Dissertation Fellowship, Princeton University; a Council for European Studies Summer Research Grant; and my mother, Mimi Coppersmith. The staffs of the

British Library, the Fawcett Library, and Firestone Library, Princeton University, located numerous obscure materials; I am especially indebted to Mary George, Reference Librarian at Princeton, for sending articles between Princeton and London.

My work on Schreiner has profited from discussions at the Feminist Reconstructions of the Self and Society Seminar, led by Alison Jagger at Douglass College in the spring of 1985, as well as from the ideas of Polly Beals, Sarah Lambert, and Mary Todd. Cherry Clayton graciously offered photographs and suggestions from her forthcoming study of Olive Schreiner, without which the *Reader* could not have been completed. I owe special thanks to Ann Scott, Patrick Brantlinger, and Henry Louis Gates, Jr. for help in finding photographs the South African government claims do not exist; and to Jayne Lewis and Laura Linke for assistance in proofreading. Candida Lacey is a superb editor; James Logenbach and Rachel Weil also read drafts of the introduction. The book owes much to their long and generous discussions, and even more to Jed Kwartler, partner and friend.

Introduction

In the summer of 1978 I discovered Olive Schreiner in Tillie
Olsen's *Silences*. I bought a copy of Schreiner's famous novel, *The
Story of an African Farm* (1883, rpt 1968), and stayed up most of
the night reading it through. Lyndall is an unforgettable
heroine. She wants to be an actress, she says, to change the
ways of men and the shape of history: her dream life fuses
maternity with images of spiritual power from a variety of
cultures: 'a Hindoo philosopher . . . a troop of Bacchanalians . . .
a mother giving bread and milk to her children' (201–2).
Lyndall imagines that education will grant her access to the
world, but her girls' 'finishing school' tries to squelch everything
she desires in herself:

> We all enter the world little plastic beings, with so much
> natural force, perhaps, but for the rest – blank! and the world
> tells us what we are to be, and shapes us by the ends it sets
> before us. To you [her male friend, Waldo] it says – *Work!*
> and to us it says – *Seem!* To you it says . . . as your arm is
> strong and your knowledge great, and the power to labour is
> with you, so you shall gain all the human heart desires. To us
> it says – Strength shall not help you, nor knowledge, nor
> labour. You shall gain what men gain, but by other means.
> And so the world makes men and women. (175)

Lyndall is seventeen, an English orphan in South Africa
dependent on the favours of her Boer guardians. Her lush,
spiritual rhetoric seems to address many situations of oppression
at once. A Lancashire working woman who read *The Story of an*

1

African Farm when it was first published remembered Lyndall's speaking to the needs of the poor and workers: 'I think there is hundreds of women what feels like that but can't speak, but *she* could speak what we feel' (Smith and Maclennan: 67). Yet Lyndall's strong words are at odds with the novel's plot: I remember being haunted for days by Lyndall's self-destruction, her apparent capitulation to a man who wishes only to master her and her pain after losing their child. Africa remained a gauzy backdrop to the heroine's journey from innocence through experience to death.

Schreiner's writing was well-known; the influence of *Dreams* (1890) and *Woman and Labour* (1911, rpt 1978) was acknowledged by many women and men in the early twentieth century.[2] But for feminism, I thought smugly in my bedroom in North America, Schreiner would have been forever lost. But while feminists in England and the United States reclaimed Schreiner's voice as their own, she was also undergoing something of a revival in South Africa, the land of her birth. In 1960 *Closer Union*, Schreiner's pamphlet opposing dehumanising racist policies and a strong central government, was reissued in Cape Town; in 1975 there were two separate dramatisations of *The Story of an African Farm*, and in 1983 a one-woman play based on her life and writings.[3] Perhaps even more significantly, Schreiner's *Trooper Peter Halket of Mashonaland*, an attack on 'the Colonial Man' originally published in 1897 and intermittently banned in South Africa, was reprinted.[4] This edition included the original frontispiece: a photograph of three black men dangling from a hanging tree while a group of white men looked on (see p. 189). This shocking picture – part of the book's political message – had been excluded from every edition but the first.

For white South Africans who favour majority rule Schreiner's is a kindred spirit. In 'The Psychology of the Boer' and 'The Problem of Slavery' (*Thoughts on South Africa*, 1923) Schreiner cuts through Afrikaners' myths about themselves, revealing them to be shamelessly backward-looking and dangerous because of their political use of religious rhetoric.[5] And, in *An English South-African's View of the Situation* (1899), Schreiner

Olive Schreiner, Edna Schreiner and Fanny Reitz in London, shortly before Olive Schreiner's return to Africa and her death

shows how the interests of capitalism and racism are intertwined in South Africa, how outsiders have conquered and often decimated the people and the land. But with Schreiner these messages are rarely so clear or so simple.

Like the rhetoric of her fictional heroine, Schreiner's own political ideas contain gaps – contradictions between her best vision of an egalitarian society and her confinement in the

3

Olive and W.P. Schreiner (at back) with elder brother Fred Schreiner and family, Eastbourne, April 1881

language and ideological structures of Victorian science. As Nadine Gordimer explains in 'The Prison-House of Colonialism', Schreiner was much better at articulating an ideal of freedom than at struggling through historical time in fiction.[6] Although Schreiner fundamentally believed in the powers of reason and progress, arguing in *Woman and Labour* that scientific and technological advances would eliminate infant mortality and free the mass of women to perform non-domestic tasks within a couple of generations, her idealism was often a way to avoid confronting the complexities and ambiguities of real political change. On the one hand Schreiner believed the New Man and Woman would evolve to a point of sexual honesty and equality (*Woman and Labour*: 289); on the other her generalised 'African woman' stands for an ideal of maternity that New Women no longer respect. Racism and transcultural motherhood are intertwined in almost all of Schreiner's works: she is able to reveal these constructs as social creations but is then unwilling to give them up.

This is how 'ideology' shapes experience – upholding conflicting positions, reflecting the contradictions of groups' as well as individuals' social and political location at those points where they are most tentative and vulnerable.[7] The paradoxes embodied in a woman who can understand and articulate sources of shared oppression, but who cannot or will not oppose them, can seem as troublesome in Schreiner's own life as in the lives of her fictional heroines.

Early life

Born in 1855 in Cape Colony, South Africa, Olive Emilie Albertina Schreiner was the ninth of Rebecca Lyndall and Gottlob Schreiner's twelve children, and named after three dead brothers.[8] Emilie, as her parents called her, was a precocious and strong-willed child. In later life she remembered being beaten several times by her dogmatically religious mother. The family was financially unstable, as her father was assigned to a series of failing frontier missions and her mother was frequently ill. When she was fifteen Schreiner began a string of demeaning, short-term jobs as nurse and governess, living – like Lyndall in *The Story of an African Farm* and Jannita in 'Dream Life and Real Life' – as an economic and emotional dependant in other people's houses. Out of a sense of frustration and loneliness Schreiner renamed herself 'Olive' and began writing novels. Her three novels – *Undine* (1929), *The Story of an African Farm*, and *From Man to Man; or, Perhaps Only* . . . (1926, rpt 1982) – cluster around the web of emotions – loss and betrayal in love, women's alienation, and guilt – to which she returned time and again. Schreiner's female characters are most often named after herself or her mother. The larger-than-life outsiders who bring solace to the constricted frontier farms in her novels remind us of how often Schreiner's childhood access to information came from magical 'strangers' who were passing through on their way to somewhere else. 'The Child's Day', the first item in this Reader, was based on Schreiner's childhood and conveys the omni-presence of religious songs and writings in those early years.

Schreiner never wholeheartedly swallowed her parents' re-ligion. She believed that the death of her younger sister catalysed her break with orthodox Christianity, her move toward free-thought and mysticism: 'I cannot conceive of either birth or death, or anything but simple changes in the endless existence. . . . I first had this feeling with regard to death clearly when my favourite little sister died when I was nine years old' (Cronwright-Schreiner, ed., *Letters*: 219). Schreiner's very physical desire for transcendence and unity informs *The Story of an African Farm*, where it is elaborated in relation to the body of a female labourer, and limited by abiding there.

When religion failed, science became Schreiner's religious and moral code, as it had for many Victorians.[9] Schreiner discussed her conversion to scientific theory in sexual terms. Repeatedly she was both empowered by men's writing and overwhelmed by the literalness of its presence. She read Herbert Spencer's *First Principles* (1862) as a young girl and described Spencer as a doctor who had cured her broken leg: 'Once it is set one may be said to have no more need of a doctor, nevertheless one always walks on his leg. . . . He helped me to believe in the unity

6

Wittebergen mission station, the birthplace of Olive Schreiner

underlying all nature; that was a great thing' (*Letters*: 82–3).
Similarly, once Schreiner began to imbibe Darwin, his writing
took her over completely. We can see Darwin's impact in
everything from Rebekah's fascination with biological and moral
evolution in *From Man to Man* to the arguments for racial
development and eugenics in *Woman and Labour* and Schreiner's
other political writings.[10]

England

In 1881 Schreiner travelled to England to become a doctor, but
she could not tolerate the stress of medical training. She tried
briefly to become a nurse, but that also brought on despair.
When *The Story of an African Farm* was published under the
pseudonym Ralph Iron in 1883, it created something of a
sensation. Treated as an exotic piece of Africa cast up on
English shores, Schreiner was courted and paraded in London's
political and intellectual circles. In 1884 she met Havelock Ellis
and Edward Carpenter and became involved with the Men and
Women's Club, an elite London group that met weekly to
discuss 'the Woman Question'.[11] The section of this Reader on
'Gender, Class and Science' presents a range of Schreiner's
writings that grew out of her involvement with the Club.

'The Woman Question' was a catch-all phrase for a wide
range of issues concerning women's social, political and sexual
status in late-Victorian England. Schreiner uses the language of
evolution to argue that women's status has fallen with the shifts
from agrarian to industrial society. Modern society devalues
women's emotional and reproductive labour, she asserts,
because industry needs women to perform onerous factory
labour outside the home. At the same time, middle-class women
have become 'sex parasites', economic and moral drains on a
society which gives them no meaningful work. 'The Policy in
Favour of Protection – ' shows the career of a 'sex parasite'; her
selfishness drains energy and love even from her woman friend.
Schreiner begins with Mary Wollstonecraft's plea for equality
from *A Vindication of the Rights of Woman* (1792, rpt 1975), but

shifts the argument away from what women have access to *knowing* to what we can actually *do*. And, unlike Wollstonecraft, Schreiner believed that women's emotional and reproductive lives should not be rationalised out of existence.[12] Schreiner's sense that women's lives were changing rapidly but the changes were not in women's control was one that was shared by many feminists in this period, and is in many ways accurate.

Women's lives were the site of a great deal of political controversy in the late nineteenth century, not least because eugenicists of all political persuasions feared that women's equality and education made us unfit to bear and raise children.[13] Although women were still disenfranchised, women's work and agitation had begun to secure higher education and some professional status for women of the upper classes.[14] Working-class women had been demanding equal rights since the 1840s, the early organisation of the women's suffrage campaign in England growing out of women's political involvement with the Independent Labour Party.[15] The Married Women's Property Act of 1870 gave women limited control of their possessions within marriage, and, in the 1880s, Josephine Butler organised feminists' protest against the Contagious Diseases Acts, a series of laws meant to regulate prostitution by requiring medical examinations of prostitutes, which Butler provocatively called 'instrumental rape'.[16]

As this wide range of women's concerns was reshaped in the popular press the discourse tended to emphasise women's victimisation, rather than their growing economic and sexual agency. In an intellectual circle like the Men and Women's Club, while women were the focus of discussion, they were often silenced or exploited by male members of the group.[17] As a woman intellectual and a colonial subject in a predominantly male community in London, there were two ways to work around this problem: one could become an object of men's investigations or one could investigate other women.

Schreiner inhabited both these positions, often at the same time. She made women the object of her own inquiry when she sought out and lived among prostitutes while writing *From Man to Man*, her unfinished novel about prostitution. Schreiner had always felt herself to be different and separate from other women, and often linked this feeling to memories of her sister's death: 'I sometimes think my great love for women and girls, *not* because they are myself, but because they are *not* myself, comes from my love for her' (*Letters*: 274). We can read a complicated lesbian fantasy behind Schreiner's 'love' for other women; she describes women as sexually other, as objects of curiosity, power and sometimes disdain. The position of a scientific investigator allows Schreiner to get physically close to other women yet maintain power over them through narrative distance and generalisation.[18]

Moreover, Schreiner made *herself* an object of scientific observation, carving up her life for the pleasure and approval of her male friends and allowing Havelock Ellis, in particular, to play the male scientist to her female patient.[19] Schreiner was attracted to Ellis's intelligence and appealed to him as an authority on her own feelings and desires. But she also balked at Ellis's conclusions and structured their relationship around redefining herself in response to his definitions of her. Schreiner wrote incessantly to Ellis, often several letters a day, allowing him to diagnose her asthma as psychosomatic in origin and to urge that she should neither write nor think when she felt even remotely ill. Ellis also assured Schreiner that she was not an 'invert', or lesbian.[20] At one point it seems that Schreiner and Ellis tried to be lovers, but that aspect of their relationship failed miserably. For both Schreiner and Ellis their intense 'scientific' relationship in letters was a way to sexualise the mind while keeping their bodies at a safe distance from actual sexual contact:

[A man thinks that when he] touches a woman it is only her body he is touching, it is really her soul, her brain, her creative power. It is putting his fingers into her brain and snapping the strings when he draws her to him physically and cannot take her mentally. (Schreiner, quoted in First and Scott: 141)

Schreiner yearned to be treated as an equal by these male intellectuals, even if that meant denying that she lived and spoke from a woman's life and body: 'I wish I was a man that I might be friends with all of you, but you know my sex must always divide. I only feel like a man but to you all I seem a woman' (Schreiner, quoted in First and Scott: 179). She kept herself at a safe distance from Karl Pearson of the Men and Women's Club by calling herself 'your man-friend, OS', but felt genuinely betrayed when he became interested in and eventually married another woman.[21] Like the central character in 'The Buddhist Priest's Wife', Schreiner must have realised that even intellectual men who advocated women's intelligence in theory might not choose an intelligent and outspoken woman as their own sexual partner.

Allegory and Africa

In the late 1880s and 1890s Schreiner wrote many short, allegorical pieces which she published in periodicals and which were later collected in *Dreams*, *Dream Life and Real Life* (1893), and *Stories, Dreams and Allegories* (1923). Some of these pieces are collected here in the section on 'Fantasy and the Female Body'. In letters to Ellis and Pearson, Schreiner emphasised the formal conflicts inherent in these writings. She sought to express the essential unity of all things, but she also wished to convey the real struggles of suffering human beings. Schreiner told her publisher that *Dreams* should be expensive – the book was aimed at the ruling classes and was intended to show 'Capitalists, Millionaires, and Middlemen in England and America' the suffering they dished out to the masses.[22]

Schreiner's allegories are compressed narratives of wish-fulfilment. *Dreams*, for instance, is dedicated to 'a small girl-child who may live to grasp somewhat of that which is yet sight, not touch'. In this dedication we sense Schreiner's desire for tactile sensation, a hope that is displaced onto vision in the present and the possibility of fulfilment in the next generation. Schreiner made the allegories more powerful by replacing historical narrative with biblical cadences and themes. Most often, if a woman must struggle or choose in the allegories, her struggle

11

Havelock Ellis

Karl Pearson

will end in triumph and her choice be revealed as not a choice at all. In 'Life's Gifts' a woman must choose between love and freedom. She chooses freedom and is offered a magical future time when freedom will include both love and freedom. Again, in 'A Dream of Wild Bees', a pregnant woman dreams Health, Wealth, Love and Talent as possible futures for her ninth child. It is predicted that the child will fail in all these realms of worldly success, but '*this shall be thy reward – that the ideal shall be real to thee*'. And in the womb the foetus feels 'a sensation of light! Light – that it never had seen. Light – that perhaps it never should see. Light – that existed somewhere!'

The allegories are rich in sexual symbolism – blood, flowers, pregnancy, pollenisation – but their resolution resides in a future time when women will not be slaves, when women's art will not be produced at the expense of women's lives. Schreiner's two early forms of narrative discourse – a history of evolutionary progress and timeless biblical allegory – remain structurally at odds. The frustration implicit in the structure of *Dreams* can be read as a provisional triumph.[23] Refusing to be contained within the limits of her society, Schreiner suggests in the allegories that women's position and women's relationship to language cannot change without much larger social organisation. In 'I Thought I Stood' she warns against any feminism that makes victims of other women; this feminist divisiveness stands for all political movements that do not treat people as equal – in practice as well as in words.

When Schreiner returned to South Africa in 1889 her own life changed dramatically. After an attempt to seduce Cecil Rhodes, who was soon to be Prime Minister of the Cape, she met Samuel Cron Cronwright in 1892, and began a painful and disappointing marriage with him soon after. In 1895, at the age of forty, Schreiner gave birth to a daughter who was apparently healthy, but who lived less than a day. Although Schreiner lived apart from her husband for long periods of time, she had at least four other miscarriages over a number of years. This painful personal experience tended to exacerbate Schreiner's sense that the European 'Woman Question' was rather frivolous in light of the wholesale racism and economic exploitation being practised by

Olive and S.C. Cronwright-Schreiner in 1895

the British in South Africa. Schreiner resigned her vice-presidency of the Cape Women's Enfranchisement League when the group failed to support black men and women's as well as white women's suffrage.

She committed herself to a multi-racial South Africa's struggle for independence from British colonial rule, and the bulk of her later writings are addressed to this political situation. Many of the shorter, journalistic writings from this period were integrated into *An English South-African's View of the Situation* (1899) and *Thoughts on South Africa* (1923), and are collected here in the section on 'Gender, Race and Politics'. In *Closer Union* (1909, rpt 1960) and 'Woman and War', Schreiner makes several claims, claims which remain true almost one hundred years later. She argues that blacks are a labouring class on which the South African economy depends, that race is a social rather than a physical reality, and that women understand what unites races better than men because of their shared experience of mothering. Schreiner's growing beliefs in pacifism and equality come across clearly in 'The Native Question' and 'The Dawn of Civilisation'.

Several years before the outbreak of the Anglo-Boer War (1899–1902) Schreiner conveyed the intensity of British-Dutch conflict in *Trooper Peter Halket of Mashonaland* (1897, rpt 1974), an allegorical novel in which a Dutch soldier rather unwillingly sacrifices his own life to free an African man who has been sentenced to death for spying on the British. Underneath that rather neat plot Schreiner shows how even the best-intentioned colonial man operates in a mental muddle of racist and sexist self-deception.[24] As Peter goes mad alone in the veld, his racism is enacted in his fragmented but uncritical memories of his own sexual abuse of African women. As readers we see Peter's unstated assumptions that African women are his property and that they should be grateful when he steals them from the men with whom they've chosen to live. Sexuality is at the center of Schreiner's exposé of colonialism. As Stephen Gray shows, the structural breaks in *Trooper Peter Halket* are essentially ideological; Schreiner 'rejects the realist novel *because she rejects the morality which the realist novel encodes*'.[25]

Schreiner felt the Boer War to be a violation of her central principles and even of her life and writing. In the introduction to *Woman and Labour* she describes how an earlier manuscript was wantonly treated by British soldiers: 'my desk had been forced open and broken up, and its contents set on fire in the centre of the room, so that the roof was blackened over the pile of burnt papers' (*Woman and Labour*: 18). The 'sex book' she had been working on since the 1880s was destroyed needlessly. Schreiner's sense of victimisation during the Boer War explains in part her identification with Boers' (Afrikaners') nostalgic depiction of themselves as African-born people with a right to freedom from British colonial rule.

In *The Political Mythology of Apartheid* (1985), Leonard Thompson describes how Afrikaners have reshaped events of the early nineteenth century into a 'political mythology' which they have used to justify their own racist policies ever since. Schreiner both participates in that mythology and challenges it in the short story 'Eighteen Ninety-Nine'. Most significantly, Schreiner shifts Afrikaners' stories from men's conquest of the frontier to *women's* role in maintaining cultural continuity in times of large-scale upheaval and change. Even when battles are 'won', people die; women suffer. Schreiner also shows in 'Eighteen Ninety-Nine' how women are the shapers of unofficial, private versions of publicly sanctioned myths. Battles take place in the background of the story, but the acts which we share as readers are domestic ones: child-bearing, farming and the passing on of stories, hopes and beliefs. Whereas Tant Sannie, a foolishly traditional Boer woman, is caricatured in *The Story of an African Farm*, her huge, ugly body figuring for her much more dangerous flaws of character, Schreiner's later depictions of Boer women are deeply reverential, linking Boer women's unselfconscious respect for traditional values with the community strength and continuity of South African society.[26]

In *Woman and Labour* – which suffragettes referred to as their 'bible' – Schreiner uses evolution to deify biological motherhood. Like many late nineteenth-century writers, including Engels (1884, rpt 1972) and Bachofen (1861, rpt 1967), Schreiner idealises a matriarchal age when motherhood was worshipped as the source of human life. In all these writers a sexual division of labour is projected onto a Golden Age when women and women's culture were central to human affairs. *Woman and Labour* traces human society through a series of sudden changes from this matriarchal time through industrialisation to the present. Paradoxically, this series of technological and ideological crises – the arrival of organised agriculture, cottage industry, and capitalism – both moves away from and justifies women's privileged maternal status. Schreiner uses 'labour' to mean both work for wages and child-bearing. Entrance into all fields of work, she argues, will enable women to refuse vanity and 'parasitism' and as mothers to lead a moral cleansing of the human race.

As Schreiner observed European women no longer asserting their 'overmastering hunger' to bear children, she used African women as the template to project her Golden Age of sexual harmony and lost maternal values; they alone feel the drumbeat of eternal motherhood in the twentieth century (*Woman and Labour*: 5). This myth of common racial motherhood was a way to gloss over vast differences of race and class, to prove middle-class women 'maternal' – even if they choose not to raise children – by way of other women's literal maternity. Like Schreiner's belief in evolution and her use of biblical allegory as a narrative form, this racial primitivism avoids confronting gender and race as cultural constructs that mediate between ideal and real. The belief in archetypal maternity and its blurring of history onto a set of transtemporal values obviates the need for political change in the present moment while justifying the rule and reproduction of 'virile' white men and women, those already in power.[27]

Schreiner's visionary and influential rhetoric is flawed, but as Virginia Woolf wrote soon after Schreiner's death, 'It would be frivolous to dismiss her as a mere crank, a piece of wreckage used and then thrown aside as the cause triumphed onwards. She remains . . . too uncompromising a figure to be disposed of'.[28] What happens if we bring together Schreiner's writings on women and South Africa, if we attempt to rethink her complicated and often conflicting political statements from our own position nearly a century later? Gender and sexuality are at the centre of South Africa's Race Laws; *sexual segregation* is both the symbol and the central justification of apartheid. Fears of miscegenation, and of women's sexual agency, translate into laws about who can have sex with whom.[29]

Generalisations about all women are a dangerous place to begin constructing feminist theory and practice. Even in the thought of one woman there are propositions that rest uneasily side-by-side: Schreiner's use of maternal ideology, her feminism, is fundamentally and unmistakably racist.[30] I suggest that we think of Schreiner as a woman who embodied radically conflicting ideological and narrative positions. Because Schreiner often compressed and revised her key concepts over time, her best and most coherent writing is often found in her shorter, but less-known pieces. The versions reprinted here are the political versions written to address specific events and problems. Although some of them were later collected in book form, most were first published separately as newspaper articles or political pamphlets. This Reader is organised to move with Schreiner between England and Africa, her two homes, and between feminism and anti-colonialism, her two separate ideologies. Each section is arranged chronologically, the Reader as a whole tracing Schreiner's movement from feminism, as a response to and elaboration of Victorian science, to pacifism and native African rights as a response to white women's racism and the futility of war.

As a white *woman* in South Africa, Schreiner was both colonised and coloniser; she experienced this political division as self-hatred and victimisation, on the one hand, and as racist condescension toward black Africans on the other.[31] Yet Schreiner believed fundamentally in unity, and always advocated political and economic equality for all people in South Africa. Both the force and the ideological ruptures of Schreiner's prose come from her attempts to bridge political divisions with the allegorical language and structure of the Bible, or even more tenuously to hold together the wide range of political demands in South Africa with the notion that all people are mothers' children after all. Schreiner's writings will not give us politically correct heroines, nor will our own lives. However, if we see Schreiner's texts enacting struggles between different discourses of power, they ask questions that cannot easily be dismissed. Schreiner both participates in a racist mythology and begins to deconstruct that mythology from women's perspective within a colonial system. For those of us who have never been to South Africa, Schreiner takes our minds part of the way there. Her contradictions remain *powerful* contradictions; they result from a flawed social order, one which still exists and which we must work together to change.

Prelude

The Child's Day (1887)

Schreiner first imagined 'The Child's Day' in Alassio, Italy, in 1887 (*Letters*: 290–1). She knew immediately that she had created the right beginning for a novel on the relationship between women's moral and sexual development that she had been working on since her days as a governess. 'I've a curious tenderness for that little bit of writing', she wrote, 'it always seemed to me the incarnation of my own childhood' (letter to Betty Molteno, quoted in Clayton, 1983: 122). Schreiner revised 'The Child's Day' many times (Beeton, 1980) and it was published posthumously as the opening chapter of *From Man to Man* (1926, rpt 1982). A description of a young girl's childhood that is both personal and general, 'The Child's Day' brings together a number of Schreiner's crucial narrative concerns: the centrality of childhood experiences of landscape, community, and alienation; the importance of early reading, in this case the Bible and hymns; and an almost overwhelming desire for unity that blends into young Rebekah's maternal fantasies. Later in the novel Rebekah marries a man whom she reveres, but who fails to satisfy her emotionally or intellectually. With the help of a friendship with another man she eventually becomes financially free from her husband and raises as her own the mulatto child her husband has fathered with their African servant. Rebekah's sister, Baby Bertie, is the victim of her own honesty and innocence. Once seduced by her tutor, she is marked as a fallen woman and begins a slow economic and physical deterioration as an imprisoned 'kept woman' and prostitute. Although Schreiner never completed the novel *From Man to Man*, she meant the sisters' moral and sexual careers to remain entwined, as their hands are at the end of 'The Child's Day'.

The little mother lay in the agony of child-birth. Outside all was still but the buzzing of the bees, some of which now and then found their way in to the half darkened room. The scent of orange trees and of the flowers from the garden beyond, came in through the partly-opened window, with the rich dry odour of a warm, African, summer morning. The little mother groaned in her anguish.

Old Ayah, the Hottentot[1] woman, stood at the bedside with her hands folded and her long fingers crooked, the veins on the back standing out like cords. She said, 'O ja, God! Wat zal ons nou zeg?'[2] and re-adjusted the little black shawl upon her shoulders. The window was open three inches, and the blind was drawn below it to keep out the heat. The mother groaned.

At the end of the passage in the dining room the father sat with his elbows on the deal table and his head in his hands, reading Swedenborg,[3] but the words had no clear meaning for him. Every now and then he looked up at the clock over the fireplace. It was a quarter before ten, and the house was very quiet.

At the back of the house, on the kitchen door step, stood Rebekah, the little five-years-old daughter. She looked up into the intensely blue sky, and then down to the ducks who were waddling before the lowest step, picking up the crusts she had thrown to them. She wore a short pink cotton dress with little white knickerbockers buttoned below the knees and a white kappie[4] with a large curtain that came almost to her waist. She took the kappie off and looked up again into the sky. There was something almost oppressive in the quiet. The Kaffir[5] maids had been sent home to their huts, except one who was heating water in the kitchen, and the little Kaffirs were playing away beyond the kraals[6] on the old kraal heap. It was like Sunday. She drew a slight sigh, and looked up again into the sapphire blue sky: it was going to be very hot. The farmhouse stood on the spur of a mountain, and the thorn trees in the flat below were already shimmering in the sunlight. After a while she put on her kappie and walked slowly down the steps and across the bare space which served for a farmyard. Beyond it she passed into the low bushes. She soon came to a spot just behind the kraal where the ground was flat and bare; the surface soil had been washed off,

24

and a circular floor of smooth, and unbroken stone was exposed, like the smooth floor of a great round room. The bushes about were just high enough to hide her from the farm house, though it was only fifty yards off. She stepped on to the stone slowly, on tiptoe. She was building a house here. It stood in the centre of the stone floor; it was a foot and a half high and about a foot across, and was built of little flat stones placed very carefully on one another; and it was round like a tower. The lower story opened on to the ground by a little doorway two inches high; in the upper story there was a small door in the wall; and a ladder made of sticks, with smaller sticks fastened across, led up to it. She stepped up to the house very softly. She was building it for mice. Once a Kaffir boy told her he had built a house of stones, and as he passed the next day a mouse ran out at the front door. She had thought a great deal of it; always, she seemed to see the mouse living in the house and going in and out at the front door; and at last she built this one. She had built it in two storeys, so that the family could live on the lower floor and keep their grain on the top. She had put a great flat stone, to roof the lower story, and another flat stone for the roof on the very top: and she had put a moss carpet in the lower floor for them to sleep on, and corn, ready for them to use, above. She stepped very softly up to the house and peeped in at the little door; there was nothing there but the brown moss. She sat down flat on the stone before it, and peered in. Half, she expected the mice to come; and half, she knew they never would!

Presently she took a few little polished flat stones out of her pocket and began to place them carefully round the top to form a turret; then she straightened the ladder a little. Then she sat, watching the house. After a while she stretched out her right hand, and drew its sides together, and made the fingers look as it were a little mouse; and moved it softly along the stone, creeping, creeping up to the door; she let it go in. Then after a minute she drew it slowly back and sat up. It was becoming intensely hot now; the sun, beating down on the stone drew little beads of perspiration on her forehead.

How still it was! She listened to hear whether anyone from the house would call her. It was long past ten o'clock and she was never allowed to be out in the sun so late. She sat listening: then she got a curious feeling that something was happening at the house and stood up quickly, and walked away towards it.

As she passed the dining room window, whose lower edge was on a level with her chin, she looked in. Her father was gone; but his glasses and his open book still lay on the table. Rebekah walked round to the kitchen door. Even the ducks were gone; no one was in the kitchen, only the flames were leaping up and crackling in the open fireplace, and the water was spluttering out of the mouth of the big black kettle. She stood for a moment to watch it. Then a sound struck her ear. She walked with quick sharp steps into the dining room, and threw her kappie on the table, and stood listening. Again the sound came, faint, and strange. She walked out into the long passage into which all the bedrooms opened. Suddenly the sound became loud and clear from her mother's bedroom. Rebekah walked quickly up the coconut matted passage and knocked at her mother's door, three short, sharp knocks with her knuckle. There was a noise of moving and talking inside; then the door opened a little.

'I want to come in! – Please, what is the matter?'

Someone said, 'Shall she come in?' and then a faint voice answered, 'Yes, let her come.'

Rebekah walked in; there was but a little light coming in under the blind through the slightly opened window. Her mother was lying in the large bed and her father standing at the bedside. A strange woman from the next farm, whom she had never seen before, sat in the elbow chair in the corner beyond the bed, with something on her lap; old Ayah stood near the drawers, folding some linen cloths.

Rebekah stood for a moment motionless and hesitating on the ox skin in the middle of the floor; then she walked straight up to the strange woman in the corner.

'Ask her to show you what she has got, Rebekah,' said her father.

The woman unfolded a large brown shawl, inside of which there was a white one. Even in the dim light in the corner you could see a little red face, with two hands doubled up on the chest, peeping out from it.

Rebekah looked.

'Was it *this* that made that noise?' she asked.

The woman smiled and nodded.

Her father came up.

'Kiss it, Rebekah; it is your little sister.'

Rebekah looked quietly at it.

'No – I won't – I don't like it,' she said slowly.

But her father had already moved across the room to speak to old Ayah.

Rebekah turned sharply on her heel and walked to the large bed. Her mother lay on it with her eyes shut. Rebekah stood at the foot, her eyes on a level with the white coverlet, looking at her mother.

As she stood there she heard old Ayah whisper to the father, and they both went out, to the spare bedroom opposite. The strange woman came and bent over the mother, and said something to her; she nodded her head without opening her eyes. The woman made a space at her side, and lay the white bundle down in it; she put the baby's head on the mother's arm. The mother opened her eyes then, and looked down at it with a half smile; and drew the quilt up a little higher to shield it. Rebekah watched them: then she walked softly to the door.

'Please open it for me,' she said. The handle was too high for her.

The woman let her out.

For a moment she stood outside the closed door looking at it, her tiny features curiously set almost with the firmness of a woman's; then she turned and walked down the passage. She saw her father and old Ayah come out of the spare room. Old Ayah locked the door and put the key into her pocket, and they went back to her mother's bedroom.

Rebekah picked up her kappie from the dining room table, put it on, and went out again on to the steps at the kitchen door. The sun was blazing in the yard now, the very stones seemed to throw up a red reflection. Standing on the top step in the shade, Rebekah shivered with heat.

Then she wandered slowly down the steps and across the yard. She could feel the ground burn under her feet, through the soles of her little shoes. She walked to her flat stone. The mouse house stood baking in the sun with all the little crystals in the rock glittering. She sat down before the house, drawing her skirts carefully under her, the rock burnt so. She drew her knees up to her chin, and folded her arms about them, and sat looking at the mouse house. She knew she ought not to be there in the hot sun; she knew it was wicked; but she liked the heat to burn her that morning.

After a while the little drops of perspiration began to gather under her eyes and on her upper lip; she would not wipe them off. Her face began to get very red, and her temples to throb; the heat was fierce. She looked out at the mouse house from under her white kappie with blinking red eyes. She could feel the heat scorching her arms through her little cotton dress, and she liked it.

By half-past eleven the heat was so intense she could not bear it, and there began to be a sound like a little cicada singing in her ears; so she got up, and walked slowly towards the house; but did not go in at the kitchen door.

She went to the back, where the wall of the house made a deep shadow, and went to the window of the spare room. It was her favourite place, to which she went whenever she wanted to be quite safe and alone. No one ever went there. The beds were generally left unmade till visitors came with only the mattresses and pillows on them, and under one bed she kept her box of specially prized playthings. She unclosed the outer shutters. The window was so low that she could easily raise the sash and climb in from the ground. She pushed it up, and stepped into the room. It was beautifully cool there and almost dark: she drew up the blind a very little to let in some light. She was walking towards the bed under which her box was, when something struck her eye. On the large table in the middle of the room there was a something with a white sheet spread over it. Rebekah walked up to it: this was something quite new.

She drew a chair to the side of the table and climbed up. She lifted the top of the sheet. Under it there was another sheet and a pillow; and, with its head on the pillow, dressed in pure white, was a little baby. Rebekah stood upright on the chair, holding the sheet in her hand.

After a while she let it down carefully, but so turning it back that the baby's face and hand were exposed. How fast it was sleeping!

She bent down and peered into its face. There was a curious resemblance between her own small, sharply marked features and those of the baby. She put out her forefinger gently and touched one of its hands. They were very cool. She watched it for some time; then she climbed down and went to the wardrobe where the best going-to-town clothes were kept hanging. With some difficulty she unhooked a little fur-trimmed red cape of her own, with this she climbed back on to the chair and laid it across the baby's feet. It was evidently not warm enough, though the day was hot.

She bent down over it again. On the top of its head was a little mass of soft, down-like curly black hair; she put her face down softly and touched the hair with her cheek and kissed it. She dared not kiss its face for fear of waking it. She sat down beside it, motionless, for a long time, on the edge of the table. Seeing it did not stir, after a time she climbed down, and taking off her shoes and leaving them at the foot of the table, went on tip-toe to the bed and drew from under it her box.

It was a large soap box with an odd collection of things in it. On the top was a dried monkey's skin and a large alphabet book with coloured pictures; below were different little boxes and bags; some held stones; one was full of brightly coloured beetles and grasshoppers she had picked up dead; in one, all by itself, was a very large bright crystal, carefully wrapped in cotton-wool and tied with string. Below, was an oblong shaped, common brown stone about eighteen inches in length; it was dressed in doll's clothes and it had a shawl wrapped round it. Beside it was a small shop-doll with pink cheeks and flaxen hair, which she had got on her last birthday; but it had no shawl and its face was turned to the wood. The stone she had had two years, and she loved it; the shop-doll was only interesting. Besides these there was a round Bushman stone[7] with a hole in the middle, which she had picked up behind the kraal, and a flat slate-coloured stone with the impression of a fossilised leaf, which she found on the path going up to the mountain; and, at the very bottom in the corner was a workbox, with a silver thimble and needles and cottons inside, which she thought very grand; and two little brightly coloured boxes with chocolates and peppermints with holes through them like whistles, which she had got on Christmas Day, but thought too pretty to eat; and there was also a head of Queen Victoria, cut out of the tinsel label of a sardine tin, and which she kept wrapped up in white paper.

She took all the things out of the box and handled them carefully, deliberating for a while. At last she selected the alphabet book, the Bushman stone, the silver thimble and a paper of needles, Queen Victoria's head, and a stick of chocolate. When she had packed the other things back, she went with them to the table. She climbed up on the chair. She lay the thimble and paper of needles on the cushion to the left of the baby's head, and the Bushman stone and the tinsel Queen Victoria head on the right. Very gently and slowly she slipped the alphabet book under the baby's doubled up arm; and then, turning back the silver paper at one end of the chocolate stick, she forced the other end very gently into its closed fist, leaving the uncovered end near to its mouth. Then she stood upright on the chair with her hands folded before her, looking down at them all, with a curious contentment about her mouth.

After a little time she got down and went to her box at the foot of the bed, and sat down upon it; to wait till the baby woke.

Her face was seamed under the eyes with lines hot perspiration and dust had left, and she was very tired. She leaned her arm on the bed and rested her head on it.

At half past one it was dinner-time, and old Ayah could not find her. She often crept in the heat of the day behind the piano or into the wagon-loft, and fell asleep there where no one could discover her. So old Ayah put some dinner for her in a tin plate in the oven to keep warm.

Then everyone went to lie down; the shutters of all the doors and windows were closed, and there was not a sound in all the house but the buzzing of the flies in the darkened rooms.

Only old Ayah did not sleep to-day, and was sewing a piece of white calico into a long, narrow, white robe with a stiff frill down the front for a tiny baby. She sat working in the dining-room with the shutters very slightly apart to let in enough light.

When she had done it she went down the passage to the door of the spare room and unlocked it.

The first thing she noticed was that the outer shutters she had left carefully closed were partly open, that the window had been raised, and the blind was an inch or two drawn up. She walked to the table. The baby lay with the sheet removed from its face, and the Bushman stone, and thimble, and needles, and a picture, on its pillow, and the alphabet book under its arm, and the chocolate stick in its hand. She glanced round. Rebekah was still sitting on her box at the foot of the bed with her stockinged feet crossed and her head resting on her arm on the mattress, fast asleep; her shoes standing side by side at the foot of the table.

Old Ayah walked up to her and shook her by the shoulder. Rebekah opened her eyes slowly and looked at her dreamily, without raising her head.

'What are you doing in here? Couldn't you see, if the door was locked, that you weren't meant to get in here?' she said in the Cape Dutch[8] she always spoke.

Rebekah sat up, still looking round vacantly; then in an instant all came back to her and she stood up.

'Aren't you a wicked, naughty, child, letting all the flies and the sun come in! What have you been doing?'

'Oh, please don't talk so loud,' whispered Rebekah, quickly, bending forward and stretching out her hand; 'please, you'll wake it!'

'O Lord!' said old Ayah, looking at her, 'what would your mother say if she knew you'd been in here playing with that blessed baby! You naughty child, how dared you touch it!'

'It's mine: *I* found it!' said Rebekah, walking softly up to the foot of the table.

Old Ayah came up too.

'Oh, please,' said Rebekah, putting out her hand again, '*don't* touch it! Don't touch it! I *don't* want it waked!'

She looked up at old Ayah with full lustrous eyes, as a bitch looks when you handle her pups.

'O my God!' said old Ayah, 'the child is mad! How can it be yours? It's your mother's.'

'It is mine;' said Rebekah slowly: 'I found it. Mietje found hers in the hut, and Katje found hers behind the kraal.[9] My mother found hers that cries so, in the bedroom. *This one* is mine!'

'O Lord, Lord!' cried old Ayah. 'I tell you this is your mother's baby; she had two, and this one is dead. I put it here myself.'

Rebekah looked at her.

'This one is dead: it'll never open its eyes again; it can't breathe.'

The old Hottentot woman began taking the alphabet book from under its arm and the stick from its hand, and took the things from the pillow.

Rebekah did not look at her; her gaze was fixed on the baby's face.

'Here, take these things!'

But Rebekah raised out her hand, and touched the baby's feet; a coldness went up her arm, even through the sheet. She dropped her hand.

'Child, what is it? Here! – take your shoes!'

She thrust the shoes into her hand. Rebekah held them, but let them slide between her fingers on to the floor; she was still staring at the table.

Old Ayah gathered up the child's apron and put into it the things she had taken from the baby, and forced the shoes back into her other hand.

'Here, take them, I say; and go away! And get your face washed and your hair done; and tell Mietje to put you on a clean dress and white pinafore. What would your mother say to see you looking such an ugly, dirty little fright!'

Rebekah turned away slowly, with the gathered apron in one hand and the shoes in the other, and walked to the door. When she got there she turned and looked dreamily back; then she went out into the passage.

After she had had her face washed and her hair brushed, and

had got on a clean starched pink dress and a white over-all pinafore, she went to the dining-room. Old Ayah had put her plate of warmed dinner on the table ready for her, and she sat down on the bench to eat it. She felt better now she was washed and had a clean starched dress on.

The heat outside was still very oppressive, and only a little light came in through the cracks in the shutter; and the blue flies were buzzing round everywhere in the dark. She did not feel very hungry, and played with her dinner; but she drank all the water in her mug. Then she pushed her plate from her, found her kappie and went out into the great front room. All was quiet there also, and almost quite dark. She took a large worn picture-book from the side table, and opened the double door and went out on to the front step. The vine leaves on the front wall hung dry and stiff, and even the orange leaves on the great orange trees before the door hung curled and flaccid.

It was nearly three o'clock, and the heat was hardly less intense than at midday, though there was already shade on that side of the house. The hollyhocks and dahlias in the flower garden beyond the orange trees, were hanging their heads, and the four o'clocks were curled up tight though the trees sheltered them.

She walked down through the flower garden, on, into the orchard beyond.

All was very still and brown there also. The little peach trees that stood in rows were shedding their half ripe fruit, which fell into the long yellow grass beneath them, and the fig trees along the wall had curled up the edges of their leaves. Rebekah followed a little winding footpath among the grass to the middle of the orchard, where a large pear tree stood, with a gnarled and knotted stem. There was a bench under the tree, and the grass grew very long all about it. She looked around to find a spot where the tree cast a deeper shade than elsewhere. Here she walked round and round on the grass, like a dog, and then lay down on her back in the place she had made. It was like a nest, with the grass standing several inches high all round.

She drew up her legs, cocking one knee over the other, so that one foot waved in the air.

It was very nice. She lay for a while with her hands clasped across the top of her head, from which she had thrown her white kappie. The pear tree leaves were so thick overhead, you could hardly see any sky through them. She yawned luxuriously. Beyond the edges of the pear branches, here and there as you looked through half closed eyes, were strips of blue sky, and some great, white masses of thunder cloud were showing in them, like ships sailing in the blue. She watched them for a while with her eyes half shut; then she took up the book that lay on the grass at her side, stood it open on her chest against her knee, and gently waved the foot that was cocked up in the air.

The book opened of itself about the middle at a certain page. On it was a picture: Peter, a great boy with a red face looking out through the top of the letter P, and at his feet was a little pig with a curled tail. Besides this there were in the picture, in the distance, fields and a stile, and a winding path leading far away over the hills; and in the foreground was a milestone with weeds growing around it; below was written 'P stands for Peter and Pig.'

She had had the book ever since she could remember; she had kept it very clean; there was no torn place or mark in it; but the page of *Peter and his Pig* was brown and worn round the edges. It was her favourite picture. Whenever she looked at it she wanted to make up stories. She had made one long story about it: how people were not kind to Peter and he had no one to love him but his pig, and how they both ran away together by that far off road that went over the hill and saw all the beautiful things on the other side. She liked this book better than her new books. She stood it up on her chest and looked into the picture. But to-day it had no meaning; it suggested nothing. Then she looked away again beyond the edges of the pear branches, where two great masses of white cloud were floating in the blue; they dazzled her eyes so she closed them.

Presently she made a story that one of those clouds was a ship and she was sailing in it (she had never seen the sea or a ship, but she was always making stories about them), and, as she sailed, she came at last to an island. The ship stopped there. And on the edge of the shore was a lady standing, dressed in beautiful clothes, all gold and silver. When she stepped on to the shore, the lady came up to her, and bowed to her, and said, 'I am Queen Victoria; who are you?'

And Rebekah answered her: 'I am the little Queen Victoria of South Africa.'

And they bowed to each other.

(The child under the tree moved her head very slightly, without opening her eyes.)

The Queen asked her where she came from. She said, 'From a country far away from here: not such a *very* nice country! Things are not always nice there – only sometimes they are.'

The Queen said, 'I have many islands that belong to me: but this island belongs to no one; why don't you come and live here? No one will ever scold you here, and you can do just what you like.'

Rebekah said, 'I should like it very much; but I must first go and fetch my books out of the ship.' And when she had brought her books, she said to the Queen, 'Here is a little box of presents I have got for all the people who live on the farm where I used to live; for my father and my mother and the servants and the little Kaffirs – and even old Ayah. Would you please give it to them as you go past?' And the Queen said she would; and she said, 'Good-bye, Little Queen Victoria!' And Rebekah said, 'Good-bye, Big Queen Victoria!' and they bowed to each other; and the old Queen went away in the ship in which she had come.

Then she was all alone on her island. (She had never seen an island except a lump of ground in the furrow, with some thyme and forget-me-nots growing on it; but when she grew up she found she had pictured that island just as a real island might have been!) The island had many large trees and bushes, and the grass and thyme and forget-me-nots grew down to the water's edge. She walked a little way, and she came to a river with trees on each side, and on it were two swans swimming, with their long white necks bent. She had had a book with the picture of a swan swimming in a lake, and she had always thought she must die of joy if she should see a real swan swimming up and down; and here were two!

35

A little further, on the bank of the river, there was a little house standing. It was as high in proportion to her as grown-up people's houses are in proportion to them. The doors were just high enough for her to go in and out at, and all things fitted her. One room was covered with books from the floor to the ceiling, with a little empty shelf for her own books, and there was a microscope on the table like her father's which she was never allowed to touch; but this one was hers!

Outside, in the garden, there were little rakes and spades that came as high as her shoulder. (Rebekah had always had to dig with a man's spade that made her arms ache.) At the side of the house there were all the things lying one uses for building houses; and a pile of bricks; and a bit of bare ground where you could make as much mud as you liked and make more bricks. But she hadn't time to stay and make bricks then. She went on further.

Presently she came to a place where the trees hung very low down over the water, and the grass was very thick; and there, from a large white bush, hanging right over, and nearly touching the water, she saw a snow-white pod, nearly as long as her arm. It was like a pea pod, but it was covered all over with a white, frosted silver. She reached down over the edge and tried to pick it. It was very heavy; at last she broke it off, and carried it away in her pinafore, and she sat on a bank with it on her lap. She pressed with her finger all up and down the joint, and slowly the pod cracked and cracked, and opened from one end to the other, like a mimosa pod does.

And there, lying inside it, like the seeds lie inside the pod of a mimosa tree – was a little baby! It was quite pink and naked. It was as long in proportion to her, as a Kaffir woman's new baby is in proportion to a Kaffir woman, when she first finds it. She tried to lift it out: but it was tied to the pod like the mimosa seeds are, with a little curled-up string. She broke the string and lifted it out, then she wrapped it up in her pinafore and skirt and put its head on her arm and carried it home.

(The book which was still standing up against her knee, here fell over softly into the breast of the child under the pear tree.)

When she got it home she fed it with milk from a tiny bottle

36

as one feeds a hand-lamb, and she wrapped it up in a soft white shawl, and put it on her bed and lay down beside it. She held it close against her with one arm, and stroked its hair softly with the other hand.

'Go to sleep, my baby,' she said; 'you must be very tired this first day. The world is so large. To-morrow you can see all the things, and I'll tell you about them.'

'If you should wake in the night, my baby,' she said presently, 'and hear anything, don't be afraid: just call to me. I'll be close by. And, if you hear the clock ticking, *don't* think it means any of those dreadful things – it doesn't! I'll stop it if it makes you sad. And, if you want to see the angels, then just shut your eyes and press on them *hard* with your two fingers, like this – ' (The child under the tree moved her hand as though to raise it to her eyes, but did not) – 'Those black things with the light all round which you see going round and round when you press your eyes, are the angels' heads; just like it says in the hymn:–

And through the hours of darkness keep
Their watch around my bed.[10]

'They are good angels, though they are black in the middle. I always used to see them when I was a little girl, and I pressed my eyes. I'll put a chocolate stick under your pillow, that you can find it and suck it if you feel lonely. *Don't* be sorry you are come into the world, my baby. *I* will take care of you!'

She was going to rise from the bed, then she remembered other things that had to be said, and lay down again.

'When you are grown older, I'll teach you the multiplication table and spelling, because you can't grow up if you don't know these things. I know how bad it is to learn them; I had to when I was little, and so at last I grew up.

'Kaffirs grow up without learning tables or spelling; that's why it would be nice to be a Kaffir. If you've something hard to learn, pray God to help you: sometimes he does and sometimes he doesn't. If he doesn't, it's because you've prayed wrong; but it's no use praying again on that same day, especially if it's hot; – wait till the next.'

Again there was a long pause.

'My baby, I shall *never* call *you* "a strange child"! You can climb trees and tear your clothes; but, if you find any birds' nests, you mustn't take the eggs; you can just put your hand in and feel; and, if it's a very little nest, you must only put one finger in. Especially cock-o-veet's eggs[11] you must *not* take! Kaffir boys take birds' eggs.'

Again there was a pause.

'My baby, shall I tell you a little story? It's one I made myself, and a rather nice little story:–

'Once there was a little girl, and she went for a walk in the bush. And when she had gone a little way, a cock-o-veet came flying up to her and took hold of her pinafore by the corner with its beak. And the little girl said, "Cock-o-veet, dear, what is it?"

'And the cock-o-veet said, "Make your hand like a little round nest."

'So she made it so — so!' (The child as she lay under the tree with her closed eyes drew the fingers of her right hand together and made a hollow.)

'And the cock-o-veet sat down in her hand; and when it got up, there — was — a little — real — blue — egg — lying there!

'And the little girl said, "O, cock-o-veet!"

'And the cock-o-veet said: "Put the egg in my nest, and I will sit on it and make a little bird come out, for you!" And the cock-o-veet showed the little girl where her nest was; and she put the egg in; and the cock-o-veet sat down on it, and said "Good-bye; I'll call you when it comes out."

'And when she had gone further, she saw some monkeys sitting up in the high trees, little, long-tail monkeys; and they put their hands out to her. And she looked up and said, "O, little monkeys, what do you want?"

'And they said, "Come up in the trees and have tea with us."

'And she said, "What kind of tea do you have, O monkeys?"

'And they said, "Nam-nams and Kaffir plums."[12]

'So she climbed up and sat with them on a branch, and they gave her of their nam-nams and Kaffir plums with their little black hands, and she gave them some cakes out of a little bag she had with her.

'And when they had finished the monkeys kissed her, and she

kissed them, and she climbed down and went on.

'And presently she came to a place where some very large rocks were lying deep in the bush, and the trees were hanging over them, and it was dark under the rock. And the little girl thought it looked rather like a tiger's sleeping-place!

'And when she looked under the rock, there *was* a great tiger lying! And she said, "O tiger!"

'And the tiger winked with its eyes – so!

'And she said, "I'm rather frightened of you, Mr Tiger!"

'But the tiger said, "Come here!"

'So she came.

'And the tiger said, "You can just play being my cub if you like!"

'So she lay down by the tiger, and the tiger rolled her over and made believe to bite her.

'And the tiger said, "Cubbie, would you like to sleep a little? You look rather tired." And it made a place for her between its front legs, where she could lie down with her head on its side, and it was nice and soft.

'And the tiger said, "If the flies trouble you, I'll just switch them away with my tail!"

'And the little girl said, "I'll just leave my little bag of cakes open so that if you like you can help yourself while I'm asleep."

'And she went to sleep on the tiger. And when she woke the tiger licked all over her face and said, "Good-bye"; and she went on.

'And by and by, as she was going up a very steep road right up on the mountain, there was a lion standing right before her.

'And the little girl said, "O Mr Lion!"

'And he said, "Come up to me!"

'So she came up; and he rubbed his head against her pinafore and she rubbed her head in his stiff curls.

'And the lion said, "Aren't you afraid to come walking in the bush alone?"

'And she said, "Oh no!"

'And he yawned.

'And she said, "Don't you open your mouth so *very* wide please! It's so *very* big!"

'And he said, "I'm only yawning a little; it's nothing."

'And the little girl gave him some of her cakes. She said, "I've made them myself."

'He licked his mouth and said they were nice cakes; and he said he would walk home with her. She said there was no need; because perhaps the people at the farm house mightn't quite like it; but that if ever he had a thorn in his foot he must just let her know and she'd take it out. He said he hadn't a thorn just then, but he'd let her know when he had. So they rubbed their heads against each other, and she went away.'

(The mouth of the child under the tree was drawn in at the corners as if half smiling, a quiet smile.)

'Then the little girl went down the mountain and into her father's garden. And, just as she was going in at the gate under the dam wall, she heard something go puff – puff – puff! And she looked round, and, there, just by her, was a great puff-adder[13] sitting up! And she said, "O, Puff-puffie!"

'And the puff-adder said, "Come with me, my dear!"

'And the little girl said, "But Puff-puffie, I'm rather afraid!"

'And the puff-adder said, "Don't be, my dear; *I* never bite little girls!" And she took the little girl to a hole in the wall, where all her little puff-adders were. And she said, "You can put your hand in and take a few out. They've all got little poison bags, but they don't use them. They only eat grass and sand; and they like a little drop of milk now and then when they can get it."

'And the little girl put her hand in and took out the little puff-adders, till her pinafore was full.

'And she said, "I shall not forget to bring them a little drop of milk when I have any!" And she put them back in the hole, and she wished good afternoon to the puff-adder, and the puff-adder wished her good afternoon and went to sleep under a stone.

'And then the little girl went down further in the garden; and she hadn't gone very far when she saw a great cobra lying on the grass, with his bright eyes looking at her.

'And she said, "O Mr Cobra!"

'And he said, "Good afternoon, my dear. Won't you take me on your lap and warm me a little? I'm so cold to-day!"

'So she held out her pinafore and the cobra climbed in: he

made her pinafore quite full. And she walked to the sod wall with him and sat down on the top, where the sun could shine on him, and she sang to the cobra; and he went to sleep in her lap. – And that's the end of the story.'

(The child under the tree seemed to be dropping asleep also; her lips had ceased to move, and her breath came evenly, but her mind went on.)

'You know that's only a story, my baby. You can't really go into the bush and do so with all the animals. They don't understand – yet. Perhaps, if you could talk to them – from a long way off; – so that they knew what you meant – ? – My father brought a tiger down from the bush once, that they had caught with a trap. I was sorry for him because he was shut up in a cage, and looked so sad. So I saved my meat for him at dinner, and I took it out to him when the others were asleep; his eyes were quite nearly shut and his head was on his feet. But just when I put my hand in with the meat he jumped up; he tried to bite me. I didn't tell anyone.

'Only dogs understand. If a great dog comes at you, my baby, don't you run away. Just say "Sibby! Sibby! Sibby!" and make – so – with your fingers; say "P-o-o-r dog, *p-o-o-r*, P-O-O-R little Sibby!" Even if he's big, you can say "little"; dogs always like to be called "little." Even if he's got his mouth on a side – so –, and you can see his one tooth; don't be afraid; just stand and talk to him. He'll understand. But other things don't. – The best thing is to feed them.

'My baby, was it a nice little story I've told you? If I tell you a secret, you mustn't tell anyone else! I'm a person that makes stories! I write *books*! When I was little I used to scribble them in a copybook with a stick, when I didn't know how to write. But when I grew up I learnt to write; – I wrote real books, a whole room full! I've written a book about birds, and about animals, and about the world; and one day I'm going to write a book something like the Bible. If you like to make up stories, I shall never let anyone laugh at *you*, when you walk up and down and talk to yourself. I know you *must*.

'There are some stories I didn't make that I like too. There's one I like best of all. Shall I tell it to you?'

(The child under the tree moved her arms a little as if drawing something closer to her.)

'It's rather a hard story because it's a grown-up people's story; I heard it one Sunday afternoon; my father read it to my mother. They thought I couldn't understand, but I did. I don't know if I tell it right, because I only heard it once, but I often looked at the picture. I'll make it as easy as I can.

'You see, it's called *What Hester Durham Lived For*[14] – Hester Durham was a woman, and she sat by the table talking; and the minister came and talked with her. And she said, "Oh, I wish I was dead! My husband isn't very kind to me, and my boy, whom I loved so much, is dead; and now I wish I was dead too."

'And the Clergyman (that is a Minister) said to her, "Oh, you mustn't say that; perhaps one day you'll have something to do for someone."

'And so the lady went away to India; – that's a land far away where black people live – and the black soldiers (they call them Sepoys) wanted to kill them. They came all round the house, calling and yelling, with swords and sticks. They were only women and children there; and all of them were very frightened; even the old black Ayah. But Hester Durham was not afraid. In the picture they are all standing round her and some of them have caught hold of her dress, and some are lying on the ground close to her; and you can see the men's faces outside, with their eyes very big, wanting to come in and kill them all, and their mouths open, screaming! Then it says in the Book: – "*Alone, like a rock in a raging sea; Hester Durham stood there.*" They hadn't been *so* afraid, because she was there to comfort them. And at last the Sepoys did come in, and killed them all; but – "*to comfort those frail women and children in their last hour of despair, that was what Hester Durham lived for*" – those are the words I heard my father read. It's rather a difficult story; but you'll know what it means when you're grown up, when you are five years old – I did – though it is difficult.

'I can teach you many things, my baby; poems; there's a nice one:

The Assyrian came down———[15]

'And another:

> Like mist on the mountains,
> Like ships on the sea——

'But the nicest of all is about a woman. The Romans came and they took away her country and they beat her till the blood ran off her back on to the ground, and they were cruel to her daughters.[16] The Romans were people who took other peoples' countries; and she got into a chariot and her two daughters and her long hair flying in the wind; and under the tree sat an old man with a long white beard; – and he said –

> "Rome shall perish; write that word
> In the blood that she hath spilt——"'

(The child under the pear tree with her eyes still fast closed raised her right hand, and her lips moved making a low sound.)

> '"Rome, for Empire far renown
> Tramps on a thousand States;
> Soon her pride shall kiss the ground:
> Hark! – The Gaul is at her gates!"'

(The child under the tree lifted her hand higher and waved it dramatically with her eyes still closed.)

'And the Gauls did come; and they knocked at the gates, and they burnt it down. "Hark! – The Gaul is at her gates!" – I'm glad they burnt it, aren't you?'

(The child's hand dropped.)

'It's a long poem. I'll teach it you. I could understand it all, except "For-Empire" and "far-renown". – I don't know what "far-renown" is – or "for-empire – "'

(The child under the tree knit her forehead a little.)

'Grown-up people's things are nicer than children's. I didn't like *Jane Taylor's Hymns for Infant Minds*.[17] You'll never have to learn them. The Bible is nice, especially about Elijah,[18] and some texts; one beautiful one; – "And instead of the thorn tree shall come up the fir tree; and instead of the briar shall come up the myrtle-tree."[19] It's just like water going – so – !! But Miss Plumtree's Bible stories[20] are horrid! My mother used to read them to me.'

(The child under the tree turned her head a little to one side and bent it, as though bringing it nearer to something that lay on her arm.)

'My baby, do you know who Charles is? – He's the boy who always plays with me. You won't mind if I love him more than you, because I've known him so very long. He always tells me stories, and I tell him stories, and we walk up and down together. He's a little older than me. He's not a *real* boy, you know! I made him up. He is the Prince Consort of South Africa, and I am the Queen.

'I don't like *real* boys. We had two come to visit us once: they were my cousins. Frank was the biggest. Before they came I meant to play with them and show them all my things; but afterwards I didn't: I wouldn't even show them my flat stone. Frank laughed at me and called me Goody-no-shoes. Well, I didn't mind that so much, it's not so bad as to be called a "Tomboy", or "a strange child!" – but he was so unkind to the cat! He held her up by her tail. I don't like cats, they eat birds; but you can't do *that* to them! He used to come after me when I wanted to be alone, and say, "Ha, ha, Miss! I've found you!" and he said I'd have to marry him when I grew up, – but I said I never would.'

She paused for a long while.

'I liked him better than John-Ferdinand – that was his brother. One day John-Ferdinand saw the little Kaffir maid break the churn stick, and he went and told old Ayah; and old Ayah beat her. Frank and I saw it too, but we didn't say anything. Frank said I ought to say to him –

You tell tale tit,
Your tongue shall be slit,
And every dog in the town
Shall have a little bit!

'It wasn't such a very nice little poem; my mother said I mustn't say it up. I just tell you what Frank said. He knew many other little poems –

Four and twenty tailors
Went to catch a snail –

44

'and

    Boobee – Boobee! Black-face!

'They are not such very nice poems; but rather funny; and you can say them up if you like, I won't mind. He could make wagons – but I was glad when they went away. I don't like live boys: they are something like Kaffirs. Jan married Mietje our Kaffir maid, and he used to beat her – I'm glad I'm not a Kaffir man's wife.

'My baby, I'm so glad you are a little girl. I'll make you a pair of thick trousers to climb trees in; these white ones tear so when you slide down, and then the people call you "Tom-boy"!

'Now put your arms tight round your mother's neck, and hold mother tight.'

(The child under the tree turned yet slightly more on to her side, and moved her left arm as though she were drawing something nearer to her.)

'Mother will tell you just one little story before you go to sleep, a very easy one.

'Once there was a little blue egg in a nest, and the mother bird sat on it. And one day out came a bird; it had no feathers and its eyes were shut, and the mother bird sat on it. By and by the feathers began to come and the eyes opened. And one night, when the mother bird was fast asleep in the nest and the little bird was under her, it put out its head from under the mother's wing and looked. And what do you think it saw? – It saw all the stars shining! – And it sat up and looked at them!

'That's the end of the story.' She paused for a while.

(The child under the tree knit her brows a little, and her hand moved softly up and down on her bosom.)

'My baby, I'm so sorry I have to give you food out of a bottle – Kaffir women have milk for their babies – and cows and sheep too – but I am like the birds.'

(She moved her hand over her little flat breast.)

'I'm so sorry. Now go to sleep, my baby. Put your arms round mother's neck. You must always try to be a good little girl: I always did when I was little – at least – I didn't always – but you must, please. Now go to sleep. Mother will sing you a little song.'

(The child under the tree made a queer piping little sound in her throat, and half-formed words came from her lips.)

London's burning!
London's burning!
Fire! Fire!
Bring some water! Bring some water!
London's burning!
London's burning!

(The song died away, and the child under the tree lay quite motionless; but her dream still went on.)

She thought when the baby had gone to sleep, that she got softly off the bed and went out. The evening air was blowing over the island, and it was near sunset. She went to the side of the house where the building materials lay. She was going to build a play room for the baby. She rolled up her sleeves and dug a foundation and filled it with stones. (She had seen the workmen build the wagon house.) Then she mixed mud, and took off her shoes and socks, and danced in it. (She had seen the Kaffirs treading the mud to build the wagon house, but she had never been allowed to help.) Then she began to build. She took the bricks in one hand and the trowel in the other; she threw the bricks round in one hand and cut off the rough points with the trowel, as the workmen did. Then she placed each brick carefully on the layer of mortar, and tap-tapped them with the end of the handle of the trowel to see if they were quite straight.

When the little wall was two layers high, she looked round. The sun was setting on the island, and over the trees a strange soft evening light shone. There was a pink glow in the sky, and it reflected itself on everything. She stood perfectly still, holding the trowel in her hand, and looked at it. The swans were swimming up and down in the quiet water, far away, with their necks bent. They left a long snow-white mark in the water, like the swans in the picture.

The swan swam in a silvery lake.
Well swam the swan!

A spasm of delight thrilled up the spine of the child under the pear-tree. When a full-grown woman, long years afterwards she could always recall that island, the little house, the bricks, the wonderful light over earth and sky and the swans swimming on the still water.

After a time she half opened her eyes and looked up. Above her was the pear-tree, with its stiff branches of dull green leaves. Slowly she raised herself into a sitting posture, and looked round.

All about lay the parched yellow grass, and the little dried peach-trees, with their shrivelled leaves and dropping yellow peaches. Everything was brown and dry: she stretched herself and yawned.

Then she stood up. Suddenly she saw a herd of little pigs a short way off, feeding under the peach trees. They had got in through a hole in the wall and were eating the fallen fruit among the grass. They would soon make their way up to the flower garden.

With a shout and whoop she rushed off after them, waving her kappie at them by one string. The little pigs squeaked and grunted and scattered in all directions. She chased them till she had got them in a herd all together, and drove them out through one of the gaps in the sod wall. Then she stood on the wall and shouted frantically after them, still waving her kappie, though they were all running as fast as they could, with their little curled-up tails. She stood on the wall and waved till they disappeared behind the kraals.

The severest heat of the afternoon was now past, and there was a certain mellow haziness beginning to creep into the afternoon air. She shaded her eyes with her hand and looked away over the flat below the homestead, where the thorn trees grew. There seemed a kind of soft, yellow, transparent veil over it all; and there were little gnats in the air. Presently, as she stood dreamily gazing, she saw some figures moving far away in the flat below the house, near the great dam with the willow-trees. The foremost figure carried something on its shoulders; it looked like Long Jan the Kaffir: then came her father, and then two Kaffir boys with something over their shoulders that looked like spades. She could not see well; they were so far away and the soft yellow haze made things dreamy. They passed through the new lands; and then they went out of sight, behind the great willow-trees which grew round the dam.

She stood still, looking out at them very drowsily thinking of nothing in particular, and hardly noting them.

Suddenly a small shrill voice called from the back steps of the house, 'Get down from that wall, child, will you! Standing there with nothing on your head! You'll be burnt as black as a Kaffir before your mother gets up. Put your kappie on!'

It was old Ayah, who had come to the back door to throw water into the pigs' wash.

Rebekah climbed from the wall on the garden side, and walked away; but she did not put her kappie on: she tied it round her waist by its long strings, and walked back to the pear tree. Everything seemed a little bald and empty; she had no wish to make more stories, and there was nothing to do. It seemed to her, all at once, that it was a very long afternoon. Then there came back to her the picture of her mother lying in the bed with the baby's head on her arm, which she had been trying to put from her all day. She saw the embroidered wrist of her mother's nightdress; and she saw her mother drawing up the cover to shield the baby's head. She tried to think of something else.

There was a strange little blind footpath among the grass under the pear tree on the left side. It was a few feet long, trodden hard, and flat, and led to nothing. She had made it by walking up and down there when she and Charles made stories and talked.

She began to walk up and down in it now, rather dragging her feet. By and by she and Charles began to talk; she talked in a quite audible voice, now for Charles, and then for herself. They told each other no stories, but they began to discuss a little about the house of stramonium[21] stalks they were going to build; he said what he thought was the best way of making the roof would be with stramonia branches, she said she thought peach branches would be stronger and better. But neither had much of interest to say that afternoon.

It began to get cooler now. The large white butterflies that had sat with folded wings during the great heat, were beginning to hover over the brown grass; and there was a faint movement in the air, which showed that the evening cool was going to begin.

Then, as she walked, her eye caught sight of a white ball sticking on the bark of the pear tree. She walked round to the stem to look at it, and broke a bit of dry bark off to get it out. It was a soft fluffy ball. She put it on the ground, and opened it carefully with two sticks, bending over it, her knees drawn up almost to her chest, and all her little white knickerbockers showing. Inside of it were little grey things that looked like tiny spiders' eggs. She examined it carefully and long, sticking her under lip out over the upper. It was very curious. She was going to examine it more closely, when she caught sight of a row of black ants walking across her own footpath, like a file of little soldiers, one after the other; each one had a pink egg in its mandibles. A few inches farther was another line of little black ants returning across the footpath, probably to fetch more of the eggs which were in some nest hidden in the grass. She wheeled round, still on her heels, with a hand on each knee to balance herself, and watched them closely. Presently a huge ant, like those running up and down the stem of the pear tree, dashed into the path from the grass and seized one of the tiny ants that were carrying the eggs. The ant dropped the egg. The large ant held it exactly in the middle with its large nippers. In an instant she started up, drew her lips tighter, and seized a stick of straw, and tried to divide them; but the large one held so tightly she found she would crush both. She took two withered leaves and softly tried to separate them. The large one caught the leaf with its nippers and the small one got free; it ran away to look for its dropped egg. The large one was clinging angrily to the leaf, and trying to bite it. She bent intently over it, watching it.

Suddenly she looked up. She had a curious feeling that someone was looking at her! She looked round and up into the pear tree, still balancing herself carefully in her half sitting position; there was nothing there but the green dried leaves, and all about nothing but the long brown grass, in some places partly trodden down, in others still standing upright.

She looked back at the ants. Then she glanced round again inquiringly. Two feet from the round spot in the grass which she had trodden down to lie in, was the head of a large yellow cobra. Most of its body was hidden in the grass; but its head was out: and it was watching her. It was the colour of the grass, pale yellow with brown marks. Had it been there all the afternoon? She stood softly upright and stared at it. It looked at her with its glittering unblinking eyes. Then it began to move. Krinkle! krinkle! krinkle! It drew its long body out over the grass, with a sound like a lady walking in a stiff starched print dress. She gazed at it in fixed horror, motionless.

She was not afraid of snakes. When she was three years old she had carried one home in her pinafore, as a great treasure, and been punished for doing so. Since she understood what they were, she was not afraid of them, but they had become a nightmare to her. They spoiled her world. Krinkle, krinkle, krinkle! – it moved away over the grass towards a hole in the sod wall, winding its long six feet of body after it.

She seized her book and ran up the path through the orchard. According to rule, she should have gone to the house and called people to look for it and kill it. But she ran quickly through the flower garden and up the steps on to the front stoep,[22] then she stood still. Her heart was beating so she could hear it; she had a sense of an abandoned wickedness somewhere: it was almost as if *she herself* were a snake, and had gone krinkle! krinkle! krinkle! over the grass. She had a sense of all the world being abandonedly wicked; and a pain in her left side. When her heart had stopped throbbing quite so loud, she opened the door slowly and went into the large front room.

No one had remembered to open the shutters that afternoon though it was almost sunset, it was dusky in the room even with the door open. On the wall hung two great framed pictures of Queen Victoria and the Prince Consort, in regal dress. She always played the Queen was herself, and the Prince, Charles; and once, when no one was about, she had put a chair on the side table and climbed up on to it, and kissed her own hand, and put it high up where she could touch Charles' face with it.

But to-night she did not look at them. The chair in which her

50

mother always sat stood empty beside the little work table, and the footstool before it was covered with dust. She opened the drawer of the table and took out a calico duster and carefully dusted the chair and stool. When she had put the duster back, she opened another drawer and took out a spelling book. She drew her own little square wooden footstool between her mother's chair and the open door and sat down on it, with her spelling book in her hand. She began to learn a short column of spelling which she should have learnt in the morning. She held up the book before her so that the light from the door might fall on the page, and spelt out –

'T-h-e-i-r – their.'

She repeated it a few score of times; then she went on to –

'T-h-o-s-e – those.'

– and then turned to her multiplication table. It was printed on the cover of the book. She was learning six-times. She repeated slowly over and over to herself –

'Six times six is – thirty-six,
And six times six is – thirty-six.'

The soft, fading evening light was creeping over the orange trees outside the door.

She drawled slower –

'And, six times six is – thirty-six,
And, six times six is – thirty-six,
And, six times six is – thirty-six,
And, six times six – is – thirty-seven,
And, six times six – is – thirty-seven.'

She repeated it slowly about a hundred times, sometimes right, and sometimes wrong, looking out dreamily all the while over the book, through the open door, her mind almost a complete blank; then she paused. In a moment, something had flashed on her! She knew now what those figures had meant which she had seen walking down in the flat in the afternoon when she stood on the sod wall. She knew now what it was Long Jan was carrying; she knew why her father walked behind him, and the two Kaffir boys had spades over their shoulders. In an instant, she knew well, and with an absolute certainty, that if she went down to the great dam behind the willow trees beyond the new lands, she would find there a little mound of earth, and that the baby from the spare room would be under it. All day she had not let herself think of that baby since old Ayah had driven her out of the room. She knew, also, something else; she knew at that moment – vaguely, but quite certainly – something of what birth and death mean, which she had not known before. She would never again look for a new little baby, or expect to find it anywhere; vaguely but quite certainly something of its genesis had flashed on her.

She stood up in the quickly darkening room; put her multiplication book back into the drawer, and walked straight to the door that opened into the dining room, and closed it behind her.

In the dining room also it was getting dark now, though it looked towards the west and the window was open, and here also it was very quiet. This was generally the noisy time of the day, when there was a stir and a bustle everywhere: her mother was generally giving out rations, and the herds and maids who had come from the huts to fetch their food stood about the storehouse door outside laughing and talking. The Kaffir maids who worked in the house were generally chatting loudly in the kitchen; and the little Kaffirs, who might not approach at any other time, often stood about the kitchen steps waiting for their mothers; and from the milking kraal you could hear the men shouting to the cows and calves, and calling to one another; and the dogs felt the excitement and barked, and above everything could always be heard old Ayah's voice, in a shrill, small key, giving orders everywhere which no one ever obeyed. But to-night it was all quiet: you could only hear the lowing of the cows and the bleating of the sheep. The men hardly shouted. The rations had been given out early in the morning, and the little Kaffirs had been told not to come about the back door.

Through the great square window the twilight was beginning to come in. She would not go to her mother's room, and she had nowhere else to go. She sat down on a deal bench without a back, that stood against the wall. No one came to light the candles; and you could see the dim outlines of the tall clock in the corner, and the wooden chairs and tables standing out as shadows from the white-washed walls. Presently, as it grew quite darker, a bat came in at the window and flapped about from side to side and went out again. Then the room grew pitch dark. Rebekah drew her legs up under her on to the form, and leaned her head back against the white-washed wall.

By and by the two Kaffir maids came in from the milk house, each carrying a bucket of milk. They had a lighted candle. They went through the dining room into the pantry; they were laughing and talking softly; the light from the open pantry door came back into the dining room.

Presently old Ayah came in from the mother's bed room.

'What are you sitting here all alone in the dark for, child?' she said.

She went into the pantry, and came out with a large basin of bread and milk sop, and a little pannikin of pure milk. She set them down on the side of the table next to the bench with a tallow candle beside them, in a low candlestick.

'Why didn't you eat your dinner, little white face?'

Rebekah sat upright; old Ayah pushed the table a little nearer to her, and she began to eat. She had not known before that she was hungry. Now she ate ravenously and drank at the milk out of her pannikin.

Old Ayah went back into the pantry and scolded the maids in Dutch because the wooden milk-pail was leaking. Very soon the maids and old Ayah came back to the dining room, and rested the pail on the end of the dining table to examine what was gone wrong. One of the maids held the lighted candle, while the other was chewing tallow to put in the cracks.

'What's the baby like, old Ayah?' asked the maid holding the light, as old Ayah examined the leak.

'A fine child,' said old Ayah, without looking up. 'She'd make four of *that* child when she was born. Its hands are nearly as large as hers now.'

The maid who was chewing the tallow pressed some down on the open seam.

'Where has *she* been all day?' she asked, nicking her head at Rebekah.

'Oh, God knows!' said old Ayah; 'I've hardly seen her. You might as well try to keep your eye on a mier-kat[23] among its holds as on *that* child.'

They talked of her to her face as if she were a stone wall.

Rebekah kept on eating her supper, gazing straight into her basin, and taking large mouthfuls.

'Look at her now!' said the first Kaffir maid, 'How she eats! She's trying to swallow the spoon!'

'Sy's 'n snaaks se kind!' said old Ayah. ('She's a strange child!')

Rebekah kept on eating steadily and looking into the basin. It hurt her so that they talked of her.

When they had done stopping the hand-pail, the two maids went to the kitchen, and old Ayah went back to the mother's room. Immediately they were gone Rebekah pushed her basin with what was left in it from her; and leaned back on the bench. She drew up one leg, leaned her elbow on the bench and rested her head against the whitewashed wall. She was very tired. She watched the tallow candle fixedly; it was burning up red, and flickering a little as the moths and night flies that came in through the open window fluttered round it. It seemed so long since she had got up in the morning. It was her bedtime, but no one came to tell her to go to bed.

Then she began to watch the wick of the tallow candle more fixedly as it burnt larger and redder. She pressed two of her fingers on her eyes, half closing them; then she saw two candles; she took them away, and there was only one. She wondered how that was, and tried it again. When she moved one finger a little, the one light went up slowly and stood over the other; she moved the other finger and they came so close, they were almost one. She took her hand away and looked at the candle, half-closing her eyes; she did not see two candles now, but only four long rays of red light, the two higher ones darker and the two lower lighter. She was slowly getting very interested in it.

She held up her hand and let the light shine through her fingers; the hand made a long dark shadow on the wall to the left of the room. Why was the shadow so much longer than the hand, she wondered, and why did it fall just where it did? She moved her hand and watched the shadow move. If only one were grown up, one would know all about these things! She dropped her hand on her side. Perhaps, even grown-up people didn't know all. – Perhaps only God knew what lights and shadows were!

She lay still watching the candle. The wick had burnt so long it was beginning to droop and turn over a little on one side. The next morning she would get up early before anyone was up, and begin learning her multiplication table and spelling: perhaps she would know it before evening. She would not play once the whole day, or make up stories. She would learn the whole day. It would all help to make you grow up quickly, and know everything!

It was half past eight now. Her eyelids began to droop; she only kept them open with a strong effort: she could not bear to go to sleep; but her head bowed, nodding even though she leaned it against the wall.

Suddenly she sat bolt upright; her eyes opened widely. They seemed to grow larger and larger at each instant. She listened intently. From her mother's bedroom there came a sound, a loud, wailing cry. Rebekah got off the bench and stood rigid and upright. Her small sharp cut face, pale before, became now a deadly white. There was silence for a moment; then another cry, then another, and another, each louder and longer than before. Her hands doubled into fists; she turned a bright pink. The crying went on. She raised her chin; her throat swelled till it looked like the full throat of a tiny woman; the veins stood out like little whipcords. She drew in the corners of her mouth. Again there was a cry, but this time, fainter. A dark purple flush came up over her forehead; her eyelids drooped. She rushed out at the door, striking herself against it. She flew up the dark passage to the door of her mother's room. She tried to reach the handle, but it was too high. With hands and feet she struck the panels of the door till they rebounded.

'Let me in! Let me in! I say, let me in! I will – I – will – I say – I will come in!'

The baby inside had left off crying.

Rebekah heard nothing but the surging of the blood in her

own ears. Old Ayah opened the door.

'Let me in! Let me in! – I will come in!'

Old Ayah tried to put her back with her hand.

'Leave me alone! – Leave me alone!' she cried. 'You are killing it like the other one! Leave me alone I say! Leave me alone!'

Old Ayah tried to hold her fast, but she caught the Hottentot woman's skirts and twisted them round with her arms and legs.

The little mother from the bed asked in a sleepy voice what was the matter.

'Don't ask me what is the matter!' cried old Ayah indignantly, in Cape Dutch. 'Ask the Father of all Evil! This child is mad!'

She wrenched her skirts free from Rebekah's grasp, and thrust her into the room. Rebekah stood on the ox skin in the centre of the floor, vibrating from the soles of her feet to her head.

The candle was on a stand beside her mother's bed, and threw its light full on her, as she lay with the baby's head on her arm, and her hand with the white frill thrown across it. On the right side of the great four-poster bed they had pinned up a red cotton quilt, with great lions and palm-trees printed on it, to keep off the draught from the open window; and the quilt reflected a soft red light over the mother and child. In the far right hand corner of the room was Rebekah's own little cot, where she had slept ever since she was born.

'God only does know what possesses this child!' said old Ayah, fixing her twinkling black eyes on Rebekah and talking at her. 'If she were my child, I wouldn't let her come into the house at all, where respectable people live who like to be indoors. I'd just tie her fast with a chain to a monkey post outside, and let her go round and round there. Then she could eat Kaffir beans like a baboon, and climb, and scream as much as she liked!'

'What did you make such a noise for, Rebekah?' the little mother said gently. 'Did you think they were hurting the baby?'

Rebekah said nothing; the blood was leaving her head and running into her heart and she felt faint.

'Twisting a person's clothes almost off their backs! Can't one even wash and dress a child without this little wild thing coming howling, and dancing round one!' Old Ayah smoothed out her crumpled skirt.

'Do you want to see the baby, Rebekah?' asked her mother.

Rebekah walked unsteadily to the foot of the bed and stood beside the great wooden bedpost.

Old Ayah took up the baby's bath and walked out of the room with it, muttering that some children ought to live with the baboons.

'If you would like to come and see the baby, you can climb up,' said her mother drowsily, with half closed eyes.

Rebekah waited a moment, then she clambered softly up on to the bed, and sat down at the foot, half kneeling, with her back against the post. Her mother who was very tired had re-closed her eyes. The baby's red face pressed against the mother's white breast. The light shone on them both.

Rebekah drew up her knees and clasped her arms round them, and sat watching.

'It's drinking, isn't it, eh, mother?' she said at last, very softly.

'Yes,' said her mother, without opening her eyes.

'It's *your* little baby? Eh, mother?' she whispered again softly, after a long pause.

Her mother nodded dreamily.

Rebekah stroked her little skirts down over her knees.

'It *must* drink!' she said after a time. 'It *must* have milk, eh, mother? – It's your little baby, eh, mother?' – she added after a long pause.

But the little mother made no answer; she had dropped away into sleep.

Rebekah sat watching them.

By and by the baby moved its hand which struck out from the white flannel wrapper about it: it opened its fingers slowly; and stretched them out one after the other and closed them up again into a fist. Rebekah watched it intently.

Presently she leaned forward, resting one elbow on the bed, and slowly stretched out her other hand, and with one forefinger touched the hand of the baby. Her mouth quivered; she sat up quickly, and watched them again. She leaned her head back against the post at the foot of the bed and sat gazing at them, her eyes never moving.

At half-past nine old Ayah came in again bringing in the hot water bottle and an etna to warm the gruel during the night.

'My fatherland's force![24] You not in bed yet! Are you going to sit up till morning?'

The mother woke up. 'Have you been sitting here all this while, Rebekah?' she asked gently.

Old Ayah put the warm water bottle at the mother's feet.

'She'd never go to bed if she could help it!' old Ayah muttered. 'It's my belief, if you came in at three o'clock in the morning, you'd find her sitting up in her bed, talking to the spiders in the dark. She'd talk to the stars if she hadn't anything else to talk to, just not to go to sleep like other children!'

'Mother,' said Rebekah in a very slow, clear voice, stroking down her knees; 'Mother, – will you let me have *your* baby to sleep by me for a little while?'

She spoke each word slowly and distinctly, as one who repeats what they have carefully prepared.

'No, dear,' said the mother, 'it's too small; you can't have it to sleep with you yet.'

'Have it to sleep with you!' said old Ayah. 'I should think not! Why, you'd kill it!'

'I should take great care of it,' said Rebekah, very slowly, still stroking her knees, her eyes very wide open and fixed steadily on her mother; 'I wouldn't lie on it, nor let it fall. I only want to take care of it, and teach it.'

'Teach it! Teach it, indeed!' said old Ayah, tucking in the mother's feet; 'You just want to teach her to be a naughty Tomboy like you. We'll take care she doesn't play with you, and learn all your wild ways.'

Rebekah stroked her knees more heavily. 'I didn't mean to teach her anything wrong,' she said slowly; – 'I wasn't even going to teach her to hate *you*.'

'Hate me! – Rather! – I should think not! What next! Why should you teach her to hate me?'

Rebekah turned her eyes on to old Ayah and gazed at her. 'Because *I* hate you so!' she said.

'Don't quarrel with her any more, Ayah,' said the mother;

'the child really doesn't know what she is talking about; she's half-asleep already. – Come, get off the bed, Rebekah, and go and undress. – You can't have the baby.'

But Rebekah sat motionless. Slowly the tears gathered under her eyelids. She closed them, and the tears lay in large heavy drops under the lashes without falling.

She raised her face with its closed eyes to the canopy of the bed.

'Oh, I can't bear it! – I can't bear it!' she said slowly. 'What shall I do? – What shall I do? – Oh, what shall I do?' She moved her upturned face with its closed eyes slowly from side to side. – 'I meant to love it so! Oh I meant – All my things – my Peter book – all my stones – .Oh, if you will let me love it!' The bed shook, but no tears fell from the closed eyes. She stroked her knees with both hands. 'It's not any use! – you see – it's not any use! – I have tried! – I have tried! – Oh, I wish I was dead – I wish I was dead – I wish I was dead!'

Even old Ayah looked at her in silence.

'The child is really three-parts asleep,' said the mother. 'It's been a long trying day for her, running about with no one to look after her. She is but a baby, though she is so old-fashioned. Get off the bed, Rebekah, and old Ayah will undress you.'

But Rebekah felt her way to the foot of the bed and slid down:

'I can undress myself,' she heaved.

She stood on the floor in the middle of the room with her eyes still closed, the lids swollen and fastened together and unbuttoned her things one by one, letting them drop on the floor, until she stood there in her little white shift, her small naked shoulders still vibrating. Old Ayah brought her her nightdress.

'Dis 'n snaaks se kind!' she muttered. (''Tis a strange child!')

Rebekah slipped it over her own head, and then, with her hand stretched out, she felt her way to the bed in the corner. She climbed up over the side of the cot and lay down. The long vibrating movement still went on; it was almost as if a man were crying.

'I can't have that,' said the little mother; 'She'll go on with it half the night in her sleep. I know the child. I think she dreams of things. Take the baby and lay it by her just for a little while. It's been a long day, and she's very tired.'

Old Ayah shook her head forebodingly; but she took up the baby, wrapped it in its shawl, and carried it across the room. She turned back the cover and made a place for it beside Rebekah. The child stretched out her arm for its head; the Hottentot woman laid it down on it, and drew the cover up over both. Then she turned and went out, to fetch the gruel and the night-light.

The elder sister slipped her hand under the shawl till she found the baby's hand; she clasped her fingers softly into its tiny fingers, and held them. With the other hand she tried to draw its body up close against her.

Presently there was a queer quavering little sound, as though some one were trying to sing; but nothing came of it; then all was quiet.

When old Ayah came back in fifteen minutes every one in the room was quiet and asleep.

She put the gruel and night light down on the drawers, and came to the bedside to remove the baby. But when she turned down the cover she found the hands of the sisters so interlocked, and the arm of the elder sister so closely round the younger, that she could not remove it without awaking both.

Old Ayah shook her head, and drew the cover up softly. She blew out the candle, and put the night light down on the floor beyond the bed, and walked softly towards the door of the room, with her naked yellow feet, her figure casting a long dark shadow on the wall. When she got to the door as she passed out she turned and looked back. Along the floor the night light shone, casting deep shadows into far corners, especially that in which the two children lay!

But they were all sleeping well.

Gender, Class and Science

The Woman Question (1899)

'The Woman Question' is one of Schreiner's many responses to a set of problems – feminism, evolution, eugenics – that were discussed at length in her intellectual community in London in the 1880s. The article reprinted here was published in two parts in *The Cosmopolitan* (New York) in 1899 and is one of several shorter articles later reworked into *Woman and Labour* (1911, rpt 1978), which Schreiner called her 'sex book' and suffragettes referred to as their 'bible'.

Schreiner writes in an imaginary voice of female experience, a prophetic voice that cuts across differences of culture and time and gives birth to social change as well as to human individuals. The ideological patterns established in this piece also inform *Woman and Labour*: Schreiner uses evolution to rethink the relationship between her own time and a variety of biblical and historical narratives. She presents a related but much more idealistic argument in 'The Boer Woman and the Modern Woman Question' (*Thoughts on South Africa*, 1923) and renders a fictional version in the short story 'Eighteen Ninety-Nine' (see this volume, pp.155–85). Schreiner's evolutionary model is derived from Darwin, her sense of modern women's powerlessness from Herbert Spencer. The thick scientific language in this piece also echoes works on sexuality and eugenics by Schreiner's friends Karl Pearson and Havelock Ellis (see bibliography for related works). Because Schreiner thought modern 'New Women' no longer able to raise children, she cast an ideal of motherhood onto black South African women, without discussing the larger economic and social pattern in which black women are often forced to perform domestic labour for minimal wages in a way that actually wrenches them out of their chosen families. In both the differences it sees between men and women, and those it fails to see between women of different race and class situations, 'The Woman Question' suggests ways in which ideals about women's maternal experience can lead to potentially racist generalisations.

Olive with a young black servant, Kimberley, 1896

Olive with a black woman servant and her baby, on her farm in 1894

I

In that clamour which has arisen in the modern world, where now this, and then that, is demanded for and by large bodies of modern women, he who listens carefully may detect as a keynote, beneath all the clamour, a demand which may be embodied in such a cry as this: *Give us labour and the training which fits for labour! We demand this, not for ourselves, alone, but for the race.*

If this demand be logically expanded, it will take such form as this: Give us labour! For countless ages, for thousands, millions it may be, we have laboured. When first man wandered, the naked, newly-erected savage, and hunted and fought, we wandered with him: each step of his was ours. Within our bodies we bore the race, on our shoulders we carried it; we sought the roots and plants for its food; and, when man's barbed arrow or hook brought the game, our hands dressed it. Side by side, the savage man and the savage woman, we wandered free together and laboured free together. And we were contented!

Then a change came.

We ceased from our wanderings, and, camping upon one spot of earth, again the labours of life were divided between us. While man went forth to hunt, or to battle with the foe who would have dispossessed us of all, we laboured on the land. We hoed the earth, we reaped the grain, we shaped the dwellings, we wove the clothing, we modelled the earthen vessels and drew the lines upon them, which were humanity's first attempt at domestic art; we studied the properties and uses of plants, and our old women were the first physicians of the race, as, often, its first priests and prophets.

We fed the race at our breast, we bore it on our shoulders; through us it was shaped, fed, and clothed. Labour more toilsome and unending than that of man was ours; yet did we never cry out that it was too heavy for us. While savage man lay in the sunshine on his skins, resting, that he might be fitted for war or the chase, or while he shaped his weapons of death, he ate and drank that which our hands had provided for him; and while we knelt over our grindstone, or hoed in the fields, with one child in our womb, perhaps, and one on our back, toiling till the young body was old before its time – did *we* ever cry out that the labour allotted to us was too hard for us? Did we not know that the woman who threw down her burden was as a man who cast away his shield in battle – a coward and a traitor to his race? Man fought – that was his work; we fed and nurtured the race – that was ours. We knew that upon our labours, even as upon man's depended the life and well-being of the people whom we bore. We endured our toil, as man bore his wounds, silently; and we were content.

Then again a change came.

Ages passed, and time was when it was no longer necessary that all men should go to the hunt or the field of war; and when only one in five, or one in ten, or but one in twenty, was needed continually for these labours. Then our fellow-man, having no longer full occupation in his old fields of labour, began to take his share in ours. He too began to cultivate the field, to build the house, to grind the corn (or make his male slaves do it); and the hoe, and the potter's tools, and the thatching-needle, and at last even the grindstones which we first had picked up and smoothed to grind the food for our children, began to pass from our hands into his. The old, sweet life of the open fields was ours no more; we moved within the gates, where the time passes more slowly and the world is sadder than in the air outside; but we had our own work still, and were content.

If, indeed, we might no longer grow the food for our people, we were still its dressers; if we did not always plant and prepare the flax and hemp, we still wove the garments for our race; if we did no longer raise the house walls, the tapestries that covered them were the work of our hands; we brewed the ale, and the simples which were used as medicines we distilled and prescribed; and, close about our feet, from birth to manhood, grew up the children whom we had borne; their voices were always in our ears. At the doors of our houses we sat with our spinning-wheels, and we looked out across the fields that were once ours to labour in – and were contented. Lord's wife, peasant's, or burgher's, we all still had our work to do!

A thousand years ago, had one gone to some great dame,

questioning her why she did not go out a-hunting or a-fighting, or enter the great hall to dispense justice and confer upon the making of laws, she would have answered: 'Am I a fool that you put to me such questions? Have I not a hundred maidens to keep at work at spinning-wheels and needles? With my own hands daily do I not dispense bread to over a hundred folk? In the great hall go and see the tapestries I with my maidens have created by the labour of years, and which we shall labour over for twenty more, that my children's children may see recorded the great deeds of their forefathers. In my store-room are there not salves and simples, that my own hands have prepared for the healing of my household and the sick in the country round? Ill would it go indeed, if when the folk came home from war and the chase of wild beasts, weary or wounded, they found all the womenfolk gone out a-hunting and a-fighting, and none there to dress their wounds, or prepare their meat, or guide and rule the household! Better far might my lord and his followers come and help us with our work, than that we should go and help them! You are surely bereft of all wit.'

And the burgher's wife, asked why she did not go to labour in her husband's workshop, or away into the market-place, or go a-trading to foreign countries, would certainly have answered: 'I am too busy to speak with such as you! The bread is in the oven (already I smell it a-burning), the winter is coming on, and my children lack good woollen hose and my husband needs a warm coat. I have six vats of ale all a-brewing, and I have daughters whom I must teach to spin and sew, and the babies are clinging round my knees. And you ask *me* why *I* do not go abroad to seek for new labours! God-sooth! Would you have me to leave my household to starve in summer and die of cold in winter, and my children to go untrained, while I gad about to seek for other work? A man must have his belly full and his back covered before all things in life. Who, think you, would spin and bake and brew, and rear and train my babes, if I went abroad? New labour, indeed, when the days are not long enough, and I have to toil far into the night! I have no time to talk with fools! Who will rear and shape the nation if I do not?'

And the young maiden at the cottage door, beside her wheel,

asked why she was content and did not seek new fields of labour, would surely have answered: 'Go away, I have no time to listen to you. Do you not see that I am spinning here that I too may have a home of my own? I am weaving the linen garments that shall clothe my household in the long years to come! I cannot marry till the chest upstairs be full. *You* cannot hear it, but as I sit here alone, spinning, far off across the hum of my spinning-wheel I hear the voices of my little unborn children calling to me – "O mother, mother, hasten on" and sometimes, when I seem to be looking out across my wheel into the sunshine, it is the blaze of my own fireside that I see, and the light shines on the faces round it; and I spin on the faster and the steadier when I think of what shall be. Do you ask *me* why I do not go out and labour in the fields with the lad whom I have chosen? Is his work, then, indeed more needed than mine for the raising of that home that shall be ours? Oh, very hard I will labour, for him and for my children, in the long years to come. But I cannot stop to talk to you now. Far off, through the hum of my spinning-wheel, I hear the voices of my children calling to me, and I must hurry on. Do you ask me why I do not seek for labour whose hands are full to bursting?'

Such would have been our answer in Europe in the ages of the past, if asked the question why we were contented with our field of labour and sought no other. Man had his work; we had ours. We knew that we upbore our world on our shoulders; and that through the labour of our hands it was sustained and strengthened – and we were contented.

But now, again a change has come.

Something that is entirely new has entered into the field of human labour, and left nothing as it was.

In man's fields of toil, change has accomplished, and is yet more accomplishing, itself.

On lands where once fifty men and youths toiled with their cattle, to-day one steam-plough, guided by but two pair of hands, passes swiftly; and an automatic reaper in one day reaps and binds and prepares for the garner the produce of fields it would have taken a hundred strong male arms to harvest in the past. The iron tools and weapons, only one of which it took an ancient father of our race long months of stern exertion to extract from ore and bring to shape and temper, now are poured forth by steam-driven machinery as a mill-pond pours forth its water; and even in war, the male's ancient and especial field of labour, a complete reversal of the ancient order has taken place. Time was when the size and strength of the muscles in a man's legs and arms, and the strength and size of his body, largely determined his fighting powers, and an Achilles or a Richard Cœur de Lion, armed only with his spear or battle-axe, made a host fly before him; to-day the puniest mannikin behind a modern Maxim gun[1] may hew down in perfect safety a phalanx of heroes whose legs and arms and physical powers a Greek god might have envied, but who, having not the modern machinery of war, fall powerless. The day of the primary import to humanity of the strength in man's extensor and flexor muscles, whether in labours of war or of peace, is gone by for ever; and the day of the all-importance of the strength, culture, and activity of man's brain and nerve has already come.

The brain of one consumptive German chemist who in his laboratory accomplishes the compounding of a new explosive, has more effect upon the wars of the modern nations than the structure of ten thousand soldierly legs and arms; and the man who invents one new labour-saving mechanical device may, through the cerebration of a few days, have performed the labour it would otherwise have taken hundreds of thousands of his lustily legged and armed fellows to perform.

Year by year, month by month, and almost hour by hour, this change is increasingly shaping itself in the field of the modern man's labour; and crude muscular force, whether in man or beast, sinks continually in its value in the field of human toil, while intellectual power, virility and activity, and that culture which leads to the mastery of the inanimate forces of nature, to the invention of machinery and to the delicate manipulative skill required in guiding it, becomes ever of greater and greater importance to the race. Already today we tremble on the verge of a discovery which may come to-morrow or the next day, when through the attainment of some simple and cheap method of controlling some widely diffused, everywhere accessible

69

natural force (such, for instance, as the force of the great tidal wave) there will at once and forever pass away even that comparatively small value which still, in our present stage of material civilisation, clings to the expenditure of mere crude, muscular human energy; and the creature, however muscularly powerful, who can merely pull, push and lift, will have no further value in the field of human labour.

Therefore, even to-day, we find that wherever that condition which we call modern civilisation prevails and in proportion as it tends to prevail – wherever steam-power, electricity, or the forces of wind or water, are compelled by man's intellectual activity to act as the motor-powers in the accomplishment of human toil; wherever the delicate adaptations of scientifically constructed machinery are taking the place of the simple manipulations of the human hand – that there has arisen, all the world over, a large body of males who find their ancient fields of labour have slipped or are slipping from them, and who discover that the modern world has no place or need for them. At the gates of our dockyards, in our streets and in our fields, are to be found everywhere, in proportion as modern civilisation is really dominant, men whose bulk and animal strength would have made them as warriors invaluable members of any primitive community, and who would have been valuable even in any simpler civilisation than our own as machines of toil, but who, owing to lack of intellectual or delicate manual training, have now no form of toil to offer society which it stands really in need of, and who therefore form our *Great Male Unemployed*, a body which finds the only powers it possesses so little needed by its fellows, that in return for its intensest physical labour life is hardly sustained. The material conditions of life have been rapidly modified, and the man has not been modified with them: machinery has largely filled his place in the old fields of labour, and he has found no new one.

It is from these men, often men who viewed from the broad humanitarian standpoint are of the most lovable and interesting type, and who might in a simpler state of society have been the heroes, leaders and chiefs of their people, that there arises in the modern world the bitter cry of the male unemployed: 'Give us labour or we die!'[2]

Yet it is only upon one, and a comparatively small, section of the males of the modern civilised world that these changes in the material conditions of life have told in such fashion as to take all useful occupation from them and render them wholly or partly dependent on society. If the modern male's field of labour has contracted at one end (the physical), at the other (the intellectual) it has immeasurably expanded! If machinery, and the command of inanimate motor-forces, have rendered of comparatively little value the male's mere muscular energy, the demand upon his intellectual faculties, the call for the expenditure of nervous energy, and the exercise of delicate manipulative skill in the labours of human life, have immeasurably increased.

In well-nigh a million new directions forms of honoured and remunerative social labour are opening up before the feet of the modern man, which his ancestors never dreamed of; and day by day they yet increase in numbers and importance. The steamship, the hydraulic lift, the patent road-maker, the railway-train, the electric tram-car, the steam-driven mill, the Maxim gun and the torpedo-boat, once made, may perform their labours with the guidance and assistance of comparatively few hands; but a whole army of men of science, engineers, clerks and highly trained workmen is necessary for their invention, construction and maintenance. In the domains of art, of science, of literature, and above all in the field of politics and government, an almost infinite extension has taken place in the fields of male labour. Where in primitive times woman was often the only builder, and patterns she daubed on her hut walls or traced on her earthen vessels were the only attempts at domestic art; and where later but an individual here and there was required to design a king's palace or a god's temple or to ornament it with statues or paintings – to-day, a mighty army of males, a million strong, is employed in producing plastic art alone, both high and low, from the traceries on wall-papers and the illustrations in penny journals, to the production of the pictures and statues which adorn the national collections, and a mighty new field of toil has opened before the anciently hunting and fighting male. Where once one ancient witch-doctress may have been the only creature in a whole land who studied the

71

nature of herbs and earths, or a solitary wizard experimenting on poisons was the only individual in a whole territory interrogating nature; and where, later, a few score of alchemists and astrologers only were engaged in examining the natures of substances or the movements of planets, to-day a hundred thousand men in every civilised community are labouring to unravel the mysteries of nature, and from the practical chemist and physician and anatomist and engineer, to the astronomer and mathematician, scientific men form a mighty and always increasingly important army of male labourers. Where once an isolated bard supplied a nation with its literature, or where later a few thousand priests and men of letters wrote and transcribed from the few to read, to-day literature gives labour to a multitude of males almost as countless as a swarm of locusts. From the penny-a-liner[3] to the poet and philosopher, the demand for their labour continually increases. Where one town-crier with stout legs and lusty lungs was once all-sufficient to spread the town news, a score of men now sit daily, pen in hand, preparing the columns of the morning's paper, and far into the night a hundred compositors are engaged in a labour which requires a higher culture of brain and finger than most ancient kings and rulers possessed. Even in the labours of war, the most brutal and primitive of the occupations lingering on into civilised life from the savage state, the new demand for intellectual male labour is enormous, and the invention, construction and working of one Krupp gun,[4] though it hardly demands more crude muscular exertion than a savage expends in shaping his boomerang, yet represents almost an infinitude of care and thought, and of well-rewarded male labour. Above all, in the domain of politics and government, where once a king or queen, aided by a handful of councillors, was alone practically concerned in the labours of national guidance or legislation, to-day, owing to the rapid means of intercommunication, and the consequent diffusion of political and social information throughout a territory, it has become possible, for the first time, for every adult in a large community to keep himself closely informed on all national affairs, and in every highly civilised state the ordinary male has been almost compelled to take his share, however small, in the duties and labours of the legislation and government, and thus has been opened before the mass of males a vast new sphere of labour undreamed of by their ancestors. Thus, in every direction, the change which modern material civilisation has wrought, while it has militated against that comparatively small section of males who have nothing to offer society but the expenditure of their untrained muscular energy (inflicting much and often completely unmerited suffering upon them), has immeasurably extended the field of male labour as a whole. Never before in the history of the earth has the male field of remunerative toil been so wide, so interesting, so complex, and in its results so all-important to society; never before has the male sex, taken as a whole, been so fully and strenuously employed.

So much is this the case, that, exactly as in the earlier conditions of society an excessive and almost crushing amount of social labour often devolved upon the female, so under modern civilised conditions among the wealthier and fully civilised classes an unduly excessive share of labour tends to devolve on the male. That almost entirely modern, morbid condition, affecting brain and nervous system, and shortening the lives of hundreds of thousands in modern civilised societies, which is vulgarly known as 'overwork' or 'nervous breakdown,' and which is immensely more common among males than females, is but one evidence of the frequently excessive share of mental labour devolving upon the modern male, who, in addition to maintaining himself, has frequently dependent upon him a larger or smaller number of entirely parasitic females. Whatever the result of the changes of modern civilisation may be with regard to the male, he certainly cannot complain that they have as a whole robbed him of his labour, diminished his share in the conduct of life, or reduced him to a condition of morbid inactivity.

In our woman's field of labour, matters have tended to shape themselves wholly otherwise! The changes which have taken place during the last centuries, and which we sum up under the compendious term 'modern civilisation,' have tended to rob woman, not merely in part but almost wholly, of her ancient domain of productive social labour, and, where there has not been a determined and conscious resistance on her part, have nowhere spontaneously tended to open out to her new and compensatory fields.

It is this fact which constitutes our modern 'Woman's Problem.'

Our spinning-wheels are all broken: in a thousand huge buildings steam-driven looms, guided by a few hundred thousand hands (often those of men), produce the garments of our race; and we dare no longer say, proudly, as of old, that we and we alone clothe our peoples.

Our hoes and our grindstones passed from us long ago, and the plowman and the miller took our toil; but we kept fast possession of the kneading-trough and the brewing-vat. To-day, steam often shapes our bread, and the loaves are set down at our very door (it may be, by a man-driven motor-car); and the history of our household drinks we know no longer till we see them set before us at our tables. Day by day machine-prepared and factory-produced viands take a larger and larger place in the dietary of rich and poor alike, till even the workingman's wife places before her household little that is of her own preparation; while among the wealthier classes, so far has domestic change gone, that males are not infrequently found labouring in our houses and kitchens, and even standing behind our chairs ready to do all but actually place the morsels of food between our feminine lips. The army of rosy milkmaids has passed away forever to give place to the cream-separator and the male- and machinery-manipulated butter-pat. In every direction the ancient saw, that it was exclusively the woman's sphere to prepare the viands of her race, has become, in proportion as civilisation has perfected itself, an antiquated lie.

Even the minor domestic operations are tending to pass out of the circle of woman's domestic labour: in modern cities our carpets are beaten, our windows cleaned, our door-steps polished, by machinery or extra-domestic and often male labour. And the change has gone much further than to the mere taking from us of the preparation of the materials from which the clothing of the race is formed. Already the domestic sewing-machine, which has supplanted almost entirely the ancient needle, begins to become antiquated and a thousand machines driven in factories by central engines are already supplying not merely the husband and son, but the woman herself, with almost every article of attire from hose to jacket; while among the wealthy classes, Worth[5] with his hundred fellow male-milliners and dressmakers is helping finally to explode the ancient myth, that it is woman's exclusive sphere as a part of her domestic toil to shape the garments of her race.

Year by year, day by day, there is a silently working but determined tendency for the sphere of woman's domestic labours to contract itself: and this contraction is marked exactly in proportion as that condition which we term modern civilisation is advanced. It manifests itself more in England and America than in Italy and Spain, more in great cities than in country places, more among the wealthier classes than the poorer, and is an unfailing indication of advancing modern civilisation.[6]

But it is not only, nor even mainly, in the sphere of woman's material domestic labours that change has touched her and shrunk her ancient field of labour.

Time was, when the woman kept her children about her knees till adult years were reached. Hers was the training and influence which shaped them. From the moment when the infant first lay on her breast, till her daughters left her for marriage and her sons took share in man's labour, they were continually under the mother's influence. To-day, so complex have become even the technical and simpler branches of education, so mighty and inexorable are the demands which modern civilisation makes for specialised instruction and training, for all individuals who are to survive and retain their usefulness under modern conditions, that from the earliest years of its life the child is of necessity largely removed from the hands of the mother, and placed in those of the specialised instructor. Among the wealthier classes, scarcely is the infant born when it passes into the hands of the trained nurse, and from hers on into the hands of the qualified teacher; till at nine or ten the son, in

75

certain countries, often leaves his home forever for the public school, to pass on to the college and university; while the daughter, in the hands of trained instructors and dependents, owes in the majority of cases hardly more of her education or formation to maternal toil. While even among our poorer classes, the infant-school, the board-school, and later on the necessity for manual training, take the son and often the daughter as completely, and always increasingly as civilisation advances, from the maternal control. So marked has this change in woman's ancient field of labour become, that a woman of almost any class may have borne many children, and yet at middle age be found sitting alone in an empty house, all her offspring gone from her to receive training and instruction at the hands of others. The ancient statement that the training and education of her offspring is exclusively the duty of the mother, however true it may have been with regard to a remote past, has already of necessity become an absolute misstatement; and the woman who should at the present day insist on entirely educating her own offspring would, in nine cases out of ten, inflict an irreparable injury on them, because she is incompetent.

But, if possible, yet more deeply and radically have the changes of modern civilisation touched our ancient field of labour in another direction – in that very portion of the field of human labour which is peculiarly and organically ours, and which can never be wholly taken from us. Here the shrinkage has been larger than in any other direction, and touches us as women more vitally.

Time was, and still is, among almost all primitive and savage folk, when the first and all-important duty of the female and her society was to bear, to bear much, and to bear unceasingly! On her adequate and persistent performance of this passive form of labour, and on her successful feeding of her young from her own breast, depended, not merely the welfare, but often the very existence, of her tribe or nation. Where, as is the case among almost all barbarous peoples, the rate of infant mortality is high: where the unceasing casualties resulting from war, the chase, and acts of personal violence tend continually to reduce the number of adult males: where, surgical knowledge being still in its infancy, most wounds are fatal; where, above all, recurrent pestilence and famine, unfailing if of irregular recurrence, decimated the people, it has been all-important that woman should employ her creative power to its very uttermost limits if the race were not at once to dwindle and die out. 'May thy wife's womb never cease from bearing,'[7] is still to-day the highest expression of good will on the part of a native African chief to his departing guest. For, not only does the prolific woman in the primitive state contribute to the wealth and strength of her nation as a whole, but to that of her own male companion and of her family. Where the social conditions of life are so simple that, in addition to bearing and suckling the child, it is reared and nourished through childhood almost entirely through the labour and care of the mother, requiring no expenditure of tribal or family wealth on its training or education, its value as an adult enormously outweighs both to the state and the male the trouble and expense of rearing it; and the man who has twenty children to become warriors or labourers is by so much the richer and the more powerful than he who has but one, while the state whose women are prolific stands so insured against destruction. Incessant and persistent child-bearing is thus truly the highest duty and the most socially esteemed occupation of the primitive woman, equaling fully in social importance the labour of the man as hunter and warrior.

Even under those conditions of civilisation which have existed in the centuries which divide primitive savagery from high civilisation, the demand for continuous child-bearing on the part of woman as her highest social duty has generally been hardly less imperious. Throughout the Middle Ages of Europe, and down almost to our own day, the rate of infant mortality was almost as large as in a savage state; medical ignorance destroyed innumerable lives; antiseptic surgery being unknown, serious wounds were almost always fatal; in the low state of sanitary science, plagues, such as those which in the reign of Justinian[8] swept across the civilised world from India to northern Europe, well-nigh depopulating the globe, or the Black Death of 1349,[9] which in England alone swept away more than half the population of the island, were but extreme forms of the destruction of population continually going on as the result of zymotic disease;[10] while wars were not merely far more common but, owing to the famines which almost invariably followed them, were far more destructive to human life than in our own days, and deaths by violence, whether at the hands of the state or as the result of personal enmity, were of daily occurrence in all lands. Under these conditions abstinence on the part of woman from incessant child-bearing might have led to almost the same serious diminution or even extinction of her people as in the savage state; while the very existence of her civilisation depended on the production of an immense number of individuals as beasts of burden, without the expenditure of whose crude muscular force in physical labour of agriculture and manufacture those intermediate civilisations would, in the absence of machinery, have been impossible. Twenty men had to be born, fed at the breast and reared by woman to perform the crude brute labour which is performed to-day by one small, well-adjusted steam-crane; and the demand for large masses of human creatures as mere reservoirs of motor-force for accomplishing the simplest processes was imperative. So strong indeed was the consciousness of the importance to society of continuous child-bearing on the part of woman, that as late as the middle of the sixteenth century Martin Luther wrote, 'If a woman becomes weary or at last dead from bearing, that matters not: let her only die from bearing, she is there to do it': and he doubtless gave expression to the profound conviction of the bulk of his contemporaries, both male and female.[11]

To-day, this condition has almost completely reversed itself.

The advance of science and the amelioration of the physical conditions of life tend rapidly toward a diminution of human mortality. The infant death-rate among the upper classes in modern civilisations has fallen by more than one-half; while among poorer classes it is already, though slowly, falling; the increased knowledge of the laws of sanitation has made among all highly civilised peoples the depopulation by plagues a thing of the past, and the discoveries of the next twenty years will probably do away forever with the danger to man of zymotic disease. Famines of the old desolating type have become an impossibility where rapid means of transportation convey the superfluity of one land to supply the lack of another; and war and deeds of violence, though still lingering among us, have already become episodal in the lives of nations as of individuals; while the vast advances in antiseptic surgery have caused even the effects of wounds and dismemberments to become only very partially fatal to human life. All these changes have tended to diminish human mortality and protract human life; and they have to-day already made it possible for a race not only to maintain its numbers, but even to increase them, with a comparatively small expenditure of woman's vitality in the passive labour of child-bearing.

But yet more seriously has the demand for woman's labour as child-bearer been diminished by change in another direction.

Every mechanical invention which lessens the necessity for rough, untrained muscular human labour, diminishes also the social demand upon woman as the producer in large masses of such labourers. Already throughout the modern civilised world, we have reached a point at which the social demand is not merely for human creatures in the bulk for use as beasts of burden, but rather, and only, for such human creatures as shall be so trained and cultured as to be fitted for the performance of the complex duties of modern life. Not now merely for many men, but rather for few, and those few well born and well instructed, is the modern demand. And the woman who to-day merely produces twelve children and suckles them, and then turns them loose on her society and family, is regarded, and rightly so, as the curse and downdraft, and not the productive labourer, of her community. Indeed, so difficult and expensive has become in the modern world the rearing and training of even one individual, in a manner suited to fit it for coping with the complexities and difficulties of civilised life, that to the family as well as to the state, unlimited fecundity on the part of the female has already in most cases become an irremediable evil: whether it be in the case of the artisan, who at the cost of immense self-sacrifice must support and train his children till their twelfth or fourteenth year, if they are ever to become even skilled manual labourers, and who if his family be large often sinks beneath the burden, allowing his offspring, untaught and untrained, to become waste-producers of human life; or in that of the professional man, who by his mental toil is compelled to support and educate at immense expense his sons till they are twenty or older, and to sustain his daughters often throughout their lives, should they not marry, and to whom a large family proves often no less disastrous: while the state whose women produce recklessly large masses of individuals in excess of those for whom they can provide training, is a state, in so far, tending toward deterioration. The commandment to the modern woman is not now simply "Thou shalt bear,'[12] but rather 'Thou shalt not bear in excess of thy power to rear and train satisfactorily'; and the woman who should to-day appear at the door of a workhouse or the tribunal of the poor-law guardians followed by her twelve infants, demanding honourable sustenance for them and herself in return for the labour she had undergone in producing them, would meet with but short shrift. While the modern man who on his wedding-day should be greeted with the ancient good wish that he might become the father of ten sons and ten daughters, would regard it as a malediction rather than a blessing. It is certain that the time is now rapidly approaching, when child-bearing will be regarded rather as a luxury, permissible only to those who have shown their power rightly to train and provide for their offspring, than as a labour, in itself, and, under whatever conditions performed, beneficial to society.[13]

Further, owing partly to the diminished demand for child-bearing, rising from the extreme difficulty and expense of child-rearing and education, and to many other complex social causes, millions of women in our modern societies are so placed as to be absolutely compelled to go through life not merely childless, but without sex-relationship in any form whatever; while another mighty army of women is reduced by the dislocations of our civilisation to accepting sexual relationships which negate child-bearing, and whose only product is physical and moral disease.

There it has come to pass that vast numbers of us are, by

modern social conditions, prohibited from child-bearing at all, and that even those among us who are child-bearers are required, in proportion as the class or race to which we belong stands high in the scale of civilisation, to produce a smaller and ever smaller number of offspring; so that even for these of us child-bearing and suckling, instead of filling the entire circle of female life from youth to age, becomes an episodal occupation, profitably employing only three or four out of the threescore and ten years which are allotted to human life. In such societies the statement (so profoundly true when made with regard to most savage societies, and even largely true with regard to those in the intermediate stages of civilisation) that the main and continuous occupation of the woman from puberty to age is the bearing and suckling of children, and that this occupation must fully satisfy all her needs for social labour and activity, becomes – an *antiquated and unmitigated* LIE.

Not only are millions of our women precluded from ever bearing a child, but for those of us who do bear the demand is ever increasingly in civilised societies coupled with the conditions that if we would act socially we must restrict our powers.[14]

Looking round then with the uttermost impartiality we can command, on the entire field of woman's ancient and traditional labours, we find that *fully three-fourths of it have shrunk away forever, and that the remaining fourth still tends to shrink!*

It is this great fact, so often and so completely overlooked, which lies as the propelling force behind that vast and restless 'Woman's movement' which marks our day. It is *this* fact, whether clearly and intellectually grasped, or, as is more often the case, vaguely and painfully *felt*, which awakes in the hearts of the ablest modern European women their passionate, and at times it would seem almost coherent, cry for new forms of labour and new fields for the exercise of their power.

Thrown into strict logical form, our demand is this: We do not ask that the wheels of time should reverse themselves, or the stream of life flow backward. We do not ask that our ancient spinning-wheels be again resuscitated and placed in our hands; we do not demand that our old grindstones and hoes be returned to us, nor that man should again betake himself to his ancient province of war and the chase, leaving to us all domestic and civil labour; nor do we even ask that society shall again so reconstruct itself, that every woman may be again a child-bearer (desirable as it might be, and deep as lies the hunger for motherhood in every virile woman's heart); still less do we ask that she be continually employed in her craft, earning thereby social approbation: neither do we demand that the children whom we bear shall again be put exclusively into our hands to train. This we know cannot be. The past material conditions of life have gone forever; no will of man can recall them. But *this* is our demand: We demand, that, in that strange new world that is arising alike upon the man and the woman, where nothing is as it was, and all things are assuming new shapes and relations – we demand that in this new world we also shall have our share of honoured and socially useful human toil, our full half of the labour of the children of woman. We demand nothing more than this, and we will take nothing less. *This is our 'WOMAN'S RIGHT!'*

II

Is it to be said that, in the future, machinery and the captive motor-forces of nature are largely to take the place of human hand and foot in the labour of clothing and feeding the nations; are these branches of industry to be no longer domestic labours? – then, we demand that in the factory and warehouse, wherever machinery has usurped our ancient field, we also have our place, as guiders, controllers and possessors. Is child-bearing to become in the future the labour of but a portion of our sex? – then we demand for those among us who are allowed to take no share in it, compensatory and equally honourable and important fields of social toil. Is the training of human creatures to become a yet more and more onerous and laborious occupation, their education and culture to become increasingly a high art, complex and scientific? – if so, then, we demand that high and complex culture and training for ourselves, which shall fit us for instructing the race which we bring into the world. Is the demand for child-bearing to become so diminished that even in the lives of those among us who are child-bearers, it shall fill no more than half a dozen years out of the three-score-and-ten of human life? – then, we demand that an additional employment be ours which shall fill up with dignity and value the tale of the years not so employed. Is intellectual labour to take ever and increasingly the place of crude muscular exertion in the labour of life? – then we demand for ourselves that culture and the freedom of action which alone can yield us the knowledge of life and the intellectual vigour and strength which will enable us to undertake the same share of mental which we have borne in the past in physical labours of life. Are the rulers of the race to be no more its kings and queens, but the mass of the peoples? – then, we, one-half of the nations, demand our full queens' share in the duties and labours of government and legislation. Slowly but determinately, as the old fields of labour close up and are submerged behind us, we demand entrance into the new.

We make this demand, not for our own sakes alone, but for the succour of the race.

A horseman, riding alone on a dark night in an unknown land, may chance to feel his horse start beneath him; rearing, it may well-nigh hurl him to the earth: in the darkness he may curse his beast, and believe its aim simply to cast him off and free itself forever of its burden. But, when the morning dawns and lights the hills and valleys he has travelled, looking backward, he may perceive that the spot where his steed reared, planting its feet into the earth, and where it refused to move farther on the old road, was indeed the edge of a mighty precipice, down which one step more would have precipitated both horse and rider. And he may then see that an instinct wiser than his own led his beast, though in the dark, to leap backward, seeking a new path along which both might travel.[15]

In the confusion and darkness of the present, it may well seem to some that woman in her desire to seek for new paths in life is guided only by an irresponsible impulse, or that she seeks selfishly only her own good, at the cost of that of the race which she has so long and faithfully borne onward. But, when a clearer future shall have arisen and the obscuring mists of the present shall have been dissipated, it may then be manifest that not for herself alone, but for the entire race, has woman sought her new path.

For let it be noted what our position exactly is, we who as women are to-day demanding new fields of labour and a reconstruction of our relationship with life.

It is often said that the labour problem before the modern woman, and that before the unemployed or partially and uselessly employed male, are absolutely identical; that therefore, when the male labour problem of our age solves itself, that of the woman will of necessity have met its solution also.

This statement, with a certain specious semblance of truth, is yet radically and fundamentally false. It is true that both the male and female problems of our age have taken their rise largely in the same rapid material changes, which during the last centuries, and more especially the last ninety years, have altered the face of the human world. Both men and women have been robbed by those changes of their ancient remunerative fields of social and rendered labour; here the resemblance stops. The male, from whom the changes of modern civilisation have taken his ancient field of labour, has but one choice before him: he must find new fields of labour, or he must perish. Society will not ultimately support him in an absolutely quiescent and useless condition nor allow him to reproduce himself endlessly in complete mental and physical inactivity. If he does not vigorously exert himself in some direction or other (the direction may even be predatory) he must ultimately be annihilated. Individual drones,[16] both among the wealthiest and the poorest classes (millionaires' sons, dukes or tramps), may in isolated cases be preserved, and allowed to reproduce themselves without any exertion or activity of mind or body, but a vast body of males who, having lost their old forms of social employment, should refuse in any way to exert themselves or seek for new, would at no great length of time become extinct. There never has been, and as far as can now be seen, there never will be, a time when the majority of the males in any society will be supported by the rest of the community in a condition of perfect mental and physical inactivity. '*Find labour or die*' is the choice ultimately put before the human male, to-day as in the past; and *this* constitutes his labour problem.[17]

The labour of the male may not always be useful in the highest sense to his society, or it may even be distinctly harmful and antisocial, as in the case of the robber-barons of the Middle Ages who lived by capturing and despoiling all who passed by their castles; or as in the case of the share speculators, stock-jobbers, ring-and-corner specialists and monopolists of the present day, who feed upon the productive labours of society without contributing anything to its welfare. But even males so occupied are compelled to expend a vast amount of energy and even a low intelligence in their callings; and however injurious to their societies, they run no personal risk of handing down effete and enervated constitutions to their race. Whether beneficially or unbeneficially, the human male must, generally speaking, employ his intellect, or his muscle, or die.

The position of the unemployed modern female is one wholly different. The choice before her, as her ancient fields of domestic labour slip from her, is not generally or often at the present day the choice between finding new fields of labour, or death; but one far more serious in its ultimate reaction on humanity as a whole – it is the choice between finding new forms of labour or sinking slowly into a condition of more or less complete and passive *sex-parasitism*![18]

Again and again in the history of the past, when among human creatures a certain stage of material civilisation has been reached, a curious tendency has manifested itself for the human female to become more or less parasitic; social conditions tend to rob her of all forms of active conscious social labour, and to reduce her, like the field-bug, to the passive exercise of her sex functions alone. And the result of this parasitism has invariably been the decay in vitality and intelligence of the female, followed after a longer or shorter period by that of her male descendants and her entire society.

Nevertheless, in the history of the past the dangers of sex-parasitism have never threatened more than a section of the females of the human race, those exclusively of some dominant race or class; the mass of women beneath them being still compelled to assume some form of strenuous activity. It is at the present day, and under the peculiar conditions of our modern civilisation, that for the first time sex-parasitism has become a danger, more or less remote, to the mass of civilised women perhaps ultimately to all.

In the early stages of human growth, the sexual parasitism and degeneration of the female formed no possible source of social danger. Where the conditions of life rendered it inevitable that all the labour of a community should be performed by the members of that community themselves, without the assistance of slaves or machinery, the tendency has always been rather to throw an excessive amount of social labour on the female. Under no conditions, at no time, in no place, in the history of the world have the males of any period, of any nation or of any class shown the slightest inclination to allow their own females to become inactive or parasitic, so long as the actual muscular labour of feeding and clothing them would in that case have devolved upon *themselves*.

The parasitism of the human female becomes a possibility only when a point in civilisation is reached (such as that which was attained in the ancient civilisations of Greece, Rome, Persia, Assyria, India, and as to-day exists in many of the civilisations of the East, such as those of China and Turkey) when, owing to the extensive employment of the labour of slaves, or of subject races or classes, the dominant race or class has become so liberally supplied with the material goods of life, that mere physical toil on the part of its own members has become unnecessary. It is when this point has been reached, and never before, that the symptoms of female parasitism have in the past almost invariably tended to manifest themselves and have become a social danger. The males of the dominant class have almost always contrived to absorb to themselves the new intellectual occupations, which the absence of necessity for the old forms of physical toil made possible, and necessary, in their societies; and the females of the dominant class or race, for whose muscular labours there was now also no longer any need, not succeeding in grasping or attaining to these new forms of labour, have sunk into a state in which, performing no species of active social duty, they have existed through the passive performance of sexual functions alone, with how much or how little of discontent will now never be known, since no literary record has been made by the woman of the past of her desires or sorrows. Then, in place of the active labouring woman, upholding society by her toil, has come the effete wife, concubine or prostitute, clad in fine raiment, the work of others' fingers; fed on luxurious viands, the result of others' toil; waited on and tended by the labour of others. The need for her physical labour having gone, and mental industry not having taken its place, she bedecked and scented her person or had it bedecked and scented for her; she lay upon her sofa or drove or was carried out in her vehicle; and loaded with jewels, she sought by dissipations and amusements to fill up the inordinate blank left by the lack of productive activity. And as the hand whitened the frame softened, till, at last, the very duties of motherhood, which were all the constitution of her life left her, became distasteful and from the instant when her infant came damp from her womb it passed into the hands of others, to be tended and reared; and from youth to age her offspring often owed nothing to her personal toil. In many cases so complete was her enervation, that at last the very joy of giving life, the glory and beatitude of a virile womanhood, became distasteful; and she sought to evade it, not because of its interference with more imperious duties toward those already born of her, or to her society, but because her existence of inactivity had robbed her of all joy in strenuous exertion in any form. Finely clad, tenderly housed, life became for her merely the gratification of her own physical and sexual appetites, and the appetites of the male, through the stimulation of which alone she could maintain herself. And whether as kept wife, kept mistress or kept prostitute, she contributed nothing to the active and sustaining labours of her society. She had attained to the full development of that type which, whether in modern Paris or New York or London, or in ancient Greece, Assyria or Rome, is essentially one in its features, its nature and its effects – she was the 'fine lady,' the human female parasite – the most deadly microbe which can make its appearance on the surface of any social organism.[19]

Wherever in the history of the past this type has reached its full development and has comprised the bulk of the females belonging to any dominant class or race, it has heralded its decay. In Assyria, Greece, Rome, Persia, as in Turkey to-day, the same material conditions have produced the same social disease among wealthy and dominant races; and again and again when the nation so affected has come into contact with nations more healthily constituted, this diseased condition has contributed to its destruction.

In ancient Greece, in its superb and virile youth, its womanhood was richly and even heavily endowed with duties and occupations. Not the mass of the women alone, but king's wife and prince's daughter do we find going to the well to bear water, cleansing the household linen in the streams, feeding and doctoring their households, manufacturing the clothing of their race, and performing even a share of highest social functions as priestesses and prophetesses. It was from the bodies of such women as these that sprang that race of heroes, thinkers and artists, who laid the foundation of Grecian greatness. These females underlay their society as the solid and deeply buried foundations underlay the more visible and ornate portions of a great temple, making its structure and persistence possible. In Greece, after a certain lapse of time, these virile labouring women were to be found no more. The accumulated wealth of the dominant race, gathered through the labour of slaves and subject peoples, had so immensely increased that there was no longer a call for physical labour on the part of the dominant womanhood: immured within the walls of their houses as wives or mistresses, waited on by slaves and dependents, they no more sustained by their exertion either their own life or the life of their people. The males absorbed the intellectual labours of life; slaves and dependents the physical. For a moment, at the end of the fifth and beginning of the fourth century, when the womanhood of Greece had already internally decayed, there was indeed a brilliant intellectual efflorescence among her males, like to the gorgeous colours in the sunset sky when the sun is already sinking; but the heart of Greece was already rotting and her vigour failing. Increasingly, division and dissimilarity arose between male and female, as the male advanced in culture and entered upon new fields of intellectual toil while the female sank passively backward and lower in the scale of life, and thus was made ultimately a chasm which even sexual love could not bridge. The abnormal institution of avowed inter-male sexual relations upon the highest plane, was one and the most serious result of this severance. The inevitable and invincible desire of all highly developed human natures, to blend with their sexual relationships their highest intellectual interests and sympathies, could find no satisfaction or response in the relationship between the immured, ignorant and helpless females of the upper class, in Greece, and the brilliant, cultured and many-sided males who formed its dominant class in the fifth and fourth centuries. Man turned toward man; and parenthood and the divine gift of imparting human life were severed from the loftiest and profoundest phases of human emotion: Xantippe fretted out her ignorant and miserable little life between the walls of her house, and Socrates lay in the Agora, discussing philosophy and morals with Alcibiades; and the race decayed at its core.[20] Here and there an Aspasia, or earlier still a Sappho,[21] burst through the confining bonds of woman's environment, and with the force of irresistible genius broke triumphantly into new fields of action and powerful mental activity, standing side by side with the male; but their cases were exceptional. Had they, or such as they, been able to tread down a pathway, along which the mass of Grecian women might have followed them; had it been possible for the bulk of the women of the dominant race in Greece at the end of the fifth century to rise from their condition of supine inaction and ignorance and to have taken their share in the intellectual labours and stern activities of their race, Greece could never have fallen supine as she fell at the end of the fourth century, instantaneously and completely, as a rotten puff-ball falls in at the touch of a healthy finger; first, before the briberies of Philip, and then yet more completely before the arms of his yet more warlike son who was also the son of the fierce, virile and indomitable Olympia.[22] Nor could she have been swept clean, a few hundred years later, from Thessaly to Sparta, from Corinth to Ephesus, her temples destroyed, her effete women captured, by the hordes of the Goths – a people less skilfully armed and less civilised than the descendants of the race of Pericles and Leonidas, but a branch of the great Teutonic folk,[23] whose monogamous domestic life was sound at the core, and whose fearless, labouring and resolute women yet bore for the men they followed to the ends of the earth, what Spartan women once said they alone bore – men.

In Rome, in the days of her virtue and vigour, the Roman matron laboured mightily, and bore on her shoulders her full half of the social burden, though her sphere of labour and influence was ever somewhat smaller than that of the Teutonic sisterhood whose descendants were finally to supplant her own. From the vestal virgin to the matron, the Roman woman in the days of the nation's health and growth fulfilled lofty functions and bore the whole weight of domestic toil. From Lucretia, the great Roman dame whom we find spinning with her hand-maidens deep into the night, and whose personal dignity was so dear that violated she sought only death, to the mother of the Gracchi,[24] one of the last of the great line, we find everywhere, erect, labouring and resolute, the Roman woman who gave birth to the men who built up Roman greatness. A few centuries later, and Rome also had reached that dangerous spot in the order of social change which Greece had reached centuries before her. Slave labour and the enjoyment of the unlimited spoils of subject races had done away forever with the demand for physical labour on the part of the members of the dominant race. Then came a period when the male still occupied himself with the duties of war and government, of legislation and self-culture; but the Roman matron had already ceased forever from her toils. Decked in jewels and fine clothing, brought at the cost of infinite human labour from the ends of the earth, nourished on the most delicate victuals, prepared by others' hands, she sought now only, with amusement, to pass away a life that no longer offered her the excitement and joy of active productive exertion. She frequented theatres and baths, or reclined on her sofa, and like her modern counterpart, painted herself, wore patches, affected an artistic walk and a handshake with the elbow raised and the fingers hanging down. Her children were reared by dependents, and in the intellectual labour and government of her age she took no part, and was fit to take none. There were not wanting writers and thinkers who saw clearly the end to which the enervation of the female was tending, and who were not sparing in their denunciations. 'Time was,' cries one Roman writer of that age, 'when the matron turned the spindle with the hand and kept at the same time the pot in her eye that the pottage might not be singed, but now,' he adds bitterly, 'when the wife loaded with jewels reposes among pillows, or seeks the dissipation of baths and theatres, all things go downward and the state decays.' Yet, neither he nor that large body of writers and thinkers who saw the condition toward which the parasitism of woman was tending to reduce society, preached any adequate remedy.[25]

Thoughtful men sighed over the present and yearned for the past, nor seem to have perceived that it was irrevocably gone; that the Roman lady who, with a hundred servants standing idle about her, should, in imitation of her ancestress, have gone out with her pitcher on her head to draw water from the well, while in all her own courtyards pipe-led streams gushed forth, would have acted the part of the pretender; that had she insisted on resuscitating her loom and had she sat up all night to spin, she could never have produced those fabrics which alone her household demanded, and would have been but a puerile actor; that it was not by attempting to return to the ancient and forever closed fields of labour, but by entering upon new, that she could alone serve her race, and retain her own dignity and virility; that not by bearing water and weaving linen, but by so training and disciplining herself that she should be fitted to bear her share in the labour necessary to the just and wise guidance of a great empire, that she should be capable of training a race of men adequate to exercise an enlightened, merciful and beneficent rule over the vast masses of subject people – that so, and so only, could she fulfil her duty toward the new society about her, and bear its burden together with man, as her ancestresses of bygone generations had borne theirs.

That in this direction and this alone, lay the only possible remedy for the evils of woman's condition, was a conception apparently grasped by none; and the female sank lower and lower, till the image of the parasitic woman of Rome – with a rag of the old Roman intensity left even in her degradation – seeking madly by pursuit of pleasure and sensuality to fill the void left by the lack of honourable activity; accepting lust in the place of love, ease in the place of exertion, and an unlimited consumption in the place of production; too enervated at last to care even to produce offspring, and shrinking from every form of endurance – remains, even to the present day, the most perfect, and therefore the most appalling picture of the parasite female that earth has produced – a picture only less terrible than it is pathetic.

We recognise that it was inevitable that this womanhood, born to guide and enlighten a world, and in place thereof feeding on it, should at last have given birth to a manhood as effete as itself, and that both should in the end have been swept away before the march of those Teutonic folk, whose women were virile, and could give birth to *men* – among whom the woman received on the morning of her marriage from the man who was to be her companion through life, no miserable trinkets to hang upon her limbs, but a shield, a spear, a sword, and a yoke of oxen, while she bestowed on him in return a suit of armour, in token that they two were henceforth to be one, in toil and in the facing of danger; that she too should dare with him in war and suffer with him in peace – and of whom another writer tells us, that these women not only bore the race and fed it at their breasts without the help of others' hands, but that they undertook the whole management of house and lands, leaving the males free for war and chase – of whom Suetonius[26] tells us, that when Augustus Cæsar demanded hostages from a tribe, he took women, not men, because he found by experience that the women were more regarded than men – of whom Strabo[27] tells us, that so highly did the Germanic races value the intellect of their women that they regarded them as inspired and entered into no war or great undertaking without their advice and counsel; while among the Cimbrian women who accompanied their husbands in the invasion of Italy were certain who marched barefooted in the midst of the lines, distinguished by their white hair and milk-white robes, and who were regarded as prophinspired – of whom Florus,[28] describing an early Roman victory, says 'the conflict was not less fierce and obstinate with the wives of the vanquished: in their carts and wagons they formed a line of battle, and from their elevated situation, as from so many turrets, annoyed the Romans with their poles and lances.'[29] Their death was as glorious as their martial spirit. Finding that all was lost, they strangled their children, and either destroyed themselves in one scene of mutual slaughter or with the sashes that bound up their hair suspended themselves by the neck to the boughs of trees or the tops of their wagons – of whom Valerius Maximus says, that 'if the gods on the day of battle had inspired the men with equal fortitude Marius would never have boasted of his Teutonic victory' – and of whom Tacitus, speaking of those women who accompanied their husbands to war, adds, 'these are the darling witnesses of his conduct, the applauders of his valour, at once beloved and valued. The wounded seek their mothers and their wives; undismayed at the sight, the women count each honourable scar and suck the gushing blood. They are even hardy enough to mix with the combatants administering refreshment and exhorting them to deeds of valour'; and adds moreover that 'to be contented with one wife was peculiar to the Germans; while the woman was contented with one husband as with one life, one mind, one body.'[30]

It was inevitable that before the sons of women such as these the sons of the parasitic Roman should be swept from existence, as the offspring of the caged canary would fall in conflict with the offspring of the free.

Again and again with wearisome reiteration, the same story repeats itself. Among the Jews in the days of their health and growth, we find their women bearing the major weight of agricultural and domestic toil, full always of labour and care – from Rachel, whom Jacob met and loved as she watered her father's flocks, to Ruth, the ancestress of a line of kings and heroes, whom her Boas first noted labouring in the harvest-fields; from Sarah, kneading and baking cakes for Abraham's prophetic visitors, to Miriam, herself prophetess and singer, and Deborah, who judging Israel from beneath her palm-tree gave rest to her land for forty years. Everywhere the ancient Jewish woman appears, an active, sustaining power among her people; and perhaps the noblest picture of the labouring woman to be found in any literature is contained in the Jewish writings, indicted possibly at the very time when the labouring woman was for the first time tending among a section of the Jews to become a thing of the past[31] – when already Solomon with his seven hundred parasite wives and three hundred parasite concubines loomed large on the horizon of the national life, to take the place of flock-tending Rachel and gleaning Ruth; and to produce, amid their palaces of cedar and gold, among them all, no Joseph or David but in way of descendant only a Rehoboam, under whose hand the kingdom was to totter to its fall.

In the East to-day, the same story has wearisomely written itself: in China, where the power of the most ancient existing civilisation may be measured accurately by the length of its woman's shoe; in Turkish harems, where one of the noblest dominant Aryan races the world has yet produced, is being slowly suffocated in the arms of a parasitic womanhood and might indeed long ago have been obliterated, had not a certain virility and strength been continually reinfused into it through the persons of purchased wives, who in early childhood and youth have been themselves active labouring peasants. Everywhere in the past as in the present the parasitism of the female heralds the decay of a nation, and as invariably indicates disease as the pustules of smallpox upon the skin indicate the existence of a purulent virus in the system.

We are indeed far from asserting that the civilisations of the past which have decayed, have decayed alone through the parasitism of their females. Vast, far-reaching social phenomena have invariably causes and reactions immeasurably too complex to be summed up under one so simple a term. Behind the phenomenon of female parasitism has always lain another and

94

yet larger social phenomenon – it has invariably been preceded, as we have seen, by the subjugation of large bodies of other human creatures, either as slaves, subject races, or classes; and as the result of the excessive labours of these classes there has always been an accumulation of unearned wealth in the hands of the dominant class or race. *It has invariably been by feeding on this wealth, the result of forced or of ill-paid labour,* that the female of the dominant race or class has lost her activity and has come to exist purely through the passive performance of her sexual functions. Without slaves or subject classes to perform the crude physical labours of life and produce superfluous wealth, the parasitism of the female would, in the past, have been an impossibility.

There is, therefore, a profound truth in that universal and ancient saw which states that the decay of the great nations and civilisations of the past has resulted from the enervation caused by wealth and luxury; and there is a further and if possible more profound truth underlying the statement that their destruction has ultimately been the result of the enervation of the entire race, male and female.

But when we come further to inquire how, exactly, this process of decay took place, we shall find that the part which the parasitism of the female has played has been fundamental. The mere use of any of the material products of the labour, which we term wealth, can never in itself produce that decay, physical or mental, which precedes the downfall of great civilisations. Salmon at ten shillings a pound can in itself no more debilitate and corrupt the moral, intellectual and physical constitution of the man consuming it, than it could enervate his naked forefathers who speared it in their rivers for food: the fact that an individual wears a robe made from the filaments of a worm, can no more deteriorate his spiritual or physical fibre, than were it made of sheep's wool: an entire race, housed in marble palaces, faring delicately and clad in silks, and surrounded by the noblest products of literature and plastic art, so those palaces, viands, garments, and products of art were the result of their *own* labours, could never be enervated by them. The debilitating effect of wealth sets in at that point exactly (and never before) at which the supply of material necessaries and comforts, and of aesthetic enjoyments, clogs the individuality, causing it to rest satisfied in the mere passive possession of the results of the labour of others, without feeling any necessity or desire for further productive activity of its own.[32]

The exact material condition at which this point will be reached, will vary, not only with the race, and the age, but with the individual. A Marcus Aurelius[33] in a palace of gold and marble was able to retain his simplicity and virility as completely as though he had lived in a cowherd's hut; while on the other hand, it is quite possible for the wife of a savage chief who has but four slaves to bring her her corn and milk and spread her skins in the sun to become almost as purely parasitic as the most delicately pampered female of fashion in ancient Rome, or modern Paris or New York; while the exact amount of unearned material wealth which will emasculate individuals in the same society, will vary exactly as their intellectual fibre and natural activity are strong or weak.[34]

The debilitating effect of wealth lies, then, not in the nature of any material adjunct to life in itself, but in the power it may possess of robbing the individual of all incentive to exertion, thus destroying the intellectual, the physical and finally, the moral fibre.

In all the civilisations of the past examination will show that almost invariably it has been the female who has tended first to reach this point, and examination will show that it has almost invariably been from the woman to the man that enervation and decay have spread.

Why this should be so is obvious. Firstly, it is in the sphere of domestic labour that slave or hired labour most easily and insidiously penetrates. The force of blows or hireling gold can far more easily supply labourers as the preparers of food and clothing, and even as the rearers of children, than it can supply labourers fitted to be intrusted with the toils of war and government, which have in the past of necessity been the especial sphere of male toil. The Roman woman had for generations been supplanted in the sphere of her domestic labours and in the toil of rearing and educating her offspring, and had long become abjectly parasitic, before the Roman male had been able to substitute the labour of the hireling and barbarian for his own in the labours of war and government.

Secondly, the female having one all-important, though passive and wholly unintelligent, form of production, which *cannot* be taken from her, and which is peculiarly connected with her own person, in the act of child-bearing, she is liable in a peculiarly insidious and gradual manner to become dependent on this one faculty for her support; and so much is this the case, that even when she does not in any way perform this function there is still a curious tendency for the kudos of the function still to hang about her, and for her mere potentiality in the direction of a duty which she may never fulfil, to be confused in her own estimation and that of society with the actual fulfilment of that function. Under the mighty ægis of the woman who bears and rears offspring and in other directions labours actively for her race, creeps in gradually and unnoticed the woman who does none of these things. From the mighty labouring woman who bears human creatures to the full extent of her power, rears her offspring unaided and performs at the same time severe social labour in other directions (and who is undoubtedly, wherever found, one of the most productive toilers known to the race), it is but one step to that still labouring woman who bears and rears herself without assistance a large number of offspring, though she may undertake no other form of social labour (for the toil of rearing from birth for the first six months, even one human creature, is one of the most exacting though ill-appreciated forms of human labour). From this woman it is again but one step, though a long one, to the woman who produces offspring freely but does not herself rear them, and performs no compensatory social labour; from this woman again, to the one who bears few or no children, and performs no productive social labour, but being married is officially regarded to be a child-bearer, the step is short; while again divided from her by an almost imperceptible line is the absolutely celibate woman, who manifestly performs no duty to her race as child-bearer, and who, when she undertakes no other form of productive social labour, lives on a sexual potentiality which is never called into active existence at all. There is but one step farther to the prostitute, who affects no form of labour, and who, in place of life, is recognised as producing death. Enormous as is the distance between the women at the two extremes of this series as regards their social functions, there is yet, in actual life, no sharp, clearly drawn line dividing the one type of woman from the other: they shade off into each other by delicate and insensible degrees. And it is down this inclined plane that the women of civilised races are peculiarly inclined unconsciously to slip, from a condition of strenuous social activity into a condition of complete helpless and inactive parasitism, without being clearly aware of the fact themselves, and without society's becoming so.[35]

These peculiarities in her condition have in all civilised societies laid the female more early open to the attacks of parasitism than the male. And while the accumulation of wealth has always been the antecedent condition, and the degeneracy and effeteness of the male the final and obvious cause, of the decay of the great dominant races of the past; yet, between these two has always lain, as a great middle term, the parasitism of the female – without which the first would have been inoperative and the last impossible.

Not slavery, nor the most vast accumulation of wealth, could destroy a nation by enervation, whose women remained active, virile and laborious.

The conception which again and again appears to have haunted successive societies, that it was a possibility for the male to advance in physical power and intellectual vigour, while his companion female became stationary and inactive, taking no share in the labours of society beyond the passive fulfilment of sexual functions, has always been negated. It has ended as would end the experiment of a man seeking to raise a breed of winning race-horses out of unexercised, short-winded, knock-kneed mares. Nay, more disastrously, for while the female animal transmits herself to her descendant only by means of germinal inheritance, and through the influence she may exert over it during gestation, the human female by producing the intellectual and moral atmosphere in which the early years of life are passed, impresses herself far more indelibly on her descendants. Only an able and labouring womanhood can permanently produce an able and labouring manhood; only an effete and inactive male can ultimately be produced by an effete and inactive womanhood. The curled darling, scented and languid, with his drawl, his delicate apparel, his devotion to the rarity and variety of his viands, whose severest labour is the search after pleasure; and for whom even the chase, which was for his remote ancestor an invigorating and manly toil essential for the meat and life of his people, becomes a luxurious and farcical amusement – this male, whether found in the later Roman empire, the Turkish harem of to-day, or in our northern civilisations, is possible only because generations of parasitic women have preceded him. More repulsive than the parasitic female herself, because a yet further product of decay, it is yet only the scent of his mother's boudoir that we smell in his hair. He is like to the bald patches and rotten wool on the back of a scabby sheep; which indeed indicate that, deep beneath the surface, a parasite insect is eating its way into the flesh, but which are not so much the cause of disease, as its final manifestation.

It is the power of the human female to impress herself on her descendants, male and female, through germinal inheritance, through influence during the period of gestation, and above all by producing the mental atmosphere in which the impression-able years of life are passed, which makes the condition of the child-bearing female the paramount interest of the race. It is this fact which causes even prostitution (in many respects the most repulsive form of female parasitism which afflicts humanity) to be, probably, not so deadly to the advance and even to the conservation of a healthy and powerful society, as the parasitism of its child-bearing females. For the prostitute, heavily as she weights society for her support, returning disease and mental and emotional disintegration for what she consumes, does not yet so immediately affect the next generation as the kept wife, or kept mistress, who impresses her effete image indelibly on the race.

No man ever yet entered life farther than the length of one

navel-cord from the body of the woman who bore him. It is the child-bearing woman who is the final standard of the race, from which there can be no departure for any distance for any length of time in any direction: as her brain weakens weakens the man's she bears; as her muscle softens softens his; as she decays decays the people.

Other causes may, and do, lead to the enervation and degeneration of a race; the parasitism of its child-bearing women MUST.

We, the European women of this age, stand to-day where again and again, in the history of the past, women of other races have stood; but our condition is yet more grave, and of wider import to humanity as a whole, than theirs ever was. Why this is so, is a subject for further consideration.

Three Dreams in a Desert (1887)

In the introduction to *Woman and Labour* Schreiner explained that 'Three Dreams in a Desert', though it appeared separately in the *Fortnightly Review* (1882), was originally conceived as part of her large-scale study of sexuality and the range of relationships between men and women: 'In addition to the prose argument I had in each chapter [of *Woman and Labour*] one or more allegories; because while it was easy clearly to express abstract thoughts in argumentative prose, whatever emotion those thoughts awaken I have not felt myself able adequately to express except in the other form' (*Woman and Labour*: 16). Along with 'The Child's Day' and 'The Woman Question', then, the following allegory grows out of Schreiner's work in London in the 1880s; it can be considered another formulation, or an articulation in another form, of 'The Woman Question', from the period when Schreiner was deciding to return from Europe to South Africa. 'Three Dreams' was also published in *Dreams* (1890).

Under a Mimosa-Tree

As I travelled across an African plain the sun shone down hotly. Then I drew my horse up under a mimosa-tree, and I took the saddle from him and left him to feed among the parched bushes. And all to right and to left stretched the brown earth. And I sat down under the tree, because the heat beat fiercely, and all along the horizon the air throbbed. And after a while a heavy drowsiness came over me, and I laid my head down against my saddle, and I fell asleep there. And, in my sleep, I had a curious dream.

I thought I stood on the border of a great desert, and the sand blew about everywhere. And I thought I saw two great figures like beasts of burden of the desert, and one lay upon the sand with its neck stretched out, and one stood by it. And I looked curiously at the one that lay upon the ground, for it had a great burden on its back, and the sand was thick about it, so that it seemed to have piled over it for centuries.

And I looked very curiously at it. And there stood one beside me watching. And I said to him, 'What is this huge creature who lies here on the sand?'

And he said, 'This is woman; she that bears men in her body.'

And I said, 'Why does she lie here motionless with the sand piled round her?'

And he answered, 'Listen, I will tell you! Ages and ages long she has lain here, and the wind has blown over her. The oldest, oldest, oldest man living has never seen her move: the oldest, oldest book records that she lay here then, as she lies here now, with the sand about her. But listen! Older than the oldest book, older than the oldest recorded memory of man, on the Rocks of Language, on the hard-baked clay of Ancient Customs, now crumbling to decay, are found the marks of her footsteps! Side by side with his who stands beside her you may trace them; and you know that she who now lies there once wandered free over the rocks with him.'

And I said, 'Why does she lie there now?'

And he said, 'I take it, ages ago the Age-of-dominion-of-muscular-force found her, and when she stooped low to give suck to her young, and her back was broad, he put his burden of subjection on to it, and tied it on with the broad band of Inevitable Necessity. Then she looked at the earth and the sky, and knew there was no hope for her; and she lay down on the sand with the burden she could not loosen. Ever since she has lain here. And the ages have come, and the ages have gone, but the band of Inevitable Necessity has not been cut.'

And I looked and saw in her eyes the terrible patience of the centuries; the ground was wet with her tears, and her nostrils blew up the sand.

And I said, 'Has she ever tried to move?'

And he said, 'Sometimes a limb has quivered. But she is wise;

she knows she cannot rise with the burden on her.'

And I said, 'Why does not he who stands by her leave her and go on?'

And he said, 'He cannot. Look – '

And I saw a broad band passing along the ground from one to the other, and it bound them together.

He said, 'While she lies there he must stand and look across the desert.'

And I said, 'Does he know why he cannot move?'

And he said, 'No.'

And I heard a sound of something cracking and I looked and I saw the band that bound the burden on to her back broken asunder; and the burden rolled on to the ground.

And I said, 'What is this?'

And he said, 'The Age-of-nervous-force has killed him with the knife he holds in his hand; and silently and invisibly he has crept up to the woman, and with that knife of Mechanical Invention he has cut the band that bound the burden to her back. The Inevitable Necessity is broken. She must rise now.'

And I saw that she still lay motionless on the sand, with her eyes open and her neck stretched out. And she seemed to look for something on the far-off border of the desert that never came. And I wondered if she were awake or asleep. And as I looked her body quivered, and a light came into her eyes, like when a sunbeam breaks into a dark room.

I said, 'What is it?'

He whispered 'Hush! the thought has come to her, "Might I not rise?"'

And I looked. And she raised her head from the sand, and I saw the dent where her neck had lain so long. And she looked at the earth, and she looked at the sky, and she looked at him who stood by her: but he looked out across the desert.

And I saw her body quiver; and she pressed her front knees to the earth, and veins stood out; and I cried, 'She is going to rise!'

But only her sides heaved, and she lay still where she was.

But her head she held up; she did not lay it down again. And he beside me said, 'She is very weak. See, her legs have been crushed under her so long.'

And I saw the creature struggle: and the drops stood out on her.

And I said, 'Surely he who stands beside her will help her?'

And he beside me answered, 'He cannot help her: *she must help herself*. Let her struggle till she is strong.'

And I cried, 'At least he will not hinder her! See, he moves farther from her, and tightens the cord between them, and he drags her down.'

And he answered, 'He does not understand. When she moves she draws the band that binds them, and hurts him, and he moves farther from her. The day will come when he will understand, and will know what she is doing. Let her once stagger on to her knees. In that day he will stand close to her, and look into her eyes with sympathy.'

And she stretched her neck, and the drops fell from her. And the creature rose an inch from the earth and sank back.

And I cried, 'Oh, she is too weak! she cannot walk! The long years have taken all her strength from her. Can she never move?'

And he answered me, 'See the light in her eyes!'

And slowly the creature staggered on to its knees.

And I awoke: and all to the east and to the west stretched the barren earth, with the dry bushes on it. The ants ran up and down in the red sand, and the heat beat fiercely. I looked up through the thin branches of the tree at the blue sky overhead. I stretched myself, and I mused over the dream I had had. And I fell asleep again, with my head on my saddle. And in the fierce heat I had another dream.

I saw a desert and I saw a woman coming out of it. And she came to the bank of a dark river; and the bank was steep and high.[1] And on it an old man met her, who had a long white beard; and a stick that curled was in his hand, and on it was written Reason. And he asked her what she wanted; and she said, 'I am woman; and I am seeking for the land of Freedom.'

And he said, 'It is before you.'

And she said, 'I see nothing before me but a dark flowing river, and a bank steep and high, and cuttings here and there with heavy sand in them.'

And he said, 'And beyond that?'

She said, 'I see nothing, but sometimes, when I shade my eyes with my hand, I think I see on the further bank trees and hills, and the sun shining on them!'

He said, 'That is the Land of Freedom.'

She said, 'How am I to get there?'

He said, 'There is one way, and one only. Down the banks of Labour, through the water of Suffering. There is no other.'

She said, 'Is there no bridge?'

He answered, 'None.'

She said, 'Is the water deep?'

He said, 'Deep.'

She said, 'Is the floor worn?'

He said, 'It is. Your foot may slip at any time, and you may be lost.'

She said, 'Have any crossed already?'

He said, 'Some have *tried!*'

She said, 'Is there a track to show where the best fording is?'

He said, 'It has to be made.'

She shaded her eyes with her hand; and she said, 'I will go.'

And he said, 'You must take off the clothes you wore in the desert: they are dragged down by them who go into the water so clothed.'

And she threw from her gladly the mantle of Ancient-received-opinions she wore, for it was worn full of holes. And she took the girdle from her waist that she had treasured so long, and the moths flew out of it in a cloud. And he said, 'Take the shoes of dependence off your feet.'

And she stood there naked, but for one white garment that clung close to her.

And he said, 'That you may keep. So they wear clothes in the Land of Freedom. In the water it buoys; it always swims.'

And I saw on its breast was written Truth; and it was white; the sun had not often shone on it; the other clothes had covered it up. And he said, 'Take this stick; hold it fast. In that day when it slips from your hand you are lost. Put it down before you; feel your way: where it cannot find a bottom do not set your foot.'

And she said, 'I am ready; let me go.'

And he said, 'No – but stay; what is that – in your breast?'
She was silent.

He said, 'Open it, and let me see.'

And she opened it. And against her breast was a tiny thing, who drank from it, and the yellow curls above his forehead pressed against it; and his knees were drawn up to her, and he held her breast fast with his hands.

And Reason said, 'Who is he, and what is he doing here?'

And she said, 'See his little wings – '

And Reason said, 'Put him down.'

And she said, 'He is asleep, and he is drinking! I will carry him to the Land of Freedom. He has been a child so long, so long, I have carried him. In the Land of Freedom he will be a man. We will walk together there, and his great white wings will overshadow me. He has lisped one word only to me in the desert – "Passion!" I have dreamed he might learn to say "Friendship" in that land.'

And Reason said, 'Put him down!'

And she said, 'I will carry him so – with one arm, and with the other I will fight the water.'

He said, 'Lay him down on the ground. When you are in the water you will forget to fight, you will think only of him. Lay him down.' He said, 'He will not die. When he finds you have left him alone he will open his wings and fly. He will be in the Land of Freedom before you. Those who reach the Land of Freedom, the first hand they see stretching down the bank to help them shall be Love's. He will be a man then, not a child. In your breast he cannot thrive; put him down that he may grow.'

And she took her bosom from his mouth, and he bit her, so that the blood ran down on to the ground. And she laid him down on the earth; and she covered her wound. And she bent and stroked his wings. And I saw the hair on her forehead turned white as snow, and she had changed from youth to age.

And she stood far off on the bank of the river. And she said, 'For what do I go to this far land which no one has ever reached? *Oh, I am alone! I am utterly alone!*'

And Reason, that old man, said to her, 'Silence! what do you hear?'

And she listened intently, and she said, 'I hear a sound of feet, a thousand times ten thousand and thousands of thousands, and they beat this way!'

He said, 'They are the feet of those that shall follow you. Lead on! make a track to the water's edge! Where you stand now, the ground will be beaten flat by ten thousand times ten thousand feet.' And he said, 'Have you seen the locusts how they cross a stream? First one comes down to the water-edge, and it is swept away, and then another comes and then another, and then another, and at last with their bodies piled up a bridge is built and the rest pass over.'

She said, 'And, of those that come first, some are swept away, and are heard of no more; their bodies do not even build the bridge?'

'And are swept away, and are heard of no more – and what of that?' he said.

'And what of that – ' she said.

'They make a track to the water's edge.'

'They make a track to the water's edge – .' And she said, 'Over that bridge which shall be built with our bodies, who will pass?'

He said, '*The entire human race.*'

And the woman grasped her staff.

And I saw her turn down that dark path to the river.

And I awoke; and all about me was the yellow afternoon light: the sinking sun lit up the fingers of the milk bushes; and my horse stood by me quietly feeding. And I turned on my side, and I watched the ants run by thousands in the red sand. I thought I would go on my way now – the afternoon was cooler. Then a drowsiness crept over me again, and I laid back my head and fell asleep.

And I dreamed a dream.

I dreamed I saw a land. And on the hills walked brave women and brave men, hand in hand. And they looked into each other's eyes, and they were not afraid.

And I saw the women also hold each other's hands.

And I said to him beside me, 'What place is this?'

And he said, 'This is heaven.'

And I said, 'Where is it?'

And he answered, 'On earth.'

And I said, 'When shall these things be?'

And he answered, 'IN THE FUTURE.'

And I awoke, and all about me was the sunset light; and on the low hills the sun lay, and a delicious coolness had crept over everything; and the ants were going slowly home. And I walked towards my horse, who stood quietly feeding. Then the sun passed down behind the hills; but I knew that the next day he would arise again.

The Buddhist Priest's Wife (1892)

Buddhist priests do not have wives. To want both a spiritual master and a sexual companion is here the woman character's central but impossible dream. This short story, written around 1891, after Schreiner had been living in South Africa again for over two years, expresses her fears and hostility about the seeming incompatibility of modern men's and women's sexual and intellectual needs. The story shows how a man can ignore in his personal life the political ideals he expounds in other contexts. The male politician in this story has certain affinities with Karl Pearson – his cold and aloof character, his ability to place the woman who is his intellectual equal in a category separate from other women yet to trivialise her ideals and ambitions when they conflict with his own. Judith Walkowitz (1986) elaborates the complicated sexual politics of Schreiner, Pearson, and the Men and Women's Club. 'The Buddhist Priest's Wife' first appeared in *Stories, Dreams and Allegories* (1923).

Cover her up! How still it lies! You can see the outline under the white. You would think she was asleep. Let the sunshine come in; it loved it so. She that had travelled so far, in so many lands, and done so much and seen so much, how she must like rest now! Did she ever love anything absolutely, this woman whom so many men loved, and so many women; who gave so much sympathy and never asked for anything in return! did she ever need a love she could not have? Was she never obliged to unclasp her fingers from anything to which they clung? Was she really so strong as she looked? Did she never wake up in the night crying for that which she could not have? Were thought and travel enough for her? Did she go about for long days with a weight that crushed her to earth? Cover her up! I do not think she would have liked us to look at her. In one way she was alone all her life; she would have liked to be alone now! . . . Life must have been very beautiful to her, or she would not look so young now. Cover her up! Let us go!

●　　　●　　　●　　　●　　　●

Many years ago in a London room, up long flights of stairs, a fire burnt up in a grate. It showed the marks on the walls where pictures had been taken down, and the little blue flowers in the wall-paper and the blue felt carpet on the floor, and a woman sat by the fire in a chair at one side.

Presently the door opened, and the old woman came in who took care of the entrance hall downstairs.

'Do you not want anything to-night?' she said.

'No, I am only waiting for a visitor; when they have been, I shall go.'

'Have you got all your things taken away already?'

'Yes, only these I am leaving.'

The old woman went down again, but presently came up with a cup of tea in her hand.

'You must drink that; it's good for one. Nothing helps one like tea when one's been packing all day.'

The young woman at the fire did not thank her, but she ran her hand over the old woman's from the wrist to the fingers.

'I'll say good-bye to you when I go out.'

The woman poked the fire, put the last coals on, and went.

When she had gone the young one did not drink the tea, but drew her little silver cigarette case from her pocket and lighted a cigarette. For a while she sat smoking by the fire; then she stood up and walked the room.

When she had paced for a while she sat down again beside the fire. She threw the end of her cigarette away into the fire, and then began to walk again with her hands behind her. Then she went back to her seat and lit another cigarette, and paced again. Presently she sat down, and looked into the fire; she pressed the palms of her hands together, and then sat quietly staring into it.

Then there was a sound of feet on the stairs and someone

knocked at the door.

She rose and threw the end into the fire and said without moving, 'Come in.'

The door opened and a man stood there in evening dress. He had a great-coat on, open in front.

'May I come in? I couldn't get rid of this downstairs; I didn't see where to leave it!' He took his coat off. 'How are you? This is a real bird's nest!'

She motioned to a chair.

'I hope you did not mind my asking you to come?'

'Oh no, I am delighted. I only found your note at my club twenty minutes ago.'

'So you really are going to India? How delightful! But what are you to do there? I think it was Grey told me six weeks ago you were going, but regarded it as one of those mythical stories which don't deserve credence. Yet I am sure I don't know! Why, nothing would surprise me.'

He looked at her in a half-amused, half-interested way.

'What a long time it is since we met! Six months, eight?'

'Seven,' she said.

'I really thought you were trying to avoid me. What have you been doing with yourself all this time?'

'Oh, been busy. Won't you have a cigarette?'

She held out the little case to him.

'Won't you take one yourself? I know you object to smoking with men, but you can make an exception in my case!'

'Thank you.' She lit her own and passed him the matches.

'But really what have you been doing with yourself all this time? You've entirely disappeared from civilised life. When I was down at the Grahams' in the spring, they said you were coming down there, and then at the last moment cried off. We were all quite disappointed. What is taking you to India now? Going to preach the doctrine of social and intellectual equality to the Hindu women and incite them to revolt? Marry some old Buddhist Priest, build a little cottage on the top of the Himalayas and live there, discuss philosophy and meditate? I believe that's what you'd like. I really shouldn't wonder if I heard you'd done it!'

She laughed and took out her cigarette case.

She smoked slowly.

'I've been here a long time, four years, and I want change. I was glad to see how well you succeeded in that election,' she said. 'You were much interested in it, were you not?'

'Oh, yes. We had a stiff fight. It tells in my favour, you know, though it was not exactly a personal matter. But it was a great worry.'

'Don't you think,' she said, 'you were wrong in sending that letter to the papers? It would have strengthened your position to have remained silent.'

'Yes, perhaps so; I think so now, but I did it under advice. However, we've won, so it's all right.' He leaned back in the chair.

'Are you pretty fit?'

'Oh, yes; pretty well; bored, you know. One doesn't know what all this working and striving is for sometimes.'

'Where are you going for your holiday this year?'

'Oh, Scotland, I suppose; I always do; the old quarters.'

'Why don't you go to Norway? It would be more change for you and rest you more. Did you get a book on sport in Norway?'

'Did you send it me? How kind of you! I read it with much interest. I was almost inclined to start off there and then. I suppose it is the kind of *vis inertiæ*[1] that creeps over one as one grows older that sends one back to the old place. A change would be much better.'

'There's a list at the end of the book,' she said, 'of exactly the things one needs to take. I thought it would save trouble; you could just give it to your man, and let him get them all. Have you still got him?'

'Oh, yes. He's as faithful to me as a dog. I think nothing would induce him to leave me. He won't allow me to go out hunting since I sprained my foot last autumn. I have to do it surreptitiously. He thinks I can't keep my seat with a sprained ankle; but he's a very good fellow; takes care of me like a mother.' He smoked quietly with the firelight glowing on his black coat. 'But what are you going to India for? Do you know anyone there?'

'No,' she said. 'I think it will be so splendid. I've always been a great deal interested in the East. It's a complex, interesting life.'

He turned and looked at her.

'Going to seek for more experience, you'll say, I suppose. I never knew a woman throw herself away as you do; a woman with your brilliant parts and attractions, to let the whole of life slip through your hands, and make nothing of it. You ought to be the most successful woman in London. Oh, yes; I know what you are going to say: "You don't care." That's just it; you don't. You are always going to get experience, going to get everything, and you never do. You are always going to write when you know enough, and you are never satisfied that you do. You ought to be making your two thousand a year, but you don't care. That's just it! Living, burying yourself here with a lot of old frumps.[2] You will never do anything. You could have everything and you let it slip.'

'Oh, my life is very full,' she said. 'There are only two things that are absolute realities, love and knowledge, and you can't escape them.'

She had thrown her cigarette end away and was looking into the fire, smiling.

'I've let these rooms to a woman friend of mine.' She glanced round the room, smiling. 'She doesn't know I'm going to leave these things here for her. She'll like them because they were mine. The world's very beautiful, I think – delicious.'

'Oh, yes. But what do you do with it? What do you make of it? You ought to settle down and marry like other women, not go wandering about the world to India and China and Italy, and God knows where. You are simply making a mess of your life. You're always surrounding yourself with all sorts of extraordinary people. If I hear any man or woman is a great friend of yours, I always say: "What's the matter? Lost his money? Lost his character? Got an incurable disease?" I believe the only way in which anyone becomes interesting to you is by having some complaint of mind or body. I believe you worship rags. To come and shut yourself up in a place like this away from everybody and everything! It's a mistake; it's idiotic, you know.'

'I'm very happy,' she said. 'You see,' she said, leaning forwards towards the fire with hands on her knees, 'what matters is that something should need you. It isn't a question of love. What's the use of being near a thing if other people could serve it as well as you can. If they could serve it better, it's pure selfishness. It's the need of one thing for another that makes the organic bond of union. You love mountains and horses, but they don't need you; so what's the use of saying anything about it! I suppose the most absolutely delicious thing in life is to feel a thing needs you, and to give at the moment it needs. Things that don't need you, you must love from a distance.'

'Oh, but a woman like you ought to marry, ought to have children. You go squandering yourself on every old beggar or forlorn female or escaped criminal you meet; it may be very nice for them, but it's a mistake from your point of view.'

He touched the ash gently with the tip of his little finger and let it fall.

'I intend to marry. It's a curious thing,' he said, resuming his pose with an elbow on one knee and his head bent forward on one side, so that she saw the brown hair with its close curls a little tinged with grey at the sides, 'that when a man reaches a certain age he wants to marry. He doesn't fall in love; it's not that he definitely plans anything; but he has a feeling that he ought to have a home and a wife and children. I suppose it is the same kind of feeling that makes a bird build nests at certain times of the year. It's not love; it's something else. When I was a young man I used to despise men for getting married; wondered what they did it for; they had everything to lose and nothing to gain. But when a man gets to be six-and-thirty his feeling changes. It's not love, passion, he wants; it's a home; it's a wife and children. He may have a house and servants; it isn't the same thing. I should have thought a woman would have felt it too.'

She was quiet for a minute, holding a cigarette between her fingers; then she said slowly:

'Yes, at times a woman has a curious longing to have a child, especially when she gets near to thirty or over it. It's something distinct from love for any definite person. But it's a thing one has to get over. For a woman, marriage is much more serious than for a man. She might pass her life without meeting a man whom she could possibly love, and, if she met him, it might not be right or possible. Marriage has become very complex now it has become so largely intellectual. Won't you have another?'

She held out the case to him. 'You can light it from mine.' She bent forward for him to light it.

'You are a man who ought to marry. You've no absorbing mental work with which the woman would interfere; it would complete you.' She sat back, smoking serenely.

'Yes,' he said, 'but life is too busy; I never find time to look for one, and I haven't a fancy for the pink-and-white prettiness so common and that some men like so. I need something else. If I am to have a wife I shall have to go to America to look for one.'

'Yes, an American would suit you best.'

'Yes,' he said, 'I don't want a woman to look after; she must be self-sustaining and she mustn't bore you. You know what I mean. Life is too full of cares to have a helpless child added to them.'

'Yes,' she said, standing up and leaning with her elbow against the fireplace. 'The kind of woman you want would be young and strong; she need not be excessively beautiful, but she must be attractive; she must have energy, but not too strongly marked an individuality; she must be largely neutral; she need not give you too passionate or too deep a devotion, but she must second you in a thoroughly rational manner. She must have the same aims and tastes that you have. No woman has the right to marry a man if she has to bend herself out of shape for him. She might wish to, but she could never be to him with all her passionate endeavour what the other woman could be to him without trying. Character will dominate over all and will come out at last.'

She looked down into the fire.

'When you marry you mustn't marry a woman who flatters you too much. It is always a sign of falseness somewhere. If a woman absolutely loves you as herself, she will criticise and understand you as herself. Two people who are to live through life together must be able to look into each other's eyes and speak the truth. That helps one through life. You would find many such women in America,' she said: 'women who would help you to succeed, who would not drag you down.'

'Yes, that's my idea. But how am I to obtain the ideal woman?'

'Go and look for her. Go to America instead of Scotland this year. It is perfectly right. A man has a right to look for what he needs. With a woman it is different. That's one of the radical differences between men and women.'

She looked downwards into the fire.

'It's a law of her nature and of sex relationship. There's nothing arbitrary or conventional about it any more than there is in her having to bear her child while the male does not. Intellectually we may both be alike. I suppose if fifty men and fifty women had to solve a mathematical problem, they would all do it in the same way; the more abstract and intellectual, the more alike we are. The nearer you approach to the personal and sexual, the more different we are. If I were to represent men's and women's natures,' she said, 'by a diagram, I would take two circular discs; the right side of each I should paint bright red; then I would shade the red away till in a spot on the left edge it became blue in the one and green in the other. That spot represents sex, and the nearer you come to it, the more the two discs differ in colour. Well then, if you turn them so that the red sides touch, they seem to be exactly alike, but if you turn them so that the green and blue paint form their point of contact, they will seem to be entirely unlike. That's why you notice the brutal, sensual men invariably believe women are entirely different from men, another species of creature; and very cultured, intellectual men sometimes believe we are exactly alike. You see, sex love in its substance may be the same in both of us; in the form of its expression it must differ. It is not man's fault; it is nature's. If a man loves a woman, he has a right to try to make her love him because he can do it openly, directly, without bending. There need be no subtlety, no indirectness. With a woman it's not so; she can take no love that is not laid openly, simply, at her feet. Nature ordains that she should never show what she feels; the woman who had told a man she loved him would have put between them a barrier once and for ever that could not be crossed; and if she subtly drew him towards her, using the woman's means – silence, finesse, the dropped handkerchief, the surprise visit, the gentle assertion she had not thought to see him when she had come a long way to meet him, then she would be damned; she would hold the love, but she would have desecrated it by subtlety; it would have no value. Therefore she must always go with her arms folded sexually; only the love which lays itself down at her feet and implores of her to accept it is love she can ever rightly take up. That is the true difference between a man and a woman. You may seek for love because you can do it openly; we cannot because we must do it subtly. A woman should always walk with her arms folded. Of course friendship is different. You are on a perfect equality with man then; you can ask him to come and see you as I asked you. That's the beauty of the intellect and intellectual life to a woman, that she drops her shackles a little; and that is why she shrinks from sex so. If she were dying perhaps, or doing something equal to death, she might. . . . Death means so much more to a woman than a man; when you knew you were dying, to look round on the world and feel the bond of sex that has broken and crushed you all your life gone, nothing but the human left, no woman any more, to meet everything on perfectly even ground. There's no reason why you shouldn't go to America and look for a wife perfectly deliberately. You will have to tell no lies. Look till you find a woman that you absolutely love, that you have not the smallest doubt suits you apart from love, and then ask her to marry you. You must have children; the life of an old childless man is very sad.'

'Yes, I should like to have children. I often feel now, what is it all for, this work, this striving, and no one to leave it to? It's a blank, suppose I succeed . . . ?'

'Suppose you get your title?'

'Yes; what is it all worth to me if I've no one to leave it to? That's my feeling. It's really very strange to be sitting and talking like this to you. But you are so different from other women. If all women were like you, all your theories of the

117

equality of men and women would work. You're the only woman with whom I never realise that she is a woman.'

'Yes,' she said.

She stood looking down into the fire.

'How long will you stay in India?'

'Oh, I'm not coming back.'

'Not coming back! That's impossible. You will be breaking the hearts of half the people here if you don't. I never knew a woman who had such power of entrapping men's hearts as you have in spite of that philosophy of yours. I don't know,' he smiled, 'that I should not have fallen into the snare myself – three years ago I almost thought I should – if you hadn't always attacked me so incontinently and persistently on all and every point and on each and every occasion. A man doesn't like pain. A succession of slaps damps him. But it doesn't seem to have that effect on other men. . . . There was that fellow down in the country when I was there last year, perfectly ridiculous. You know his name . . . .' He moved his fingers to try and remember it – 'big, yellow moustache, a major, gone to the east coast of Africa now; the ladies unearthed it that he was always carrying about a photograph of yours in his pocket; and he used to take out little scraps of things you printed and show them to people mysteriously. He almost had a duel with a man one night after dinner because he mentioned you; he seemed to think there was something incongruous between your name and – '

'I do not like to talk of any man who has loved me,' she said. 'However small and poor his nature may be, he has given me his best. There is nothing ridiculous in love. I think a woman should feel that all the love men have given her which she has not been able to return is a kind of crown set up above her which she is always trying to grow tall enough to wear. I can't bear to think that all the love that has been given me has been wasted on something unworthy of it. Men have been very beautiful and greatly honoured me. I am grateful to them. If a man tells you he loves you,' she said, looking into the fire, 'with his breast uncovered before you for you to strike him if you will, the least you can do is to put out your hand and cover it up from other people's eyes. If I were a deer,' she said, 'and a stag got hurt following me, even though I could not have him for a companion, I would stand still and scrape the sand with my foot over the place where his blood had fallen; the rest of the herd should never know he had been hurt there following me. I would cover the blood up, if I were a deer,' she said, and then she was silent.

Presently she sat down in her chair and said, with her hand before her: 'Yet, you know, I have not the ordinary feeling about love. I think the one who is loved confers the benefit on the one who loves, it's been so great and beautiful that it should be loved. I think the man should be grateful to the woman or the woman to the man whom they have been able to love, whether they have been loved back or whether circumstances have divided them or not.' She stroked her knee softly with her hand.

'Well, really, I must go now.' He pulled out his watch. 'It's so fascinating sitting here talking that I could stay all night, but I've still two engagements.' He rose; she rose also and stood before him looking up at him for a moment.

'How well you look! I think you have found the secret of perpetual youth. You don't look a day older than when I first saw you just four years ago. You always look as if you were on fire and being burnt up, but you never are, you know.'

He looked down at her with a kind of amused face as one does at an interesting child or a big Newfoundland dog.

'When shall we see you back?'

'Oh, not at all!'

'Not at all! Oh, we must have you back; you belong here, you know. You'll get tired of your Buddhist and come back to us.'

'You didn't mind my asking you to come and say good-bye?' she said in a childish manner unlike her determinateness when she discussed anything impersonal. 'I wanted to say good-bye to everyone. If one hasn't said good-bye one feels restless and feels one would have to come back. If one has said good-bye to all one's friends, then one knows it is all ended.'

'Oh, this isn't a final farewell! You must come in ten years' time and we'll compare notes – you about your Buddhist Priest, I about my fair ideal American; and we'll see who succeeded best.'

She laughed.

'I shall always see your movements chronicled in the newspapers, so we shall not be quite sundered; and you will hear of me perhaps.'

'Yes, I hope you will be very successful.'

She was looking at him, with her eyes wide open, from head to foot. He turned to the chair where his coat hung.

'Can't I help you put it on?'

'Oh, no, thank you.'

He put it on.

'Button the throat,' she said, 'the room is warm.'

He turned to her in his great-coat and with his gloves. They were standing near the door.

'Well, good-bye. I hope you will have a very pleasant time.'

He stood looking down upon her, wrapped in his great-coat.

She put up one hand a little in the air. 'I want to ask you something,' she said quickly.

'Well, what is it?'

'Will you please kiss me?'

For a moment he looked down at her, then he bent over her.

In after years he could never tell certainly, but he always thought she put up her hand and rested it on the crown of his head, with a curious soft caress, something like a mother's touch when her child is asleep and she does not want to wake it. Then he looked round, and she was gone. The door had closed noiselessly. For a moment he stood motionless, then he walked to the fireplace and looked down into the fender at a little cigarette end lying there, then he walked quickly back to the door and opened it. The stairs were in darkness and silence. He rang the bell violently. The old woman came up. He asked her where the lady was. She said she had gone out, she had a cab waiting. He asked when she would be back. The old woman said, 'Not at all'; she had left. He asked where she had gone. The woman said she did not know; she had left orders that all her letters should be kept for six or eight months till she wrote and sent her address. He asked whether she had no idea where he might find her. The woman said no. He walked up to a space in the wall where a picture had hung and stood staring at it as though the picture were still hanging there. He drew his mouth as though he were emitting a long whistle, but no sound came. He gave the old woman ten shillings and went downstairs.

That was eight years ago.

How beautiful life must have been to it that it looks so young still!

'The Policy in Favour of Protection – ' (1892)

First published in the *New Review* in 1892, '"The Policy in Favour of Protection – "' was reprinted in *Dream Life and Real Life* (1893). In the later nineteenth century the liberal government of Victoria, Australia, enacted a series of controversial 'protective' tariffs meant to develop domestic industry and raise the standard of living. This story compares two women – one a 'sex parasite' and one an independent journalist, and the title draws our attention to the implicit parallel between individual and community forms of dependency, which Schreiner clearly opposed in both areas.

Was it Right? – Was it Wrong?

A woman sat at her desk in the corner of a room; behind her a fire burnt brightly.

Presently a servant came in and gave her a card.

'Say I am busy and can see no one now. I have to finish this article by two o'clock.'

The servant came back. The caller said she would only keep her a moment: it was necessary she should see her.

The woman rose from her desk. 'Tell the boy to wait. Ask the lady to come in.'

A young woman in a silk dress, with a cloak reaching to her feet, entered. She was tall and slight, with fair hair.

'I knew you would not mind. I wished to see you so!'

The woman offered her a seat by the fire. 'May I loosen your cloak? – the room is warm.'

'I wanted so to come and see you. You are the only person in the world who could help me! I know you are so large, and generous, and kind to other women!' She sat down. Tears stood in her large blue eyes: she was pulling off her little gloves unconsciously.

'You know Mr – ' (she mentioned the name of a well-known writer): 'I know you meet him often in your work. I want you to do something for me!'

The woman on the hearthrug looked down at her.

'I couldn't tell my father or my mother, or any one else; but I can tell you, though I know so little of you. You know, last summer he came and stayed with us a month. I saw a great deal of him. I don't know if he liked me; I know he liked my singing, and we rode together – I liked him more than any man I have ever seen. Oh, you know it isn't true that a woman can only like a man when he likes her; and I thought, perhaps, he liked me a little. Since we have been in town we have asked, but he has never come to see us. Perhaps people have been saying something to him about me. You know him, you are always meeting him, couldn't you say or do anything for me?' She looked up with her lips white and drawn. 'I feel sometimes as if I were going mad! Oh, it is so terrible to be a woman!' The woman looked down at her. 'Now I hear he likes another woman. I don't know who she is, but they say she is so clever, and writes. Oh, it is so terrible, I can't bear it.'

The woman leaned her elbow against the mantelpiece, and her face against her hand. She looked down into the fire. Then she turned and looked at the younger woman. 'Yes,' she said, 'it is a very terrible thing to be a woman.' She was silent. She said with some difficulty: 'Are you sure you love him? Are you sure it is not only the feeling a young girl has for an older man who is celebrated, and of whom every one is talking?'

'I have been nearly mad. I haven't slept for weeks!' She knit her little hands together, till the jewelled ring almost cut into the fingers. He is everything to me; there is nothing else in the world. You, who are so great, and strong, and clever, and who care only for your work, and for men as your friends, you cannot understand what it is when one person is everything to you, when there is nothing else in the world!'

'And what do you want me to do?'

'Oh, I don't know!' She looked up. 'A woman knows what she can do. Don't tell him that I love him.' She looked up again. 'Just say something to him. Oh, it's so terrible to be a woman; I can't do anything. You won't tell him exactly that I love him? That's the thing that makes a man hate a woman, if you tell it him plainly.'

'If I speak to him I must speak openly. He is my friend. I cannot fence with him. I have never fenced with him in my own affairs.' She moved as though she were going away from the fireplace, then she turned and said: 'Have you thought of what love is between a man and a woman when it means marriage? That long, long life together, day after day, stripped of all romance and distance, living face to face: seeing each other as a man sees his own soul? Do you realise that the end of marriage is to make the man and woman stronger than they were; and that if you cannot, when you are an old man and woman and sit by the fire, say, "Life has been a braver and a freer thing for us, because we passed it hand in hand, than if we had passed through it alone," it has failed? Do you care for him enough to live for him, not to-morrow, but when he is an old, faded man, and you an old, faded woman? Can you forgive him his sins and his weaknesses, when they hurt you most? If he were to lie a querulous invalid for twenty years, would you be able to fold him in your arms all that time, and comfort him, as a mother comforts her little child?' The woman drew her breath heavily.

'Oh, I love him absolutely! I would be glad to die, if only I could once know that he loved me better than anything in the world!'

The woman stood looking down at her. 'Have you never thought of that other woman; whether *she* could not perhaps make his life as perfect as you?' she asked, slowly.

'Oh, no woman ever could be to him what I would be. I would live for him. He belongs to me.' She bent herself forward, not crying, but her shoulders moving. 'It is such a terrible thing to be a woman, to be able to do nothing and say nothing!'

The woman put her hand on her shoulder; the younger woman looked up into her face; then the elder turned away and stood looking into the fire. There was such quiet, you could hear the clock tick above the writing-table.

The woman said: 'There is one thing I can do for you. I do not know if it will be of any use – I will do it.' She turned away.

'Oh, you are so great and good, so beautiful, so different from other women, who are always thinking only of themselves! Thank you so much. I know I can trust you. I couldn't have told my mother, or any one but you.'

'Now you must go; I have my work to finish.'

The younger woman put her arms round her. 'Oh, you are so good and beautiful!'

The silk dress and the fur cloak rustled out of the room.

The woman who was left alone walked up and down, at last faster and faster, till the drops stood on her forehead. After a time she went up to the table: there was written illegibly in a man's hand on a fragment of manuscript paper: '*Can I come to see you this afternoon?*' Near it was a closed and addressed envelope. She opened it. In it were written the words: '*Yes, please, come.*'

She tore it across and wrote the words: '*No, I shall not be at liberty.*'

She closed them in an envelope and addressed them. Then she rolled up the manuscript on the table and rang the bell. She gave it to the servant. 'Tell the boy to give this to his master, and say the article ends rather abruptly; they must state it is to be continued; I will finish it to-morrow. As he passes No. 20 let him leave this note there.'

The servant went out. She walked up and down with her hands folded above her head.

Two months after, the older woman stood before the fire. The door opened suddenly, and the younger woman came in.

'I had to come – I couldn't wait. You have heard, he was married this morning? Oh, do you think it is true? Do help me!' She put out her hands.

'Sit down. Yes, it is quite true.'

'Oh, it is so terrible, and I didn't know anything! Did you ever say anything to him?' She caught the woman's hands.

'I never saw him again after the day you were here – so I could not speak to him – but I did what I could.' She stood looking passively into the fire.

'And they say she is quite a child, only eighteen. They say he only saw her three times before he proposed to her. Do you think it is true?'

'Yes, it is quite true.'

'He can't love her. They say he's only marrying her for her rank and her money.'

The woman turned quickly. 'What right have you to say that? No one but me knows him. What need has he of any one's rank or wealth? He is greater than them all! Older women may have failed him; he has needed to turn to her beautiful, fresh young life to compensate him. She is a woman whom any man might have loved, so young and beautiful; her family are famed for their intellect. If he trains her, she may make him a better wife than any other woman would have done.'

'Oh, but I can't bear it – I can't bear it!' The younger woman sat down in the chair. 'She will be his wife, and have his children.'

'Yes.' The elder woman moved quickly. 'One wants to have the child, and lay its head on one's breast and feed it.' She moved quickly. 'It would not matter if another woman bore it, if one had it to take care of.' She moved restlessly.

'Oh, no, I couldn't bear it to be hers. When I think of her I feel as if I were dying; all my fingers turn cold; I feel dead. Oh, you were only his friend; you don't know!'

The older spoke softly and quickly. 'Don't you feel a little gentle to her when you think she's going to be his wife and the mother of his child? I would like to put my arms round her and touch her once, if she would let me. She is so beautiful, they say.'

'Oh, I could never bear to see her; it would kill me. And they are so happy together to-day! He is loving her so!'

'Don't you want him to be happy?' The older woman looked down at her. 'Have you *never* loved him, at all?'

The younger woman's face was covered with her hands. 'Oh, it's so terrible, so dark! and I shall go on living year after year, always in this awful pain! Oh, if I could only die!'

The older woman stood looking into the fire; then slowly and measuredly she said: 'There are times, in life, when everything seems dark, when the brain reels; and we cannot see that there is anything but death. But, if we wait long enough, after long, long years, calm comes. It may be we cannot say it was well; but we are contented, we accept the past. The struggle is ended. That day may come for you, perhaps sooner than you think.' She spoke slowly, and with difficulty.

'No, it can never come for me. If once I have loved a thing, I love it for ever. I can never forget.'

'Love is not the only end in life. There are other things to live for.'

'Oh yes, for you! To me love is everything!'

'Now, you must go, dear.'

The younger woman stood up. 'It has been such a comfort to talk to you. I think I should have killed myself if I had not come. You help me so. I shall always be grateful to you.'

The older woman took her hand.

'I want to ask something of you.'

'What is it?'

'I cannot quite explain to you. You will not understand. But there are times when something more terrible can come into a life than that it should lose what it loves. If you have had a dream of what life ought to be, and you try to make it real, and you fail; and something you have killed out in your heart for long years wakes up and cries, "Let each man play his own game, and care nothing for the hand of his fellow! Each man for himself. *So* the game must be played!" and you doubt all you have lived for, and the ground seems washing out under your feet – ' She paused. 'Such a time has come to me now. If you would promise me that if ever another woman comes to seek your help, you will give it to her, and try to love her for my sake, I think it will help me. I think I should be able to keep my faith.'

'Oh, I will do anything you ask me to. You are so good and great.'

'Oh, good and great! – if you knew! Now go, dear.'

'I have not kept you from your work, have I?'

'No; I have not been working lately. Goodbye, dear.'

The younger woman went; and the elder knelt down by the chair, and wailed like a little child when you have struck it and it does not dare to cry loud.

A year after; it was early spring again.

The woman sat at her desk writing; behind her the fire burnt brightly. She was writing a leading article on the causes which in differing peoples lead to the adoption of Free Trade or Protectionist principles.

The woman wrote on quickly. After a while the servant entered and laid a pile of letters on the table. 'Tell the boy I shall have done in fifteen minutes.' She wrote on. Then she caught sight of the writing on one of the letters. She put down her pen, and opened it. It ran so:–

'Dear Friend, – I am writing to you, because I know you will rejoice to hear of my great happiness. Do you remember how you told me that day by the fire to *wait*, and after long, long years I should see that all was for the best? That time has come sooner than we hoped. Last week in Rome I was married to the best, noblest, most large-hearted of men. We are now in Florence together. You don't know how beautiful all life is to me. I know now that the old passion was only a girl's foolish dream. My husband is the first man I have ever truly loved. He loves me and understands me as no other man ever could. I am thankful that my dream was broken; God had better things in store for me. I don't have that woman any more; I love every one! How are you, dear? We shall come and see you as soon as we arrive in England. I always think of you so happy in your great work and helping other people. I don't think *now* it is terrible to be a woman; it is lovely.

'I hope you are enjoying this beautiful spring weather.

'Yours always full of gratitude and love,

'E – '

The woman read the letter: then she stood up and walked towards the fire. She did not re-read it, but stood with it open in her hand, looking down into the blaze. Her lips were drawn in at the corners. Presently she tore the letter up slowly, and watched the bits floating down one by one into the grate. Then she went back to her desk, and began to write, with her mouth still drawn in at the corners. After a while she laid her arm on the paper and her head on her arm, and seemed to go to sleep there.

Presently the servant knocked; the boy was waiting. 'Tell him to wait ten minutes more.' She took up her pen – 'The policy of the Australian Colonies in favour of Protection is easily understood – ' she waited – 'when one considers the fact – the fact – '; then she finished the article.

Cape Town, South Africa, 1892.

Fantasy and the Female Body

Dream Life and Real Life: a Little African Story (1880)

This short story, first published in *The New College Magazine* in 1881, is a transitional piece between the children's stories Schreiner wrote as a governess ('The Wax Doll and the Stepmother' and 'The Adventures of Master Towser', in *Stories, Dreams and Allegories*) and her three novels: *Undine* (1929), *The Story of an African Farm* (1883, rpt 1968), and *From Man to Man; or, Perhaps Only . . .* (1926, rpt 1982). More importantly, it is the only story Schreiner tells from the point of view of the labouring class: Jannita may be a white or black indentured servant; in either case she is economically dependent and at the absolute bottom of the family from which she initially flees. We should remember that the 'navvy' (English), 'Hottentot' (Khoikhoi), and 'Bushman' (San) workers who abuse and betray her are of the same class, but structurally in control of her because they are older and are men.

Little Jannita sat alone beside a milk-bush. Before her and behind her stretched the plain, covered with red sand and thorny Karroo[1] bushes; and here and there a milk-bush, looking like a bundle of pale green rods tied together. Not a tree was to be seen anywhere, except on the banks of the river, and that was far away, and the sun beat on her head. Round her fed the Angora goats she was herding; pretty things, especially the little ones, with white silky curls that touched the ground. But Jannita sat crying. If an angel should gather up in his cup all the tears that have been shed, I think the bitterest would be those of children.

By and by she was so tired, and the sun was so hot, she laid her head against the milk-bush, and dropped asleep.

She dreamed a beautiful dream. She thought that when she

went back to the farmhouse in the evening, the walls were covered with vines and roses, and the kraals were not made of red stone, but of lilac-trees full of blossom. And the fat old Boer[2] smiled at her, and the stick he held across the door for the goats to jump over was a lily rod with seven blossoms at the end. When she went to the house her mistress gave her a whole roaster-cake for her supper, and the mistress's daughter had stuck a rose in the cake; and her mistress's son-in-law said 'Thank you!' when she pulled off his boots, and did not kick her.

It was a beautiful dream.

While she lay thus dreaming, one of the little kids came and licked her on her cheek, because of the salt from her dried-up tears. And in her dream she was not a poor indentured child any more, living with Boers. It was her father who kissed her. He said he had only been asleep – that day when he lay down under the thorn-bush; he had not really died. He felt her hair, and said it was grown long and silky, and he said they would go back to Denmark now. He asked her why her feet were bare, and what the marks on her back were. Then he put her head on his shoulder, and picked her up, and carried her away, away! She laughed – she could feel her face against his brown beard. His arms were so strong.

As she lay there dreaming with the ants running over her naked feet, and with her brown curls lying in the sand, a Hottentot came up to her. He was dressed in ragged yellow trousers, and a dirty shirt, and torn jacket. He had a red handkerchief round his head, and a felt hat above that. His nose was flat, his eyes like slits, and the wool on his head was gathered into little round balls. He came to the milk-bush, and looked at the little girl lying in the hot sun. Then he walked off, and caught one of the fattest little Angora goats, and held its mouth fast, as he stuck it under his arm. He looked back to see that she was still sleeping, and jumped down into one of the sluits.[3] He walked down the bed of the sluit a little way and came to an overhanging bank, under which, sitting on the red sand, were two men. One was a tiny, ragged old Bushman,[4] four feet high; the other was an English navvy[5] in a dark blue blouse. They cut the kid's throat with the navvy's long knife, and covered up the blood with sand, and buried the entrails and skin. Then they talked, and quarrelled a little; and then they talked quietly again.

The Hottentot man put a leg of the kid under his coat and left the rest of the meat for the two in the sluit, and walked away.

When little Jannita awoke it was almost sunset. She sat up very frightened, but her goats were all about her. She began to drive them home. 'I do not think there are any lost,' she said.

Dirk, the Hottentot, had brought his flock home already, and stood at the kraal door with his ragged yellow trousers. The fat old Boer put his stick across the door, and let Jannita's goats jump over, one by one. He counted them. When the last jumped over: 'Have you been to sleep to-day?' he said; 'there is one missing.'

Then little Jannita knew what was coming, and she said, in a low voice, 'No.' And then she felt in her heart that deadly sickness that you feel when you tell a lie; and again she said, 'Yes.'

'Do you think you will have any supper this evening?' said the Boer.

'No,' said Jannita.

'What do you think you will have?'

'I don't know,' said Jannita.

'Give me your whip,' said the Boer to Dirk, the Hottentot.

•　　　•　　　•　　　•　　　•

The moon was all but full that night. Oh, but its light was beautiful!

The little girl crept to the door of the outhouse where she slept, and looked at it. When you are hungry, and very, very sore, you do not cry. She leaned her chin on one hand, and looked, with her great dove's eyes – the other hand was cut open, so she wrapped it in her pinafore. She looked across the plain at the sand and the low karroo-bushes, with the moonlight on them.

Presently, there came slowly, from far away, a wild spring-buck. It came close to the house, and stood looking at it in wonder, while the moonlight glinted on its horns, and in its great eyes. It stood wondering at the red brick walls, and the girl watched it. Then, suddenly, as if it scorned it all, it curved its beautiful back and turned; and away it fled over the bushes and sand, like a sheeny streak of white lightning. She stood up to watch it. So free, so free! Away, away! She watched, till she could see it no more on the wide plain.

Her heart swelled, larger, larger, larger: she uttered a low cry; and without waiting, pausing, thinking, she followed on its track. Away, away, away! 'I – I also!' she said, 'I – I also!'

When at last her legs began to tremble under her, and she stopped to breathe, the house was a speck behind her. She dropped on the earth, and held her panting sides.

She began to think now.

If she stayed on the plain they would trace her footsteps in the morning and catch her; but if she waded in the water in the bed of the river they would not be able to find her footmarks; and she would hide, there where the rocks and the kopjes[6] were.

So she stood up and walked towards the river. The water in the river was low; just a line of silver in the broad bed of sand, here and there broadening into a pool. She stepped into it, and bathed her feet in the delicious cold water. Up and up the stream she walked, where it rattled over the pebbles, and past where the farmhouse lay; and where the rocks were large, she leaped from one to the other. The night wind in her face made her strong – she laughed. She had never felt such night wind before. So the night smells to the wild bucks, because they are free! A free thing feels as a chained thing never can.

At last she came to a place where the willows grew on each side of the river, and trailed their long branches on the sandy bed. She could not tell why, she could not tell the reason, but a feeling of fear came over her.

On the left bank rose a chain of kopjes and a precipice of rocks. Between the precipice and the river bank there was a narrow path covered by the fragments of fallen rock. And upon the summit of the precipice a kippersol-tree grew, whose palm-like leaves were clearly cut out against the night sky. The rocks cast a deep shadow, and the willow-trees, on either side of the river. She paused, looked up and about her, and then ran on, fearful.

'What was I afraid of? How foolish I have been!' she said, when she came to a place where the trees were not so close together. And she stood still and looked back and shivered.

At last her steps grew wearier and wearier. She was very sleepy now, she could scarcely lift her feet. She stepped out of the river-bed. She only saw that the rocks about her were wild, as though many little kopjes had been broken up and strewn upon the ground, lay down at the foot of an aloe, and fell asleep.

· · · · ·

But, in the morning, she saw what a glorious place it was. The rocks were piled on one another, and tossed this way and that. Prickly pears grew among them, and there were no less than six kippersol-trees scattered here and there among the broken kopjes. In the rocks there were hundreds of homes for the coneys,[7] and from the crevices wild asparagus hung down. She ran to the river, bathed in the clear cold water, and tossed it over her head. She sang aloud. All the songs she knew were sad, so she could not sing them now, she was glad, she was so free; but she sang the notes without the words, as the cock-o-veets do. Singing and jumping all the way, she went back, and took a sharp stone, and cut at the root of a kippersol, and got out a large piece, as long as her arm, and sat to chew it. Two coneys came out on the rock above her head and peeped at her. She held them out a piece, but they did not want it, and ran away.

It was very delicious to her. Kippersol is like raw quince, when it is very green; but she liked it. When good food is thrown at you by other people, strange to say, it is very bitter; but whatever you find yourself is sweet!

When she had finished she dug out another piece, and went to look for a pantry to put it in. At the top of a head of rocks up which she clambered she found that some large stones stood apart but met at the top, making a room.

'Oh, this is my little home!' she said.

At the top and all round it was closed, only in the front it was open. There was a beautiful shelf in the wall for the kippersol, and she scrambled down again. She brought a great branch of prickly pear, and stuck it in a crevice before the door, and hung wild asparagus over it, till it looked as though it grew there. No one could see that there was a room there, for she left only a tiny opening, and hung a branch of feathery asparagus over it. Then she crept in to see how it looked. There was a glorious soft green light. Then she went out and picked some of those purple little ground flowers – you know them – those that keep their faces close to the ground, but when you turn them up and look at them they are deep blue eyes looking into yours! She took them with a little earth, and put them in the crevices between the rocks; and so the room was quite furnished. Afterwards she went down to the river and brought her arms full of willow, and made a lovely bed; and because the weather was very hot, she lay down to rest upon it.

She went to sleep soon, and slept long, for she was very weak. Late in the afternoon she was awakened by a few cold drops falling on her face. She sat up. A great and fierce thunderstorm had been raging, and a few of the cool drops had fallen through the crevice in the rocks. She pushed the asparagus branch aside, and looked out, with her little hands folded about her knees. She heard the thunder rolling, and saw the red torrents rush among the stones on their way to the river. She heard the roar of the river as it now rolled, angry and red, bearing away stumps and trees on its muddy water. She listened and smiled, and pressed closer to the rock that took care of her. She pressed the palm of her hand against it. When you have no one to love you, you love the dumb things very much. When the sun set, it cleared up. Then the little girl ate some kippersol, and lay down again to sleep. She thought there was nothing so nice as to sleep. When one has had no food but kippersol juice for two days, one doesn't feel strong.

'It is so nice here,' she thought, as she went to sleep, 'I will stay here always.'

Afterwards the moon rose. The sky was very clear now, there was not a cloud anywhere; and the moon shone in through the bushes in the door, and made a lattice-work of light on her face. She was dreaming a beautiful dream. The loveliest dreams of all are dreamed when you are hungry. She thought she was walking in a beautiful place, holding her father's hand, and they both had crowns on their head, crowns of wild asparagus. The people

138

whom they passed smiled and kissed her; some gave her flowers, and some gave her food, and the sunlight was everywhere. She dreamed the same dream over and over, and it grew more and more beautiful; till, suddenly, it seemed as though she were standing quite alone. She looked up: on one side of her was the high precipice, on the other was the river, with the willow-trees, drooping their branches into the water; and the moonlight was over all. Up, against the night sky the pointed leaves of the kippersol-trees were clearly marked, and the rocks and the willow-trees cast dark shadows.

In her sleep she shivered, and half awoke.

'Ah! I am not there, I am here,' she said; and she crept closer to the rock, and kissed it, and went to sleep again.

It must have been about three o'clock, for the moon had begun to sink towards the western sky, when she woke, with a violent start. She sat up, and pressed her hand against her heart.

'What can it be? A coney must surely have run across my feet and frightened me!' she said, and she turned to lie down again; but soon she sat up. Outside, there was the distinct sound of thorns crackling in a fire.

She crept to the door and made an opening in the branches with her fingers.

A large fire was blazing in the shadow, at the foot of the rocks. A little Bushman sat over some burning coals that had been raked from it, cooking meat. Stretched on the ground was an Englishman, dressed in a blouse, and with a heavy, sullen face. On the stone beside him was Dirk, the Hottentot, sharpening a bowie knife.

She held her breath. Not a coney in all the rocks was so still.

'They can never find me here,' she said; and she knelt, and listened to every word they said. She could hear it all.

'You may have all the money,' said the Bushman; 'but I want the cask of brandy. I will set the roof alight in six places, for a Dutchman burnt my mother once alive in a hut, with three children.'

'You are sure there is no one else on the farm?' said the navvy.

'No, I have told you till I am tired,' said Dirk; 'the two

139

Kaffirs have gone with the son to town; and the maids have gone to a dance; there is only the old man and the two women left.'

'But suppose,' said the navvy, 'he should have the gun at his bedside, and loaded!'

'He never has,' said Dirk; 'it hangs in the passage, and the cartridges too. He never thought when he bought it what work it was for! I only wish the little white girl was there still,' said Dirk; 'but she is drowned. We traced her footmarks to the great pool that has no bottom.'

She listened to every word, and they talked on.

Afterwards, the little Bushman, who crouched over the fire, sat up suddenly, listening.

'Ha! what is that?' he said.

A Bushman is like a dog: his ear is so fine he knows a jackal's tread from a wild dog's.

'I heard nothing,' said the navvy.

'I heard,' said the Hottentot; 'but it was only a coney on the rocks.'

'No coney, no coney,' said the Bushman; 'see, what is that there moving in the shade round the point?'

'Nothing! you idiot,' said the navvy. 'Finish your meat; we must start now.'

There were two roads to the homestead. One went along the open plain, and was by far the shortest; but you might be seen half a mile off. The other ran along the river bank, where there were rocks, and holes, and willow-trees to hide among. And all down the river bank ran a little figure.

The river was swollen by the storm full to its banks, and the willow-trees dipped their half-drowned branches into its water. Wherever there was a gap between them, you could see it flow, red and muddy, with the stumps upon it. But the little figure ran on and on; never looking, never thinking; panting, panting! There, where the rocks were the thickest; there, where on the open space the moonlight shone; there, where the prickly pears were tangled, and the rocks cast shadows, on it ran; the little hands clenched, the little heart beating, the eyes fixed always ahead.

It was not far to run now. Only the narrow path between the high rocks and the river.

At last she came to the end of it, and stood for an instant. Before her lay the plain, and the red farmhouse, so near, that if persons had been walking there you might have seen them in the moonlight. She clasped her hands. 'Yes, I will tell them, I will tell them!' she said; 'I am almost there!' She ran forward again, then hesitated; she shaded her eyes from the moonlight, and looked. Between her and the farm-house there were three figures moving over the low bushes.

In the sheeny moonlight you could see how they moved on, slowly and furtively; the short one, and the one in light clothes, and the one in dark.

'I cannot help them now!' she cried, and sank down on the ground, with her little hands clasped before her.

·　　　·　　　·　　　·　　　·

'Awake, awake!' said the farmer's wife; 'I hear a strange noise; something calling, calling, calling!'

The man rose and went to the window.

'I hear it also,' he said; 'surely some jackal's at the sheep. I will load my gun and go and see.'

'It sounds to me like the cry of no jackal,' said the woman; and when he was gone she woke her daughter.

'Come, let us go and make a fire, I can sleep no more,' she said; 'I have heard a strange thing to-night. Your father said it was a jackal's cry, but no jackal cries so. It was a child's voice, and it cried, "Master, master, wake!"'

The women looked at each other; then they went to the kitchen, and made a great fire; and they sang psalms all the while.

At last the man came back; and they asked him, 'What have you seen?' 'Nothing,' he said, 'but the sheep asleep in their kraals, and the moonlight on the walls. And yet, it did seem to me,' he added, 'that far away near the krantz[8] by the river, I saw three figures moving. And afterwards – it might have been fancy – I thought I heard the cry again; but since that, all has been still there.'

·　　　·　　　·　　　·　　　·

Next day a navvy had returned to the railway works.

'Where have you been so long?' his comrades asked.

'He keeps looking over his shoulder,' said one, 'as though he thought he should see something there.'

'When he drank his grog to-day,' said another, 'he let it fall, and looked round.'

Next day, a small old Bushman and a Hottentot, in ragged yellow trousers, were at a wayside canteen. When the Bushman had had brandy, he began to tell how something (he did not say whether it was man, woman, or child) had lifted up its hands and cried for mercy; had kissed a white man's hands, and cried to him to help it. Then the Hottentot took the Bushman by the throat, and dragged him out.

Next night, the moon rose up, and mounted the quiet sky. She was full now, and looked in at the little home; at the purple flowers stuck about the room, and the kippersol on the shelf. Her light fell on the willow-trees, and on the high rocks, and on a little new-made heap of earth and round stones. Three men knew what was under it: and no one else ever will.

Lily Kloof, South Africa.

Five Pieces from *Dreams* (1890)

The following items are all from *Dreams*, published in 1890. In a Preface to *The Story of an African Farm* that responded to initial criticisms of that novel, Schreiner wrote that novels 'may be painted' according to either the 'stage method' or 'the method of the life we all lead'. She continues, 'Should one sit down to paint the scenes among which [she] has grown, [she] will find that the facts creep in upon [her]. Those brilliant phases and shapes which the imagination sees in far off lands are not for [her] to portray. Sadly [she] must squeeze the colour from [her] brush, and dip it into the grey pigments around [her]. [She] must paint what lies before [her]'. If, from an English vantage point, Schreiner's novels and short stories seemed to have an excess of 'grey pigments', of fidelity to the pain and suffering of all black and indeed of many white South Africans in the late nineteenth century, her 'creative imagination' remained 'untrammelled' in the short, visionary pieces she wrote in the late 1880s and collected in *Dreams*. Schreiner's allegories are a bit like New Testament parables, but filled with the ideals and the materialism of Emerson, Goethe and the English Romantic poets. After Schreiner's death Arnold Bennett wrote that there was 'nothing like [*Dreams*] before in English literature! Nor have they been even tolerably imitated.' At the end of each of these allegories, Schreiner notes the place where it was written, drawing the reader's attention back to the physical and historical person who is dreaming and writing of other places and other times.

The Gardens of Pleasure

She walked upon the beds, and the sweet rich scent arose; and she gathered her hands full of flowers. Then Duty, with his white clear features, came and looked at her. Then she ceased from gathering, but she walked away among the flowers, smiling, and with her hands full.

Then Duty, with his still white face, came again, and looked at her; but she, she turned her head away from him. At last she saw his face, and she dropped the fairest of the flowers she had held, and walked silently away.

Then again he came to her. And she moaned, and bent her head low, and turned to the gate. But as she went out she looked back at the sunlight on the faces of the flowers, and wept in anguish. Then she went out, and it shut behind her for ever; but still in her hand she held of the buds she had gathered, and the scent was very sweet in the lonely desert.

But he followed her. Once more he stood before her with his still, white, death-like face. And she knew what he had come for: she unbent the fingers, and let the flowers drop out, the flowers she had loved so, and walked on without them, with dry, aching eyes. Then for the last time he came. And she showed him her empty hands, the hands that held nothing now. But still he looked. Then at length she opened her bosom and took out of it one small flower she had hidden there, and laid it on the sand. She had nothing more to give now, and she wandered away, and the grey sand whirled about her.

A Dream of Wild Bees
(Written in a letter to a friend)

A mother sat alone at an open window. Through it came the
voices of the children as they played under the acacia-trees, and
the breath of the hot afternoon air. In and out of the room flew
the bees, the wild bees, with their legs yellow with pollen, going
to and from the acacia-trees, droning all the while. She sat on a
low chair before the table and darned. She took her work from
the great basket that stood before her on the table: some lay on
her knee and half covered the book that rested there. She
watched the needle go in and out; and the dreary hum of the
bees and the noise of the children's voices became a confused
murmur in her ears, as she worked slowly and more slowly.
Then the bees, the long-legged wasp-like fellows who make no
honey, flew closer and closer to her head, droning. Then she
grew more and more drowsy, and she laid her hand, with the
stocking over it, on the edge of the table, and leaned her head
upon it. And the voices of the children outside grew more and
more dreamy, came now far, now near; then she did not hear
them, but she felt under her heart where the ninth child[1] lay.
Bent forward and sleeping there, with the bees flying about her
head, she had a weird brain-picture; she thought the bees
lengthened and lengthened themselves out and became human
creatures and moved round and round her. Then one came to
her softly, saying, 'Let me lay my hand upon thy side where the
child sleeps. If I shall touch him he shall be as I.'

She asked, 'Who are you?'

And he said, 'I am Health. Whom I touch will have always
the red blood dancing in his veins; he will not know weariness
nor pain; life will be a long laugh to him.'

'No,' said another, 'let me touch; for I am Wealth. If I touch
him material care shall not feed on him. He shall live on the
blood and sinews of his fellow-men, if he will; and what his eye
lusts for, his hand will have. He shall not know "I want."' And
the child lay still like lead.

And another said, 'Let me touch him: I am Fame. The man I touch, I lead to a high hill where all men may see him. When he dies he is not forgotten, his name rings down the centuries, each echoes it on to his fellows. Think – not to be forgotten through the ages!'

And the mother lay breathing steadily, but in the brain-picture they pressed closer to her.

'Let me touch the child,' said one, 'for I am Love. If I touch him he shall not walk through life alone. In the greatest dark, when he puts out his hand he shall find another hand by it. When the world is against him, another shall say, "*You and I*."' And the child trembled.

But another pressed close and said, 'Let me touch; for I am Talent. I can do all things – that have been done before. I touch the soldier, the statesman, the thinker, and the politician who succeed; and the writer who is never before his time, and never behind it. If I touch the child he shall not weep for failure.'

About the mother's head the bees were flying, touching her with their long tapering limbs; and, in her brain-picture, out of the shadow of the room came one with sallow face, deep-lined, the cheeks drawn into hollows, and a mouth smiling quiveringly. He stretched out his hand. And the mother drew back, and cried, 'Who are you?' He answered nothing; and she looked up between his eyelids. And she said, 'What can you give the child – health?' And he said, 'The man I touch, there wakes up in his blood a burning fever, that shall lick his blood as fire. The fever that I will give him shall be cured when his life is cured.'

'You give wealth?'

He shook his head. 'The man whom I touch, when he bends to pick up gold, he sees suddenly a light over his head in the sky; while he looks up to see it, the gold slips from between his fingers, or sometimes another passing takes it from them.'

'Fame?'

He answered, 'Likely not. For the man I touch there is a path traced out in the sand by a finger which no man sees. That he must follow. Sometimes it leads almost to the top, and then turns down suddenly into the valley. He must follow it, though none else sees the tracing.'

'Love?'

He said, 'He shall hunger for it – but he shall not find it. When he stretches out his arms to it, and would lay his heart against a thing he loves, then, far off along the horizon he shall see a light play. He must go towards it. The thing he loves will not journey with him; he must travel alone. When he presses somewhat to his burning heart, crying, "Mine, mine, my own!" he shall hear a voice – "Renounce! renounce! this is not thine!"'

'He shall succeed?'

He said, 'He shall fail. When he runs with others they shall reach the goal before him. For strange voices shall call to him and strange lights shall beckon him, and he must wait and listen. And this shall be the strangest: far off across the burning sands where, to other men, there is only the desert's waste, he shall see a blue sea! On that sea the sun shines always, and the water is blue as burning amethyst, and the foam is white on the shore. A great land rises from it, and he shall see upon the mountain-tops burning gold.'

The mother said, 'He shall reach it?'

And he smiled curiously.

She said, 'It is real?'

And he said, 'What *is* real?'

And she looked up between his half-closed eyelids, and said, 'Touch.'

And he leaned forward and laid his hand upon the sleeper, and whispered to it, smiling; and this only she heard – '*This shall be thy reward – that the ideal shall be real to thee.*'

And the child trembled; but the mother slept on heavily and her brain-picture vanished. But deep within her the antenatal thing that lay here had a dream. In those eyes that had never seen the day, in that half-shaped brain was a sensation of light! Light – that it never had seen. Light – that perhaps it never should see. Light – that existed somewhere!

And already it had its reward: the Ideal was real to it.

London, 1886.

Life's Gifts

I saw a woman sleeping. In her sleep she dreamt Life stood before her, and held in each hand a gift – in the one Love, in the other Freedom. And she said to the woman, 'Choose!'

And the woman waited long: and she said, 'Freedom!'

And Life said, 'Thou hast well chosen. If thou hadst said, "Love," I would have given thee that thou didst ask for; and I would have gone from thee, and returned to thee no more. Now, the day will come when I shall return. In that day I shall bear both gifts in one hand.'

I heard the woman laugh in her sleep.

London, 1886.

The Artist's Secret

There was an artist once, and he painted a picture. Other artists had colours richer and rarer, and painted more notable pictures. He painted his with one colour, there was a wonderful red glow on it; and the people went up and down saying, 'We like the picture, we like the glow.'

The other artists came and said, 'Where does he get his colour from?' They asked him; and he smiled and said, 'I cannot tell you'; and worked on with his head bent low.

And one went to the far East and bought costly pigments, and made a rare colour and painted, but after a time the picture faded. Another read in the old books, and made a colour rich and rare, but when he had put it on the picture it was dead.

But the artist painted on. Always the work got redder and redder, and the artist grew whiter and whiter. At last one day they found him dead before his picture, and they took him up to bury him. The other men looked about in all the pots and crucibles, but they found nothing they had not.

And when they undressed him to put his grave-clothes on him, they found above his left breast the mark of a wound – it was an old, old wound, that must have been there all his life, for the edges were old and hardened; but Death, who seals all things, had drawn the edges together, and closed it up.

And they buried him. And still the people went about saying, 'Where did he find his colour from?'

And it came to pass that after a while the artist was forgotten – but the work lived.

St Leonards-on-Sea, 1887.

'I Thought I Stood'

I

I thought I stood in Heaven before God's throne, and God asked me what I had come for. I said I had come to arraign my brother, Man.

God said, 'What has he done?'

I said, 'He has taken my sister, Woman, and has stricken her, and wounded her, and thrust her out into the streets; she lies there prostrate. His hands are red with blood. *I* am here to arraign him; that the kingdom be taken from him, because he is not worthy, and given unto me. My hands are pure.'

I showed them.

God said, 'Thy hands are pure – Lift up thy robe.'

I raised it; my feet were red, blood-red, as if I had trodden in wine.

God said, 'How is this?'

I said, 'Dear Lord, the streets on earth are full of mire. If I should walk straight on in them my outer robe might be bespotted, you see how white it is! Therefore I pick my way.'

God said, '*On what?*'

I was silent, and I let my robe fall. I wrapped my mantle about my head. I went out softly. I was afraid that the angels would see me.

II

Once more I stood at the gate of Heaven, I and another. We held fast by one another; we were very tired. We looked up at the great gates; the angels opened them, and we went in. The mud was on our garments. We walked across the marble floor, and up to the great throne. Then the angels divided us. Her, they set upon the top step, but me, upon the bottom; for, they said, 'Last time this woman came here she left red foot-marks on the floor; we had to wash them out with our tears. Let her not go up.'

Then she, with whom I came, looked back and stretched out her hand to me; and I went and stood beside her. And the angels, they, the shining ones who never sinned and never suffered, walked by us to and fro and up and down; I think we should have felt a little lonely there if it had not been for one another, the angels were so bright.

God asked me what I had come for; and I drew my sister forward a little that he might see her.

God said, 'How is it you are here together to-day?'

I said, 'She was upon the ground in the street, and they passed over her; I lay down by her, and she put her arms around my neck, and so I lifted her, and we two rose together.'

God said, 'Whom are you now come to accuse before me?'

I said, 'We are come to accuse no man.'

And God bent, and said, 'My children – what is it that ye seek?'

And she beside me drew my hand that I should speak for both.

I said, 'We have come to ask that thou shouldst speak to Man, our brother, and give us a message for him that he might understand, and that he might – '

God said, 'Go, take the message down to him!'

I said, 'But what *is* the message?'

God said, 'Upon your hearts it is written; take it down to him.'

And we turned to go; the angels went with us to the door. They looked at us.

And one said – 'Ai! but their dresses are beautiful!'

And the other said, 'I thought it was mire when they came in, but see, it is all golden!'

But another said, 'Hush, it is the light from their faces!'

And we went down to him.

Alassio, Italy, 1887.

Gender, Race
and Politics

Eighteen Ninety-Nine (1904)

Schreiner wrote 'Eighteen Ninety-Nine' between 1901 and 1904 (First and Scott: 370, 375); the story was first published in *Stories, Dreams and Allegories* (1923). The title is allegorical; the date marks the beginning of the Anglo-Boer War (1899–1902), but neither the beginning nor the bulk of the story, which takes place in the 1880s (a period Schreiner spent in England and Europe) and in the early reaches of the protagonist's memory in the 1830s. In 'Eighteen Ninety-Nine' Schreiner describes a set of events – the Afrikaners' 'Great Trek' north and their resistance both to attacks by native South Africans and to British colonial rule – which were (and are) central to Afrikaner 'political mythology', Afrikaners' justification of their own racist policies and ideology (Thompson: esp. 144–80). The central character's memories of 'Dingaan's Day' and 'Slachters Nek', which she teaches to her grandson, should be seen in this light: they are collective, impressionistic memories used narratively to frame the events of the later Anglo-Boer War. These memories emphasise British imperialism and Zulu violence, all but ignoring Afrikaners' shameless decimation of native peoples and their violent takeover of these peoples' lands. In the notes I have attempted to sort out the gaps between the old woman's memories (both what she remembers and the formulaic tales she passes along to her grandson) and the actual events; see Leonard Thompson, *The Political Mythology of Apartheid*, for a full account. The story's conclusion and epigraph may suggest an ironic and critical stance towards the old woman's religious beliefs and her fragmented, racially biased memories. Told from the perspective of nameless women who do not fight, but who repeatedly lose their lovers and children to war, 'Eighteen Ninety-Nine' echoes several of Schreiner's other works in linking child-bearing, loss, and potential (but muted) feminism: 'The Artist's Secret' (1887), 'The Cry of South Africa' (1900), and especially *Woman and Labour* (1911).

Thou fool, that which thou sowest is not quickened unless it die.[1]

I

It was a warm night: the stars shone down through the thick soft air of the Northern Transvaal[2] into the dark earth, where a little daub-and-wattle house[3] of two rooms lay among the long, grassy slopes.

A light shone through the small window of the house, though it was past midnight. Presently the upper half of the door opened and then the lower, and the tall figure of a woman stepped out into the darkness. She closed the door behind her and walked towards the back of the house where a large round hut stood; beside it lay a pile of stumps and branches quite visible when once the eyes grew accustomed to the darkness. The woman stopped and broke off twigs till she had her apron full, and then returned slowly, and went into the house.

The room to which she returned was a small, bare room, with brown earthen walls and a mud floor; a naked deal table stood in the centre, and a few dark wooden chairs, home-made, with seats of undressed leather, stood round the walls. In the corner opposite the door was an open fireplace, and on the earthen hearth stood an iron three-foot, on which stood a large black kettle, under which coals were smouldering, though the night was hot and close. Against the wall on the left side of the room hung a gun-rack with three guns upon it, and below it a large hunting-watch hung from two nails by its silver chain.

In the corner by the fireplace was a little table with a coffee-pot upon it and a dish containing cups and saucers covered with water, and above it were a few shelves with crockery and a large Bible; but the dim light of the tallow candle which burnt on the table, with its wick of twisted rag, hardly made the corners visible. Beside the table sat a young woman, her head resting on her folded arms, the light of the tallow candle falling full on her head of pale flaxen hair, a little tumbled, and drawn behind into a large knot. The arms crossed on the table, from which the cotton sleeves had fallen back, were the full, rounded arms of one very young.

The older woman, who had just entered, walked to the fireplace, and kneeling down before it took from her apron the twigs and sticks she had gathered and heaped them under the kettle till a blaze sprang up which illumined the whole room. Then she rose up and sat down on a chair before the fire, but facing the table, with her hands crossed on her brown apron.

She was a woman of fifty, spare and broad-shouldered, with black hair, already slightly streaked with grey; from below high, arched eyebrows, and a high forehead, full dark eyes looked keenly, and a sharply cut aquiline nose gave strength to the face; but the mouth below was somewhat sensitive, and not overfull. She crossed and recrossed her knotted hands on her brown apron.

The woman at the table moaned and moved her head from side to side.

'What time is it?' she asked.

The older woman crossed the room to where the hunting-watch hung on the wall.

It showed a quarter-past one, she said, and went back to her seat before the fire, and sat watching the figure beside the table, the firelight bathing her strong upright form and sharp aquiline profile.

Nearly fifty years before her parents had left the Cape Colony,[4] and had set out on the long trek northward,[5] and she, a young child, had been brought with them. She had no remembrance of the colonial home. Her first dim memories were of travelling in an ox-wagon; of dark nights when a fire was lighted in the open air, and people sat round it on the ground, and some faces seemed to stand out more than others in her memory which she thought must be those of her father and mother and of an old grandmother; she could remember lying awake in the back of the wagon while it was moving on, and the stars were shining down on her; and she had a vague memory of great wide plains with buck on them, which she thought must have been in the Free State.[6] But the first thing which sprang out sharp and clear from the past was a day when she and another child, a little boy cousin of her own age, were playing among the bushes on the bank of a stream; she remembered how, suddenly, as they looked through the bushes, they saw black men leap out, and mount the ox-wagon outspanned[7] under the trees; she remembered how they shouted and dragged people along, and stabbed them; she remembered how the blood gushed, and how they, the two young children among the bushes, lay flat on their stomachs and did not move or breathe, with that strange self-preserving instinct found in the young of animals or men who grow up in the open.

She remembered how black smoke came out at the back of the wagon and then red tongues of flame through the top; and even that some of the branches of the tree under which the wagon stood caught fire. She remembered later, when the black men had gone, and it was dark, that they were very hungry, and crept out to where the wagon had stood, and that they looked about on the ground for any scraps of food they might pick up, and that when they could not find any they cried. She remembered nothing clearly after that till some men with large beards and large hats rode up on horseback: it might have been next day or the day after. She remembered how they jumped off their horses and took them up in their arms, and how they cried; but that they, the children, did not cry, they only asked for food. She remembered how one man took a bit of thick, cold roaster-cake out of his pocket, and gave it to her, and how nice it tasted. And she remembered that the men took them up before them on their horses, and that one man tied her close to him with a large red handkerchief.

In the years that came she learnt to know that that which she remembered so clearly was the great and terrible day when, at Weenen, and in the country round, hundreds of women and children and youths and old men fell before the Zulus, and the assegais of Dingaan's braves drank blood.[8]

She learnt that on the day all of her house and name, from the grandmother to the baby in arms, fell, and that she only and the boy cousin, who had hidden with her among the bushes, were left of all her kin in that Northern world. She learnt, too, that the man who tied her to him with the red handkerchief took them back to his wagon, and that he and his wife adopted them, and brought them up among their own children.

She remembered, though less clearly than the day of the fire, how a few years later they trekked away from Natal,[9] and went through great mountain ranges, ranges in and near which lay those places the world was to know later as Laings Nek, and Amajuba, and Ingogo; Elands-laagte, Nicholson Nek, and Spion Kop.[10] She remembered how at last after many wanderings they settled down near the Witwaters Rand,[11] where game was plentiful and wild beasts were dangerous, but there were no natives, and they were far from the English rule.

There the two children grew up among the children of those who had adopted them, and were kindly treated by them as though they were their own; it yet was but natural that these two of the same name and blood should grow up with a peculiar tenderness for each other. And so it came to pass that when they were both eighteen years old they asked consent of the old people, who gave it gladly, that they should marry. For a time the young couple lived on in the house with the old, but after three years they gathered together all their few goods and in their wagon, with their guns and ammunition and a few sheep and cattle, they moved away northwards to found their own home.

For a time they travelled here and travelled there, but at last they settled on a spot where game was plentiful and the soil good, and there among the low undulating slopes, near the bank of a dry sloot, the young man built at last, with his own hands, a little house of two rooms.

On the long slope across the sloot before the house, he ploughed a piece of land and enclosed it, and he built kraals for his stock and so struck root in the land and wandered no more. Those were brave, glad, free days to the young couple. They lived largely on the game which the gun brought down, antelope and wildebeest[12] that wandered even past the doors at night; and now and again a lion was killed: one no farther than the door of the round hut behind the house where the meat and the milk were stored, and two were killed at the kraals. Sometimes, too, traders came with their wagons and in exchange for skins and fine horns sold sugar and coffee and print and tan-cord, and such things as the little household had need of. The lands yielded richly to them, in maize, and pumpkins, and sweet-cane, and melons; and they had nothing to wish for. Then in time three little sons were born to them, who grew as strong and vigorous in the free life of the open veld[13] as the young lions in the long grass and scrub near the river four miles away. Those were joyous, free years for the man and woman, in which disease, and carking care, and anxiety played no part.

Then came a day when their eldest son was ten years old, and the father went out a-hunting with his Kaffir servants: in the evening they brought him home with a wound eight inches long in his side where a lioness had torn him; they brought back her skin also, as he had shot her at last in the hand-to-throat struggle. He lingered for three days and then died. His wife buried him on the low slope to the left of the house; she and her Kaffir servants alone made the grave and put him in it, for there were no white men near. Then she and her sons lived on there; a new root driven deep into the soil and binding them to it through the grave on the hill-side. She hung her husband's large hunting-watch up on the wall, and put three of his guns over it on the rack, and the gun he had in his hand when he met his death she took down and polished up every day; but one gun she always kept loaded at the head of her bed in the inner room. She counted the stock every night and saw that the Kaffirs ploughed the lands, and she saw to the planting and watering of them herself.

Often as the years passed men of the country-side, and even from far off, heard of the young handsome widow who lived alone with her children and saw to her own stock and lands; and they came a-courting. But many of them were afraid to say anything when once they had come, and those who had spoken to her, when once she had answered them, never came again. About this time too the country-side began to fill in; and people came and settled as near as eight and ten miles away; and as people increased the game began to vanish, and with the game the lions, so that the one her husband killed was almost the last ever seen there. But there was still game enough for food, and when her eldest son was twelve years old, and she gave him his father's smallest gun to go out hunting with, he returned home almost every day with meat enough for the household tied behind his saddle. And as time passed she came also to be known through the country-side as a 'wise woman.' People came to her to ask advice about their illnesses, or to ask her to dress old wounds that would not heal; and when they questioned her whether she thought the rains would be early, or the game plentiful that year, she was nearly always right. So they called her a 'wise woman' because neither she nor they knew any word in that up-country speech of theirs for the thing called 'genius.' So all things went well till the eldest son was eighteen, and the dark beard was beginning to sprout on his face, and his mother began to think that soon there might be a daughter in the house; for on Saturday evenings, when his work was done, he put on his best clothes and rode off to the next farm eight miles away, where was a young daughter. His mother always saw that he had a freshly ironed shirt waiting for him on his bed, when he came home from the kraals on Saturday nights, and she made plans as to how they would build on two rooms for the new daughter. At this time he was training young horses to have them ready to sell when the traders came round: he was a fine rider and it was always his work. One afternoon he mounted a young horse before the door and it bucked and threw him. He had often fallen before, but this time his neck was broken. He lay dead with his head two feet from his mother's doorstep. They took up his tall, strong body and the next day the neighbours came from the next farm and they buried him beside his father, on the hill-side, and another root was struck into the soil. Then the three who were left in the little farm-house lived and worked on as before, for a year and more.

Then a small native war broke out, and the young burghers of the district were called out to help. The second son was very young, but he was the best shot in the district, so he went away with the others. Three months after the men came back, but among the few who did not return was her son. On a hot sunny afternoon, walking through a mealie field[14] which they thought was deserted and where the dried yellow stalks stood thick, an assegai thrown from an unseen hand found him, and he fell there. His comrades took him and buried him under a large thorn tree, and scraped the earth smooth over him, that his grave might not be found by others. So he was not laid on the rise to the left of the house with his kindred, but his mother's heart went often to that thorn tree in the far north. And now again there were only two in the little mud-house; as there had been years before when the young man and wife first settled there. She and her young lad were always together night and day, and did all that they did together, as though they were mother and daughter. He was a fair lad, tall and gentle as his father had been before him, not huge and dark as his two elder brothers; but he seemed to ripen towards manhood early. When he was only sixteen the thick white down was already gathering heavy on his upper lip; his mother watched him narrowly, and had many thoughts in her heart. One evening as they sat twisting wicks for the candles together, she said to him, 'You will be eighteen on your next birthday, my son, that was your father's age when he married me.' He said, 'Yes,' and they spoke no more then. But later in the evening when they sat before the door she said to him: 'We are very lonely here. I often long to hear the feet of a little child about the house, and to see one with your father's blood in it play before the door as you and your brothers played. Have you ever thought that you are the last of your father's name and blood left here in the north; that if you died there would be none left?' He said he had thought of it. Then she told him she thought it would be well if he went away, to the part of the country where the people lived who had brought her up: several of the sons and daughters who had grown up with her had now grown up children. He might go down and from among them seek out a young girl whom he liked and who liked him; and if he found her, bring her back as a wife. The lad thought very well of his mother's plan. And when three months were passed, and the ploughing season was over, he rode away one day, on the best blackhorse they had, his Kaffir boy riding behind him on another, and his mother stood at the gable watching them ride away. For three months she heard nothing of him, for trains were not in those days, and letters came rarely and by chance, and neither he nor she could read or write. One afternoon she stood at the gable end as she always stood when her work was done, looking out along the road that came over the rise, and she saw a large tent-wagon coming along it, and her son walking beside it. She walked to meet it. When she had greeted her son and climbed into the wagon she found there a girl of fifteen with pale flaxen hair and large blue eyes whom he had brought home as his wife. Her father had given her the wagon and oxen as her wedding portion. The older woman's heart wrapt itself about the girl as though she had been the daughter she had dreamed to bear of her own body, and had never borne.

The three lived joyfully at the little house as though they were one person. The young wife had been accustomed to live in a larger house, and down south, where they had things they had not here. She had been to school, and learned to read and write, and she could even talk a little English; but she longed for none of the things which she had had; the little brown house was home enough for her.

After a year a child came, but, whether it were that the mother was too young, it only opened its eyes for an hour on the world and closed them again. The young mother wept bitterly, but her husband folded his arms about her, and the mother comforted both. 'You are young, my children, but we shall yet hear the sound of children's voices in the house,' she said; and after a little while the young mother was well again and things went on peacefully as before in the little home.

But in the land things were not going on peacefully. That was the time that the flag to escape from which the people had left their old homes in the Colony, and had again left Natal when it followed them there, and had chosen to face the spear of the savage, and the conflict with wild beasts, and death by hunger and thirst in the wilderness rather than live under, had by force and fraud unfurled itself over them again. For the moment a great sullen silence brooded over the land. The people, slow of thought, slow of speech, determined in action, and unforgetting, sat still and waited. It was like the silence that rests over the land before an up-country thunderstorm breaks.

Then the words came, 'They have not even given us the free government they promised' – then acts – the people rose. Even in that remote country-side the men began to mount their horses, and with their guns ride away to help. In the little mud-house the young wife wept much when he said that he too was going. But when his mother helped him pack his saddle-bags she helped too; and on the day when the men from the next farm went, he rode away also with his gun by his side.

No direct news of the one they had sent away came to the waiting women at the farm-house; then came fleet reports of the victories of Ingogo and Amajuba.[15] Then came an afternoon after he had been gone two months. They had both been to the gable end to look out at the road, as they did continually amid their work, and they had just come in to drink their afternoon coffee when the Kaffir maid ran in to say she saw someone coming along the road who looked like her master. The women ran out. It was the white horse on which he had ridden away, but they almost doubted if it were he. He rode bending on his saddle, with his chin on his breast and his arm hanging at his side. At first they thought he had been wounded, but when they had helped him from his horse and brought him into the house they found it was only a deadly fever which was upon him. He had crept home to them by small stages. Hardly had he any spirit left to tell them of Ingogo, Laings Nek, and Amajuba. For fourteen days he grew worse and on the fifteenth day he died. And the two women buried him where the rest of his kin lay on the hill-side.

And so it came to pass that on that warm starlight night the two women were alone in the little mud-house with the stillness of the veld about them; even their Kaffir servants asleep in their huts beyond the kraals; and the very sheep lying silent in the starlight. They two were alone in the little house, but they knew that before morning they would not be alone, they were awaiting the coming of the dead man's child.

The young woman with her head on the table groaned. 'If only my husband were here still,' she wailed. The old woman rose and stood beside her, passing her hard, work-worn hand gently over her shoulder as if she were a little child. At last she induced her to go and lie down in the inner room. When she had grown quieter and seemed to have fallen into a light sleep the old woman came to the front room again. It was almost two o'clock and the fire had burned low under the large kettle. She scraped the coals together and went out of the front door to fetch more wood, and closed the door behind her. The night air struck cool and fresh upon her face after the close air of the house, the stars seemed to be growing lighter as the night advanced, they shot down their light as from a million polished steel points. She walked to the back of the house where, beyond the round hut that served as a store-room, the wood-pile lay. She bent down gathering sticks and chips till her apron was full, then slowly she raised herself and stood still. She looked upwards. It was a wonderful night. The white band of the Milky Way crossed the sky overhead, and from every side stars threw down their light, sharp as barbed spears, from the velvety blue-black of the sky. The woman raised her hand to her forehead as if pushing the hair farther off it, and stood motionless, looking up. After a long time she dropped her hand and began walking slowly towards the house. Yet once or twice on the way she paused and stood looking up. When she went into the house the woman in the inner room was again moving and moaning. She laid the sticks down before the fire and went into the next room. She bent down over the bed where the younger woman lay, and put her hand upon her. 'My daughter,' she said slowly, 'be comforted. A wonderful thing has happened to me. As I stood out in the starlight it was as though a voice came down to me and spoke. The child which will be born of you to-night will be a man-child and he will live to do great things for his land and for his people.'

Before morning there was the sound of a little wail in the mud-house: and the child who was to do great things for his land and for his people was born.

II

Six years passed; and all was as it had been at the little house among the slopes. Only a new piece of land had been ploughed up and added to the land before the house, so that the ploughed land now almost reached to the ridge.

The young mother had grown stouter, and lost her pink and white; she had become a working-woman, but she still had the large knot of flaxen hair behind her head and the large wondering eyes. She had many suitors in those six years, but she sent them all away. She said the old woman looked after the farm as well as any man might, and her son would be grown up by and by. The grandmother's hair was a little more streaked with grey, but it was as thick as ever, and her shoulders as upright; only some of her front teeth had fallen out, which made her lips close more softly.

The great change was that wherever the women went there was the flaxen-haired child to walk beside them holding on to their skirts or clasping their hands.

The neighbours said they were ruining the child: they let his hair grow long, like a girl's, because it curled; and they never let him wear velschoens[16] like other children but always shop boots; and his mother sat up at night to iron his pinafores as if the next day were always a Sunday.

But the women cared nothing for what was said; to them he was not as any other child. He asked them strange questions they could not answer, and he never troubled them by wishing to go and play with the little Kaffirs as other children trouble. When neighbours came over and brought their children with them he ran away and hid in the sloot to play by himself till they were gone. No, he was not like other children!

When the women went to lie down on hot days after dinner sometimes, he would say that he did not want to sleep; but he would not run about and make a noise like other children – he would go and sit outside in the shade of the house, on the front doorstep, quite still, with his little hands resting on his knees, and stare far away at the ploughed lands on the slope, or the shadows nearer; the women would open the bedroom window, and peep out to look at him as he sat there.

The child loved his mother and followed her about to the milk house, and to the kraals; but he loved his grandmother best.

She told him stories.

When she went to the lands to see how the Kaffirs were ploughing he would run at her side holding her dress; when they had gone a short way he would tug gently at it and say, 'Grandmother, tell me things!'

And long before day broke, when it was yet quite dark, he would often creep from the bed where he slept with his mother into his grandmother's bed in the corner; he would put his arms round her neck and stroke her face till she woke, and then whisper softly, 'Tell me stories!' and she would tell them to him in a low voice not to wake the mother, till the cock crowed and it was time to get up and light the candle and the fire.

But what he liked best of all were the hot, still summer nights, when the women put their chairs before the door because it was too warm to go to sleep; and he would sit on the stoof at his grandmother's feet and lean his head against her knees, and she would tell him on and on of the things he liked to hear; and he would watch the stars as they slowly set along the ridge, or the moonlight, casting bright-edged shadows from the gable as she talked. Often after the mother had got sleepy and gone in to bed the two sat there together.

The stories she told him were always true stories of the things she had seen or of things she had heard. Sometimes they were stories of her own childhood: of the day when she and his grandfather hid among the bushes, and saw the wagon burnt; sometimes they were of the long trek from Natal to the Transvaal; sometimes of the things which happened to her and his grandfather when first they came to that spot among the ridges, of how there was no house there nor lands, only two bare grassy slopes when they outspanned their wagon there the first night; she told of a lion she once found when she opened the door in the morning, sitting, with paws crossed, upon the threshold, and how the grandfather jumped out of bed and reopened the door two inches, and shot it through the opening; the skin was kept in the round storehouse still, very old and mangy.

Sometimes she told him of the two uncles who were dead, and of his own father, and of all they had been and done. But sometimes she told him of things much farther off: of the old

Colony where she had been born, but which she could not remember, and of the things which happened there in the old days. She told him of how the British had taken the Cape over, and of how the English had hanged their men at the 'Slachters Nek' for resisting the English Government, and of how the friends and relations had been made to stand round to see them hanged whether they would or no, and of how the scaffold broke down as they were being hanged, and the people looking on cried aloud, 'It is the finger of God! They are saved!' but how the British hanged them up again.[17] She told him of the great trek in which her parents had taken part to escape from under the British flag; of the great battles with Moselikatse; and the murder of Retief and his men by Dingaan, and of Dingaan's Day. She told him how the British Government followed them into Natal, and of how they trekked north and east to escape from it again; and she told him of the later things, of the fight at Laings Nek, and Ingogo, and Amajuba, where his father had been. Always she told the same story in exactly the same words over and over again, till the child knew them all by heart, and would ask for this and then that.

The story he loved best, and asked for more often than all the others, made his grandmother wonder, because it did not seem to her the story a child would best like; it was not a story of lion-hunting, or wars, or adventures. Continually when she asked what she should tell him, he said, 'About the mountains!'

It was the story of how the Boer women in Natal when the English Commissioner came to annex their country, collected to meet him and pointing toward the Drakens Berg Mountains said, 'We go across those mountains to freedom or to death!'[18]

More than once, when she was telling him the story, she saw him stretch out his little arm and raise his hand, as though he were speaking.

One evening as he and his mother were coming home from the milking kraals, and it was getting dark, and he was very tired, having romped about shouting among the young calves and kids all the evening, he held her hand tightly.

'Mother,' he said suddenly, 'when I am grown up, I am going to Natal.'

'Why, my child?' she asked him; 'there are none of our family living there now.'

He waited a little, then said, very slowly, 'I am going to go and try to get our land back!'

His mother started; if there were one thing she was more firmly resolved on in her own mind than any other it was that he should never go to the wars. She began to talk quickly of the old white cow who had kicked the pail over as she was milked, and when she got to the house she did not even mention to the grandmother what had happened; it seemed better to forget.

One night in the rainy season when it was damp and chilly they sat round the large fireplace in the front room.

Outside the rain was pouring in torrents and you could hear the water rushing in the great dry sloot before the door. His grandmother, to amuse him, had sprung some dried mealies in the great black pot and sprinkled them with sugar, and now he sat on the stoof at her feet with a large lump of the sticky sweetmeat in his hand, watching the fire. His grandmother from above him was watching it also, and his mother in her elbow-chair on the other side of the fire had her eyes half closed and was nodding already with the warmth of the room and her long day's work. The child sat so quiet, the hand with the lump of sweetmeat resting on his knee, that his grandmother thought he had gone to sleep too. Suddenly he said without looking up, 'Grandmother?'

'Yes.'

He waited rather a long time, then said slowly, 'Grandmother, did God make the English too?'

She also waited for a while, then she said, 'Yes, my child; He made all things.'

They were silent again, and there was no sound but of the rain falling and the fire cracking and the sloot rushing outside. Then he threw his head backwards on to his grandmother's knee and looking up into her face said, 'But, grandmother, why did He make them?'

Then she too was silent for a long time. 'My child,' at last she said, 'we cannot judge the ways of the Almighty. He does that which seems good in His own eyes.'

The child sat up and looked back at the fire. Slowly he tapped his knee with the lump of sweetmeat once or twice; then he began to munch it; and soon the mother started wide awake and said it was time for all to go to bed.

The next morning his grandmother sat on the front doorstep cutting beans in an iron basin; he sat beside her on the step pretending to cut too, with a short, broken knife. Presently he left off and rested his hands on his knees, looking away at the hedge beyond, with his small forehead knit tight between the eyes.

'Grandmother,' he said suddenly in a small, almost shrill voice, 'do the English want *all* the lands of *all* the people?'

The handle of his grandmother's knife as she cut clinked against the iron side of the basin. 'All they can get,' she said.

After a while he made a little movement almost like a sigh, and took up his little knife again and went on cutting.

Some time after that, when a trader came by, his grandmother bought him a spelling-book and a slate and pencils, and his mother began to teach him to read and write. When she had taught him for a year he knew all she did. Sometimes when she was setting him a copy and left a letter out in a word, he would quietly take the pencil when she set it down and put the letter in, not with any idea of correcting her, but simply because it must be there.

Often at night when the child had gone to bed early, tired out with his long day's play, and the two women were left in the front room with the tallow candle burning on the table between them, then they talked of his future.

Ever since he had been born everything they had earned had been put away in the wagon chest under the grandmother's bed. When the traders with their wagons came round the women bought nothing except a few groceries and clothes for the child; even before they bought a yard of cotton print for a new apron they talked long and solemnly as to whether the old one might not be made to do by repatching; and they mixed much more dry pumpkin and corn with their coffee than before he was born. It was to earn more money that the large new piece of land had been added to the lands before the house.

They were going to have him educated. First he was to be taught all they could at home, then to be sent away to a great school in the old Colony, and then he was to go over the sea to Europe and come back an advocate or a doctor or a parson. The grandmother had made a long journey to the next town, to find out from the minister just how much it would cost to do it all.

In the evenings when they sat talking it over the mother generally inclined to his becoming a parson. She never told the grandmother why, but the real reason was because parsons do not go to the wars. The grandmother generally favoured his becoming an advocate, because he might become a judge. Sometimes they sat discussing these matters till the candle almost burnt out.

'Perhaps, one day,' the mother would slowly refold her hands across her apron and say softly, 'Who knows? – who knows?'

Often they would get the box out from under the bed (looking carefully across to the corner to see he was fast asleep) and would count out all the money, though each knew to a farthing how much was there; then they would make it into little heaps, so much for this, so much for that, and then they would count on their fingers how many good seasons it would take to make the rest, and how old he would be.

When he was eight and had learnt all his mother could teach him, they sent him to school every day on an adjoining farm six miles off, where the people had a schoolmaster. Every day he rode over on the great white horse his father went to the wars with; his mother was afraid to let him ride alone at first, but his grandmother said he must learn to do everything alone. At four o'clock when he came back one or other of the women was always looking out to see the little figure on the tall horse coming over the ridge.

When he was eleven they gave him his father's smallest gun; and one day not long after he came back with his first small buck. His mother had the skin dressed and bound with red, and she laid it as a mat under the table, and even the horns she did not throw away, and saved them in the round house, because it was his first.

When he was fourteen the schoolmaster said he could teach

171

him no more; that he ought to go to some larger school where they taught Latin and other difficult things; they had not yet money enough and he was not quite old enough to go to the old Colony, so they sent him first to the High-veld, where his mother's relations lived and where there were good schools, where they taught the difficult things; he could live with his mother's relations and come back once a year for the holidays.

They were great times when he came.

His mother made him koekies and sasarties[19] and nice things every day; and he used to sit on the stoof at her feet and let her play with his hair like when he was quite small. With his grandmother he talked. He tried to explain to her all he was learning, and he read the English newspapers to her (she could neither read in English nor Dutch), translating them. Most of all she liked his Atlas. They would sometimes sit over it for half an hour in the evening tracing the different lands and talking of them. On the warm nights he used still to sit outside on the stoof at her feet with his head against her knee, and they used to discuss things that were happening in other lands and in South Africa; and sometimes they sat there quite still together.

It was now he who had the most stories to tell; he had seen Krugersdorp, and Johannesburg, and Pretoria;[20] he knew the world; he was at Krugersdorp when Dr. Jameson made his raid.[21] Sometimes he sat for an hour, telling her of things, and she sat quietly listening.

When he was seventeen, nearly eighteen, there was money enough in the box to pay for his going to the Colony and then to Europe; and he came home to spend a few months with them before he went.

He was very handsome now; not tall, and very slight, but with fair hair that curled close to his head, and white hands like a town's man. All the girls in the country-side were in love with him. They all wished he would come and see them. But he seldom rode from home except to go to the next farm where he had been at school. There lived little Aletta, who was the daughter of the woman his uncle had loved before he went to the Kaffir war and got killed. She was only fifteen years old, but they had always been great friends. She netted him a purse of green silk. He said he would take it with him to Europe, and would show it her when he came back and was an advocate; and he gave her a book with her name written in it, which she was to show to him.

These were the days when the land was full of talk; it was said the English were landing troops in South Africa, and wanted to have war. Often the neighbours from the nearest farms would come to talk about it (there were more farms now, the country was filling in, and the nearest railway station was only a day's journey off), and they discussed matters. Some said they thought there would be war; others again laughed, and said it would be only Jameson and his white flag again. But the grandmother shook her head, and if they asked her, 'Why,' she said, 'it will not be the war of a week, nor of a month; if it comes it will be the war of years,' but she would say nothing more.

Yet sometimes when she and her grandson were walking along together in the lands she would talk.

Once she said: 'It is as if a great heavy cloud hung just above my head, as though I wished to press it back with my hands and could not. It will be a great war – a great war. Perhaps the English Government will take the land for a time, but they will not keep it. The gold they have fought for will divide them, till they slay one another over it.'

Another day she said: 'This land will be a great land one day with one people from the sea to the north – but we shall not live to see it.'

He said to her: 'But how can that be when we are all of different races?'

She said: 'The land will make us one. Were not our fathers of more than one race?'

Another day, when she and he were sitting by the table after dinner, she pointed to a sheet of exercise paper, on which he had been working out a problem and which was covered with algebraical symbols, and said, 'In fifteen years' time the Government of England will not have one piece of land in all South Africa as large as that sheet of paper.'

One night when the milking had been late and she and he were walking down together from the kraals in the starlight she

173

said to him: 'If this war comes let no man go to it lightly, thinking he will surely return home, nor let him go expecting victory on the next day. It will come at last, but not at first.' 'Sometimes,' she said, 'I wake at night and it is as though the whole house were filled with smoke – and I have to get up and go outside to breathe. It is as though I saw my whole land blackened and desolate. But when I look up it is as though a voice cried out to me, "Have no fear!"'

They were getting his things ready for him to go away after Christmas. His mother was making him shirts and his grandmother was having a kaross of jackals' skins[22] made that he might take it with him to Europe where it was so cold. But his mother noticed that whenever the grandmother was in the room with him and he was not looking at her, her eyes were always curiously fixed on him as though they were questioning something. The hair was growing white and a little thin over her temples now, but her eyes were as bright as ever, and she could do a day's work with any man.

One day when the youth was at the kraals helping the Kaffir boys to mend a wall, and the mother was kneading bread in the front room, and the grandmother washing up the breakfast things, the son of the Field Cornet[23] came riding over from his father's farm, which was about twelve miles off. He stopped at the kraal and Jan and he stood talking for some time, then they walked down to the farm-house, the Kaffir boy leading the horse behind them. Jan stopped at the round store, but the Field Cornet's son went to the front door. The grandmother asked him in, and handed him some coffee, and the mother, her hands still in the dough, asked him how things were going at his father's farm, and if his mother's young turkeys had come out well, and she asked if he had met Jan at the kraals. He answered the questions slowly, and sipped his coffee. Then he put the cup down on the table; and said suddenly in the same measured voice, staring at the wall in front of him, that war had broken out, and his father had sent him round to call out all fighting burghers.

The mother took her hands out of the dough and stood upright beside the trough as though paralysed. Then she cried in a high, hard voice, unlike her own, 'Yes, but Jan cannot go! He is hardly eighteen! He's got to go and be educated in other lands! You can't take the only son of a widow!'

'Aunt,' said the young man slowly, 'no one will make him go.'

The grandmother stood resting the knuckles of both hands on the table, her eyes fixed on the young man. 'He shall decide himself,' she said.

The mother wiped her hands from the dough and rushed past them and out at the door; the grandmother followed slowly.

They found him in the shade at the back of the house, sitting on a stump; he was cleaning the belt of his new Mauser[24] which lay across his knees.

'Jan,' his mother cried, grasping his shoulder, 'you are not going away? You can't go! You must stay. You can go by Delagoa Bay[25] if there is fighting on the other side! There is plenty of money!'

He looked softly up into her face with his blue eyes. 'We have all to be at the Field Cornet's at nine o'clock to-morrow morning,' he said. She wept aloud and argued.

His grandmother turned slowly without speaking, and went back into the house. When she had given the Field Cornet's son another cup of coffee, and shaken hands with him, she went into the bedroom and opened the box in which her grandson's clothes were kept, to see which things he should take with him. After a time the mother came back too. He had kissed her and talked to her until she too had at last said it was right he should go.

All day they were busy. His mother baked him biscuits to take in his bag, and his grandmother made a belt of two strips of leather; she sewed them together herself and put a few sovereigns between the stitchings. She said some of his comrades might need the money if he did not.

The next morning early he was ready. There were two saddle-bags tied to his saddle and before it was strapped the kaross his grandmother had made; she said it would be useful when he had to sleep on damp ground. When he had greeted them, he rode away towards the rise: and the women stood at the gable of the house to watch him.

When he had gone a little way he turned in his saddle, and they could see he was smiling; he took off his hat and waved it in the air; the early morning sunshine made his hair as yellow as the tassels that hang from the head of ripening mealies. His mother covered her face with the sides of her kappie and wept aloud; but the grandmother shaded her eyes with both her hands and stood watching him till the figure passed out of sight over the ridge; and when it was gone and the mother returned to the house crying, she still stood watching the line against the sky.

The two women were very quiet during the next days, they worked hard, and seldom spoke. After eight days there came a long letter from him (there was now a post once a week from the station to the Field Cornet's). He said he was well and in very good spirits. He had been to Krugersdorp, and Johannesburg, and Pretoria; all the family living there were well and sent greetings. He had joined a corps that was leaving for the front the next day. He sent also a long message to Aletta, asking them to tell her he was sorry to go away without saying good-bye; and he told his mother how good the biscuits and biltong[26] were she had put into his saddle-bag; and he sent her a piece of vierkleur ribbon[27] in the letter, to wear on her breast.

The women talked a great deal for a day or two after this letter came. Eight days after there was a short note from him, written in pencil in the train on his way to the front. He said all was going well, and if he did not write soon they were not to be anxious; he would write as often as he could.

For some days the women discussed that note too.

Then came two weeks without a letter, the two women became very silent. Every day they sent the Kaffir boy over to the Field Cornet's, even on the days when there was no post, to hear if there was any news.

Many reports were flying about the country-side. Some said that an English armoured train had been taken on the western border; that there had been fighting at Albertina, and in Natal. But nothing seemed quite certain.

Another week passed. . . . Then the two women became very quiet.

The grandmother, when she saw her daughter-in-law left the food untouched on her plate, said there was no need to be anxious; men at the front could not always find paper and pencils to write with and might be far from any post office. Yet night after night she herself would rise from her bed saying she felt the house close, and go and walk up and down outside.

Then one day suddenly all their servants left them except one Kaffir and his wife, whom they had had for years, and the servants from the farms about went also, which was a sign there had been news of much fighting; for the Kaffirs hear things long before the white man knows them.

Three days after, as the women were clearing off the breakfast things, the youngest son of the Field-Cornet, who was only fifteen and had not gone to the war with the others, rode up. He hitched his horse to the post, and came towards the door. The mother stepped forward to meet him and shook hands in the doorway.

'I suppose you have come for the carrot seed I promised your mother? I was not able to send it, as our servants ran away,' she said, as she shook his hand. 'There isn't a letter from Jan is there?' The lad said no, there was no letter from him, and shook hands with the grandmother. He stood by the table instead of sitting down.

The mother turned to the fireplace to get coals to put under the coffee to rewarm it; but the grandmother stood leaning forward with her eyes fixed on him from across the table. He felt uneasily in his breast pocket.

'Is there no news?' the mother said without looking round, as she bent over the fire.

'Yes, there is news, Aunt.'

She rose quickly and turned towards him, putting down the brazier on the table. He took a letter out of his breast pocket. 'Aunt, my father said I must bring this to you. It came inside one to him and they asked him to send one of us over with it.'

The mother took the letter; she held it, examining the address.

'It looks to me like the writing of Sister Annie's Paul,' she said. 'Perhaps there is news of Jan in it' – she turned to them

177

with a half-nervous smile — 'they were always such friends.'

'All is as God wills, Aunt,' the young man said, looking down fixedly at the top of his riding-whip.

But the grandmother leaned forward motionless, watching her daughter-in-law as she opened the letter.

She began to read to herself, her lips moving slowly as she deciphered it word by word.

Then a piercing cry rang through the roof of the little mud-farm-house.

'He is dead! My boy is dead!'

She flung the letter on the table and ran out at the front door.

Far out across the quiet ploughed lands and over the veld to where the kraals lay the cry rang. The Kaffir woman who sat outside her hut beyond the kraals nursing her baby heard it and came down with her child across her hip to see what was the matter. At the side of the round house she stood motionless and open-mouthed, watching the woman, who paced up and down behind the house with her apron thrown over her head and her hands folded above it, crying aloud.

In the front room the grandmother, who had not spoken since he came, took up the letter and put it in the lad's hands. 'Read,' she whispered.

And slowly the lad spelled it out.

'My Dear Aunt,

'I hope this letter finds you well. The Commandant has asked me to write it.

'We had a great fight four days ago, and Jan is dead. The Commandant says I must tell you how it happened. Aunt, there were five of us first in a position on that koppie, but two got killed, and then there were only three of us — Jan, and I, and Uncle Peter's Frikkie. Aunt, the khakies[28] were coming on all round just like locusts, and the bullets were coming just like hail. It was bare on that side of the koppie where we were, but we had plenty of cartridges. We three took up a position where there were some small stones and we fought, Aunt; we had to. One bullet took off the top of my ear, and Jan got two bullets, one through the flesh in the left leg and one through his arm, but he could still fire his gun. Then we three meant to go to the top of the koppie, but a bullet took Jan right through his chest. We knew he couldn't go any farther. The khakies were right at the foot of the koppie just coming up. He told us to lay down, Aunt. We said we would stay by him, but he said we must go. I put my jacket under his head and Frikkie put his over his feet. We threw his gun far away from him that they might see how it was with him. He said he hadn't much pain, Aunt. He was full of blood from his arm, but there wasn't much from his chest, only a little out of the corners of his mouth. He said we must make haste or the khakies would catch us; he said he wasn't afraid to be left there.

'Aunt, when we got to the top, it was all full of khakies like the sea on the other side, all among the koppies and on our koppie too. We were surrounded, Aunt; the last I saw of Frikkie he was sitting on a stone with the blood running down his face, but he got under a rock and hid there; some of our men found him next morning and brought him to camp. Aunt, there was a khakie's horse standing just below where I was, with no one on it. I jumped on and rode. The bullets went this way and the bullets went that, but I rode! Aunt, the khakies were sometimes as near me as that tent-pole, only the Grace of God saved me. It was dark in the night when I got back to where our people were, because I had to go round all the koppies to get away from the khakies.

'Aunt, the next day we went to look for him. We found him where we left him; but he was turned over on to his face; they had taken all his things, his belt and his watch, and the pugaree[29] from his hat, even his boots. The little green silk purse he used to carry we found on the ground by him, but nothing in it. I will send it back to you whenever I get an opportunity.

'Aunt, when we turned him over on his back there were four bayonet stabs in his body. The doctor says it was only the first three while he was alive; the last one was through his heart and killed him at once.

'We gave him Christian burial, Aunt; we took him to the camp.

'The Commandant was there, and all of the family who are

with the Commando were there, and they all said they hoped
God would comfort you . . .'

The old woman leaned forward and grasped the boy's arm.
'Read it over again,' she said, 'from where they found him.' He
turned back and re-read slowly. She gazed at the page as though
she were reading also. Then, suddenly, she slipped out at the
front door.

At the back of the house she found her daughter-in-law still
walking up and down, and the Kafir woman with a red
handkerchief bound round her head and the child sitting across
her hip, sucking from her long, pendulous breast, looking on.

The old woman walked up to her daughter-in-law and
grasped her firmly by the arm.

'He's dead! You know, my boy's dead!' she cried, drawing the
apron down with her right hand and disclosing her swollen and
bleared face. 'Oh, his beautiful hair – Oh, his beautiful hair!'

The old woman held her arm tighter with both hands; the
younger opened her half-closed eyes, and looked into the keen,
clear eyes fixed on hers, and stood arrested.

The old woman drew her face closer to hers. 'You . . . do . . .
not . . . know . . . what . . . has . . . happened!' she spoke slowly,
her tongue striking her front gum, the jaw moving stiffly,
as though partly paralysed. She loosed her left hand and held
up the curved work-worn fingers before her daughter-in-law's
face. 'Was it not told me . . . the night he was born . . . here
. . . at this spot . . . that he would do great things . . . great
things . . . for his land and his people?' She bent forward till her
lips almost touched the other's. 'Three . . . bullet . . . wounds
. . . and four . . . bayonet . . . stabs!' She raised her left hand
high in the air. 'Three . . . bullet . . . wounds . . . and four . . .
bayonet . . . stabs! . . . Is it given to many to die so for their land
and their people!'

The younger woman gazed into her eyes, her own growing
larger and larger. She let the old woman lead her by the arm in
silence into the house.

The Field-Cornet's son was gone, feeling there was nothing
more to be done; and the Kaffir woman went back with her

baby to her hut beyond the kraals. All day the house was very silent. The Kaffir woman wondered that no smoke rose from the farm-house chimney, and that she was not called to churn, or wash the pots. At three o'clock she went down to the house. As she passed the grated window of the round out-house she saw the buckets of milk still standing unsifted[30] on the floor as they had been set down at breakfast time, and under the great soap-pot beside the wood pile the fire had died out. She went round to the front of the house and saw the door and window shutters still closed, as though her mistresses were still sleeping. So she rebuilt the fire under the soap-pot and went back to her hut.

It was four o'clock when the grandmother came out from the dark inner room where she and her daughter-in-law had been lying down; she opened the top of the front door, and lit the fire with twigs, and set the large black kettle over it. When it boiled she made coffee, and poured out two cups and set them on the table with a plate of biscuits, and then called her daughter-in-law from the inner room.

The two women sat down one on each side of the table, with their coffee cups before them, and the biscuits between them, but for a time they said nothing, but sat silent, looking out through the open door at the shadow of the house and the afternoon sunshine beyond it. At last the older woman motioned that the younger should drink her coffee. She took a little, and then folding her arms on the table rested her head on them, and sat motionless as if asleep.

The older woman broke up a biscuit into her own cup, and stirred it round and round; and then, without tasting, sat gazing out into the afternoon's sunshine till it grew cold beside her.

It was five, and the heat was quickly dying; the glorious golden colouring of the later afternoon was creeping over everything when she rose from her chair. She moved to the door and took from behind it two large white calico bags hanging there, and from nails on the wall she took down two large brown cotton kappies. She walked round the table and laid her hand gently on her daughter-in-law's arm. The younger woman raised her head slowly and looked up into her mother-in-law's face; and then, suddenly, she knew that her mother-in-law was an old, old woman. The little shrivelled face that looked down at her was hardly larger than a child's, the eyelids were half closed and the lips worked at the corners and the bones cut out through the skin in the temples.

'I am going out to sow – the ground will be getting too dry to-morrow; will you come with me?' she said gently.

The younger woman made a movement with her hand, as though she said 'What is the use?' and redropped her hand on the table.

'It may go on for long, our burghers must have food,' the old woman said gently.

The younger woman looked into her face, then she rose slowly and taking one of the brown kappies from her hand, put it on, and hung one of the bags over her left arm; the old woman did the same and together they passed out of the door. As the older woman stepped down the younger caught her and saved her from falling.

'Take my arm, mother,' she said.

But the old woman drew her shoulders up. 'I only stumbled a little!' she said quickly. 'That step has been always too high'; but before she reached the plank over the sloot the shoulder had drooped again, and the neck fallen forward.

The mould in the lands was black and soft; it lay in long ridges, as it had been ploughed up a week before, but the last night's rain had softened it and made it moist and ready for putting in the seed.

The bags which the women carried on their arms were full of the seed of pumpkins and mealies. They began to walk up the lands, keeping parallel with the low hedge of dried bushes that ran up along the side of the sloot almost up to the top of the ridge. At every few paces they stopped and bent down to press into the earth, now one and then the other kind of seed from their bags. Slowly they walked up and down till they reached the top of the land almost on the horizon line; and then they turned, and walked down, sowing as they went. When they had reached the bottom of the land before the farm-house it was almost sunset, and their bags were nearly empty; but they turned to go up once more. The light of the setting sun cast long, gaunt shadows from their figures across the ploughed land, over the low hedge and the sloot, into the bare veld beyond; shadows that grew longer and longer as they passed slowly on pressing in the seeds. . . . The seeds! . . . that were to lie in the dank, dark, earth, and rot there, seemingly, to die, till their outer covering had split and fallen from them . . . and then, when the rains had fallen, and the sun had shone, to come up above the earth again, and high in the clear air to lift their feathery plumes and hang out their pointed leaves and silken tassels! To cover the ground with a mantle of green and gold through which sunlight quivered, over which the insects hung by thousands, carrying yellow pollen on their legs and wings and making the air alive with their hum and stir, while grain and fruit ripened surely . . . for the next season's harvest!

When the sun had set, the two women with their empty bags turned and walked silently home in the dark to the farm-house.

Nineteen Hundred and One

Near one of the camps in the Northern Transvaal are the graves of two women. The older one died first, on the twenty-third of the month, from hunger and want; the younger woman tended her with ceaseless care and devotion till the end. A week later when the British Superintendent came round to inspect the tents, she was found lying on her blanket on the mud-floor dead, with the rations of bread and meat she had got four days before untouched on a box beside her. Whether she died of disease, or from inability to eat the food, no one could say. Some who had seen her said she hardly seemed to care to live after the old woman died; they buried them side by side.

There is no stone and no name upon either grave to say who lies there . . . our unknown . . . our unnamed . . . our forgotten dead.[31]

In the Year Nineteen Hundred and Four

If you look for the little farm-house among the ridges you will not find it there to-day.

The English soldiers burnt it down. You can only see where the farm-house once stood, because the stramonia and weeds grow high and very strong there; and where the ploughed lands were you can only tell, because the veld never grows quite the same on land that has once been ploughed. Only a brown patch among the long grass on the ridge shows where the kraals and huts once were.

In a country house in the north of England the owner has upon his wall an old flint-lock gun. He takes it down to show his friends. It is a small thing he picked up in the war in South Africa, he says. It must be at least eighty years old and is very valuable. He shows how curiously it is constructed; he says it must have been kept in such perfect repair by continual polishing for the steel shines as if it were silver. He does not tell that he took it from the wall of the little mud house before he burnt it down.

It was the grandfather's gun, which the women had kept polished on the wall.

In a London drawing-room the descendant of a long line of titled forefathers entertains her guests. It is a fair room, and all that money can buy to make life soft and beautiful is there.

On the carpet stands a little dark wooden stoof. When one of her guests notices it, she says it is a small curiosity which her son brought home to her from South Africa when he was out in the war there; and how good it was of him to think of her when he was away in the back country. And when they ask what it is, she says it is a thing Boer women have as a footstool and to keep their feet warm; and she shows the hole at the side where they put the coals in, and the little holes at the top where the heat comes out.

And the other woman puts her foot out and rests it on the stoof just to try how it feels, and drawls 'How f-u-n-n-y!'

It is grandmother's stoof, that the child used to sit on.

The wagon chest was found and broken open just before the thatch caught fire, by three private soldiers, and they divided the money between them; one spent his share in drink, another had his stolen from him, but the third sent his home to England to a girl in the East End of London. With part of it she bought a gold brooch and ear-rings, and the rest she saved to buy a silk wedding-dress when he came home.

A syndicate of Jews in Johannesburg and London have bought the farm.[32] They purchased it from the English Government, because they think to find gold on it. They have purchased it and paid for it . . . but they do not possess it.

Only the men who lie in their quiet graves upon the hill-side, who lived on it, and loved it, possess it; and the piles of stones above them, from among the long waving grasses, keep watch over the land.

The Native Question (1908)

'The Native Question' is the final section of a long letter to the *Transvaal Leader* in answer to twelve questions posed to Schreiner by the newspaper's editors. Written in the autumn of 1908, the letter was published the following year as a pamphlet, *Letter on the South African Union and the Principles of Government* and reprinted by the Cape Town Constitutional Reform Association as *Closer Union* in 1960. Sometimes with her husband but most often alone, Schreiner had spent twenty years writing and lecturing in favour of a multi-racial, democratic federation of states as the only just form of government for the land of her birth; 'The Native Question' remains her most cogent statement in this area. Like her younger brother, William Philip Schreiner, who had been Prime Minister of the Cape from 1898–1900 and who opposed a union of South African states because of the colour bar in the proposed constitution, Schreiner refuses to be limited by the available political choices; she directs her attention to the central questions of freedom and equality for all South Africans. In the earlier sections of this essay she argues that it is of primary importance for the South African government to be free from British economic and political control. The states should be slow to unify, she goes on, because it is harder to untie a strong central government later than to live without it for a time. And she concludes, just before this excerpt begins, 'Unless the foundations be laid in justice and wisdom, they labour in vain who build the state'.

(. . .)

I hold this to be the root question in South Africa; and as is our wisdom in dealing with it, so will be our future.

No exact census exists of the population of South Africa, but it is roughly calculated that there are about nine millions of inhabitants, eight million of dark men and one million of white.

The white race consists mainly of two varieties, of rather mixed European descent, but both largely Teutonic,[1] and though partly divided at the present moment by traditions and the use of two forms of speech, the Taal[2] and the English, they are so essentially one in blood and character that within two generations they will be inextricably blended by inter-marriage and common interests, as would, indeed, long ago have been the case had it not been for external interference. They constitute, therefore, no great problem for the future, though at the present moment their differences loom large. Our vast, dark native population consists largely of Bantus, who were already in South Africa when we came here; of a few expiring yellow varieties of African races, and a small but important number of half-castes, largely the descendants of imported slaves whose blood was mingled with that of their masters, as is always the case where slavery exists, and a very small body of Asiatics. It is out of this great heterogeneous mass of humans that the South African nation of the future will be built. For the dark man is with us to stay. Not only does the Bantu increase and flourish greatly, as is natural in his native continent, and under the climatic conditions which are best suited to him; not only does he refuse to die out in contact with our civilisation, as the yellow races have largely done, and rather tries to grasp and make it his own; not only can we not exterminate him – but, we cannot even transport him, because we want him! We desire him as thirsty oxen in an arid plain desire water, or miners hunger for the sheen of gold. We want more and always more of him – to labour in our mines, to build our railways, to work in our fields, to perform our domestic labours, and to buy our goods. We desire to import more of him when we can. It has more than once happened in a House of Legislature that bitter complaints have been brought against the Government of the day for employing too many natives on public works, and so robbing the landowner of what he most desires – native labour.

They are the makers of our wealth, the great basic rock on which our State is founded – our vast labouring class.

Diamond mine in Kimberley, 1872

'The Hanging Tree'. The original frontispiece of *Trooper Peter Halket* (1897), protesting against the summary execution of black political prisoners in Mashonaland

Every great nation of the past or present has contributed something to the sum total of things beautiful, good, or useful, possessed by humanity: therein largely lies its greatness. We in South Africa can never hope exactly to repeat the records of the past. We can never hope, like Greece, to give to the world its noblest plastic art; we can never hope, like Rome, to shape the legal institutions of half the world; the chief glory of England, that wherever she goes, whether she will or not, and even against her will, she spreads broadcast among the nations the seeds of self-governing institutions – may never be ours. But the great national parts are not exhausted; and there lies before us in South Africa a part as great and inspiring as any which any nation has ever been called upon to play – if we are strong enough to grasp it.

The problem of the twentieth century will not be a repetition of those of the nineteenth or those which went before it. The walls dividing continents are breaking down; everywhere European, Asiatic and African will interlard. The world on which the twenty-first century will open its eyes will be one widely different from that which the twentieth sees at its awaking. And the problem which this century will have to solve is the accomplishment of this interaction of distinct human varieties on the largest and most beneficent lines, making for the development of humanity as a whole, and carried out in a manner consonant with modern ideals and modern social wants. It will not always be the European who forms the upper layer; but in its essentials the problem will be everywhere the same.

We in South Africa are one of the first peoples in the modern world, and under the new moral and material conditions of civilisation, to be brought face to face with this problem in its acutest form. On our power to solve it regally and heroically depends our greatness. If it be possible for us out of our great complex body of humanity (its parts possibly remaining racially distinct for centuries) to raise up a free, intelligent, harmonious nation, each part acting with and for the benefit of the others, then we shall have played a part as great as that of any nation in the world's record. And as we to-day turn our eyes towards Greece or Rome or England for models in those things wherein they have excelled, nations in the future, whatever their dominant class may be, will be compelled to turn their eyes towards us and follow our lead, saying, 'Hers was the first and true solution of the problem.'

I have said we to-day have to face the problem in its acutest form; but we have also exceptional advantages for solving it.

In our small, to-day dominant, European element we have the descendants of some of the most virile of the northern races, races which, at least for themselves, have always loved freedom and justice; in our vast Bantu element we possess one of the finest breeds of the African stock. A grave and an almost fatal error is sometimes made when persons compare our native question with the negro question in the Southern States of America. Not only is the South African Bantu (a race probably with a large admixture of Arab blood!) as distinct from the West Coast negro, who was the ancestor of the American slave, as the Norwegian is from the Spaniard, but he has never been subjected to the dissolving and desocialising ordeal of slavery. We find him in the land of his growth with all the instincts of the free man intact; with all the instincts of loyalty to his race and its chiefs still warm in his heart; with his social instincts almost abnormally developed and fully active; we have only with wisdom and patient justice slowly to transfer them to our own larger society – they are there! Every man and woman who has studied the Bantu in his native state – before we have indoctrinated him with those vices which dog everywhere the feet of our civilisation, and have compelled his women to graduate in our brothels and his men in our canteens or have dragged him into our city slums, where even our own races rot – knows that the proudest of us may envy many of the social virtues which the Bantu displays. We have a great material here, wisely handled.

In our small, permanent, and largely South African born, Asiatic population we have a section of people sober, industrious, and intelligent, rich with those deep staying-powers which have made many Asiatic peoples so persistent, and often dominant, in the past and present. Even in the most disorganised element of our population, often without definite race or social traditions, I believe that careful study will show it to compare favourably, and often most favourably, with analogous classes in Europe (and I speak from a wide personal knowledge of those European classes).

This is the material from which our nation must be shaped; and we, the small and for the moment absolutely dominant white aristocracy on whom the main weight of duty of social reconstruction rests, have reason to be thankful it is what it is.

If by entering on a long and difficult course of strictly just and humane treatment, as between man and man, we can bind our dark races to us through their sense of justice and gratitude; if we, as a dominant class, realise that the true wealth of a nation is the health, happiness, intelligence, and content of every man and woman born within its borders; if we do not fail to realise that the true crown of honour on the head of a dominant class is that it leads and teaches, not uses and crushes; if, as the years pass, we can point with pride to our native peoples as the most enlightened and the most free, the most devoted to the welfare of its native land of all African races; if our labouring class can in the end be made to compare favourably with that of all other countries; and if for the men of genius or capacity who are born among them there be left open a free path, to take their share in the higher duties of life and citizenship, their talents expended for the welfare of the community and not suppressed to become its subterraneous and disruptive forces; if we can make our State as dear to them, as the matrix in which they find shelter for healthy life and development, as it is to us; then I think the future of South Africa promises greatness and strength.

But if we fail in this? – If, blinded by the gain of the moment, we see nothing in our dark man but a vast engine of labour; if to us he is not man, but only a tool; if dispossessed entirely of the land for which he now shows that large aptitude for peasant proprietorship for the lack of which among their masses many great nations are decaying; if we force him permanently in his millions into the locations and compounds and slums of our cities, obtaining his labour cheaper, but to lose what the wealth of five Rands[3] could not return to us; if, uninstructed in the highest forms of labour, without the rights of citizenship, his own social organisation broken up, without our having aided him to participate in our own; if, unbound to us by gratitude and sympathy, and alien to us in blood and colour, we reduce this vast mass to the condition of a great seething, ignorant proletariat – then I would rather draw a veil over the future of this land.

For a time such a policy may pay us admirably both as to labour and lands; we may work gold mines where the natives' corn now stands, and the dream of a labourer at two-pence a day which has haunted the waking visions of some men may be realised – but can it pay ultimately?

Even in the commercial sense, will it pay us in the direction of manufacture and trade, if, when the labouring classes of other countries are steadily increasing in skill and intelligence, ours remain in the mass mere hewers of wood and drawers of water, without initiative or knowledge? Will it even pay us to have him robbed of his muscular strength and virility by a sudden change to unhealthy conditions of life? Considered as a mere engine of labour, is not his muscle one of our commercial assets? If we doctor him with our canteens and cheap wines, and immerse him in city-slum life, will he even as a machine of labour remain what he is?

Are we to spend all our national existence with a large, dark shadow looming always in the background – a shadow-which-we-fear?

I would not willingly appeal to the lowest motives of self-interest, yet it may be permitted to say this: as long as the population of South Africa is united, and the conditions of warfare remain what they are, we need fear no foe. With our inaccessible coast, and few harbours, our mighty mountain ranges and desolate plains, into which the largest armies might be led and left to starve, we are as unassailable as Northern Russia behind her steppes and icefields; it would take more than a Napoleon to walk over us; we are, indeed, an impregnable fortress in these Southern seas – if the entire population is united.

But what if we are not united? What if, when the day comes, as it must, when hostile fleets – perhaps not European – gather round our shores, and the vast bulk of our inhabitants should cast eyes of indifference, perhaps of hope, towards them? Having no share in the life of our State, being bound to us by no ties of sympathy, having nothing to lose, might not the stranger even appear in the guise of a deliverer, and every bush hide a possible guide, and the bulk of the men and women in our land whisper, 'It is no business of ours; let them fight it out'?

As long as nine-tenths of our community have no permanent stake in the land, and no right or share in our government, can we ever feel safe? Can we ever know peace?

One dissatisfied man or woman who feel themselves wronged is a point of weakness in a community; but when this condition animates the vast majority of the inhabitants of a State, there is a crack down the entire height of the social structure. In times of peace it may be covered over by whitewash and plaster, and one may profess that all is well; but when the time of conflict and storm comes, that is where the social structure will give way.

But a far more subtle and inevitable form of evil must ultimately overtake us. It is ordained by the laws of human life that a Nemesis[4] should follow the subjection and use, purely for purposes of their own, of any race by another which lives among them. Spain fell before it in America; Rome felt it; it has dogged the feet of all conquering races. In the end the subjected people write their features on the face of the conquerors.

We cannot hope ultimately to equal the men of our own race living in more wholly enlightened and humanised communities, if our existence is passed among millions of non-free subjected peoples. The physical labour we despise and refuse because they do it for us; the continual association with human creatures who are not free, will ultimately take from us our strength and our own freedom; and men will see in our faces the reflection of that on which we are always treading and looking down. If we raise the dark man we shall rise with him; if we kick him under our feet he will hold us fast by them.

It was recently reported in one of our Houses of Legislature, in a speech by one of our leading men, that once when discussing the question of the light and dark races with a Bantu, the latter had said: 'When you do well to us, you do well to yourselves.'

This seems to me to sum up the philosophy of the whole matter. The dark man is the child the gods have given us in South Africa for our curse or our blessing; we shall rise with him, and we shall also sink with him.

To-day we in South Africa stand at the parting of the ways; and there is no man and no woman, however small and without influence their voice may be, and though themselves devoid of citizen rights, who, believing that the future of South Africa depends on our taking in this matter the higher and more difficult path, can absolve them to themselves, if they do not speak the word which weighs on them.

Lastly, if I were asked what in South Africa is our great need at the present moment, I should answer, 'Great men to lead us.'

In an ordinary household, where a woman brings up the children she herself has borne, who share her blood and to whom her instincts bind her, she needs no exceptionally great or rare qualities to rear her children and govern her house in harmony. But if a woman, having children born of her own body, should marry a man already having children by another wife, and they two should again have children of their own, and even receive into their family one or two children by adoption, then, to make her work a success, that woman would require altogether wider and more exceptional gifts. The animal instinct which binds us to what is ours by blood would not suffice; and unless carefully watched and controlled might totally unfit her for the work she had to do. She would need not merely those high intellectual powers which enable us to understand types of mind widely distinct from our own, but those still rarer graces of the spirit allied to intellectual gifts but distinct from them, which make the love of justice inherent in an individual which would enable her to stretch maternal sympathies out, far beyond the limits of mere instinct. If she possessed these qualities in balanced proportions, the domestic world she ruled over might become a centre of unity and desirable human relations; if she possessed none of them, it would become a hell.

So the man fitted to be the national leader of a great heterogeneous people requires certain qualities not asked for in the leaders, even the great leaders, of a homogeneous race. Our call in South Africa to-day is not for a Cavour or a Talleyrand, nor even at the moment for à William Wallace or a Robert Bruce.[5] The man who should help to guide us toward the path of true union and a beneficent organisation must be more than the great party leader, the keen diplomatist, far-seeing politician, or even the renowned soldier. He may be some of these, but he must be much more.

He must be a man able to understand, and understanding to sympathise with, all sections of our people; loving his own race and form of speech intensely, he will never forget it is only one among others, and deserving of no special favour because it is his; he will value the diverse virtues of our two great white classes which almost, as much as their faults, have brought them into collision, and seek to harmonise them; he will understand the really colossal difficulties which a white race has to face in dealing with a labouring class which is severed from it by colour (difficulties often not understood by those across the seas; who condemn conduct which they themselves would probably follow if brought face to face with the same difficulties); he will realise to the full the difficulties the dark man faces when, his old ideals and order of life suddenly uprooted, he is thrown face to face with a foreign civilisation which he must grasp and rise to, or under which he must sink; and he will seek by every means in his power to help him bridge the transition without losing his native virtues. At all costs to himself he will persist in holding up before us the ideal, by which he is himself dominated, of a great South Africa, in which each element of our population, while maintaining its own individuality, shall subserve the interests of others as well as its own; till from this sense of mutual service and from that passionate love for our physical Mother Earth, which is common to all South Africans, shall grow up the wide and deep South African feeling that alone can transform us into a 'great nation.' In spite of many mistakes and many failures, and the sorrow which walks beside all who strike out new paths for the feet of men, such a man would form the true centre of our national life, and, however fitfully and slowly, would lead our national conscience to shape itself in harmony with that ideal.

For beneath the self-seeking and animal instinct which covers the surface of our lives lies that which in its saner moments does recognise singleness of purpose where it finds it, and knows only that a wide justice and humanity between men is righteousness – the righteousness that exalteth a nation.

(...)

The States and territories of South Africa will ultimately combine in some form of union. It is inevitable; no man can stay it.

If among those things which fate still holds hidden from us in the hollow of her hand there be such a man, or such men, loving justice and freedom, not only for themselves or their own race, but for all their fellow-countrymen, and able to imbue us with their own larger conception of the national life, and lead us towards it, then I see light where the future of South Africa rises; if not, we shall still attain to a political unification in some form or other, but it will be a poor, peddling thing when we have it – perhaps bloody.

De Aar, 1908.

Woman and War (1911)

This chapter from *Woman and Labour* was printed separately as a political pamphlet in 1914. Although Schreiner never supported violent militancy as a feminist political strategy, over the course of her life she had known and corresponded with women of almost every turn-of-the-century feminist persuasion (Stanley). *Woman and Labour* was dedicated to Lady Constance Lytton, one of the early leaders of the English women's suffrage campaign. As Schreiner initially molded her own feminism from an amalgam of Victorian science and her situation as a colonial subject, in the last years of her life she pushed her idealistic, eugenicist feminism to answer the questions posed by other political struggles. The relations sketched here, between women, maternity and peace, are further developed in her last work, 'The Dawn of Civilisation', reprinted below (pp. 212–20). 'Woman and War' asks a question that may bridge contemporary feminism to the liberation struggle in South Africa: how do we as human beings cultivate both difference and equality?

It may be said, 'Granting fully that you are right, that, as woman's old fields of labour slip from her, she must grasp the new, or must become wholly dependent on her sexual function alone, all the other elements of human nature in her becoming atrophied and arrested through lack of exercise: and, granting that her evolution being arrested, the evolution of the whole race will be also arrested in her person: granting all this to the full, and allowing that the bulk of human labour tends to become more and more intellectual and less and less purely mechanical, as perfected machinery takes the place of crude human exertion; and that therefore if woman is to be saved from degeneration and parasitism, and the body of humanity from arrest, she must receive a training which will cultivate all the intellectual and all the physical faculties with which she is endowed, and be allowed freely to employ them; nevertheless, would it not be possible, and perhaps be well, that a dividing line of some kind should be drawn between the occupations of men and of women? Would it not, for example, be possible that woman should retain agriculture, textile manufacture, trade, domestic management, the education of youth, and medicine, in addition to child-bearing, as her exclusive fields of toil; while to the male should be left the study of abstract science, law, and war, and statecraft; as of old, man took war and the chase, and woman absorbed the further labours of life? Why should there not be again a fair and even division in the field of social labour?'

Superficially, this suggestion appears rational, having at least this to recommend it – that it appears to harmonize with the course of human evolution in the past; but closely examined, it will, we think, be found to have no practical or scientific basis, and to be out of harmony with the conditions of modern life. In ancient and primitive societies, the mere larger size and muscular strength of man, and woman's incessant physical activity in child-bearing and suckling and rearing the young, made almost inevitable a certain sexual division of labour in almost all countries, save perhaps in ancient Egypt.[1] Woman naturally took the heavy agricultural and domestic labours, which were yet more consistent with the continual dependence of infant life on her own, than those of man in war and the chase. There was nothing artificial in such a division; it threw the heaviest burden of the most wearying and unexciting forms of social labour on woman, but under it both sexes laboured in a manner essential to the existence of society, and each transmitted to the other, through inheritance, the fruit of its slowly expanding and always exerted powers; and the race progressed.

Individual women might sometimes, and even often, become the warrior chief of a tribe; the King of Ashantee might train his terrible regiment of females; and men might now and again plant and weave for their children: but in the main, and in most societies, the division of labour was just, natural, beneficial; and

199

it was inevitable that such a division should take place. Were to-day a band of civilized men, women, and infants thrown down absolutely naked and defenceless in some desert, and cut off hopelessly from all external civilized life, undoubtedly very much of the old division of labour would, at least for a time, reassert itself; men would look about for stones and sticks with which to make weapons to repel wild beasts and enemies, and would go a-hunting meat and fighting savage enemies and tend the beasts when tamed:[2] women would suckle their children, cook the meat men brought, build shelters, look for roots and if possible cultivate them; there certainly would be no parasite in the society; the woman who refused to labour for her offspring, and the man who refused to hunt or defend society, would not be supported by their fellows, would soon be extinguished by want. As wild beasts were extinguished and others tamed and the materials for war improved, fewer men would be needed for hunting and war; then they would remain at home and aid in building and planting; many women would retire into the house to perfect domestic toil and handicrafts, and on a small scale the common ancient evolution of society would practically repeat itself. But for the present, we see no such natural and spontaneous division of labour based on natural sexual distinctions in the new fields of intellectual or delicately skilled manual labour, which are taking the place of the old.

It is possible, though at present there is nothing to give indication of such a fact, and it seems highly improbable, that, in some subtle manner now incomprehensible, there might tend to be a subtle correlation between that condition of the brain and nervous system which accompanies ability in the direction of certain modern forms of mental, social labour, and the particular form of reproductive function possessed by an individual. It may be that, inexplicable as it seems, there may ultimately be found to be some connection between that condition of the brain and nervous system which fits the individual for the study of the higher mathematics, let us say, and the nature of their sex attributes. The mere fact that, of the handful of women who, up to the present, have received training and been allowed to devote themselves to abstract study, several have excelled in the higher mathematics, proves of necessity no pre-eminent tendency on the part of the female sex in the direction of mathematics, as compared to labour in the fields of statesmanship, administration, or law; as into these fields there has been practically no admittance for women. It is sometimes stated, that as several women of genius in modern times have sought to find expression for their creative powers in the art of fiction, there must be some inherent connection in the human brain between the ovarian sex function and the art of fiction. The fact is, that modern fiction being merely a description of human life in any of its phases, and being the only art that can be exercised without special training or special appliances, and produced in the moments stolen from the multifarious, brain-destroying occupations which fill the average woman's life, they have been driven to find this outlet for their powers as the only one presenting itself. How far otherwise might have been the directions in which their genius would naturally have expressed itself can be known only partially even to the women themselves; what the world has lost by that compulsory expression of genius, in a form which may not have been its most natural form of expression, or only one of its forms, no one can ever know. Even in the little third-rate novelist whose works cumber the ground, we see often a pathetic figure, when we recognize that beneath that failure in a complex and difficult art, may lie buried a sound legislator, an able architect, an original scientific investigator, or a good judge. Scientifically speaking, it is as unproven that there is any organic relation between the brain of the female and the production of art in the form of fiction, as that there is an organic relation between the hand of woman and a typewriting machine. Both the creative writer and the typist, in their respective spheres, are merely finding outlets for their powers in the direction of least resistance. The tendency of women at the present day to undertake certain forms of labour, proves only that in the crabbed, walled-in, and bound conditions surrounding woman at the present day, these are the lines along which action is most possible to her.

It may possibly be that in future ages, when the male and

female forms have been placed in like intellectual conditions, with like stimuli, like training, and like rewards, that some aptitudes may be found running parallel with the line of sex function when humanity is viewed as a whole. It may possibly be that, when the historian of the future looks back over the history of the intellectually freed and active sexes for countless generations, that a decided preference of the female intellect for mathematics, engineering, or statecraft may be made clear; and that a like marked inclination in the male to excel in acting, music, or astronomy may by careful and large comparison be shown. But, for the present, we have no adequate scientific data from which to draw any conclusion, and any attempt to divide the occupations in which male and female intellects and wills should be employed, must be to attempt a purely artificial and arbitrary division: a division not more rational and scientific than an attempt to determine by the colour of his eyes and the shape and strength of his legs, whether a lad should be an astronomer or an engraver. Those physical differences among mankind which divide races and nations – not merely those differences, enormously greater as they are generally, than any physical differences between male and female of the same race, which divide the Jew and the Swede, the Japanese and the Englishman, but even those subtle physical differences which divide closely allied races such as the English and German – often appear to be allied with certain subtle differences in intellectual aptitudes. Yet even with regard to these differences, it is almost impossible to determine scientifically in how far they are the result of national traditions, environment, and education, and in how far the result of real differences in organic conformation.[3]

No study of the mere physical differencs between individuals of different races would have enabled us to arrive at any knowledge of their mental aptitude; nor does the fact that certain individuals of a given human variety have certain aptitudes form a rational ground for compelling all individuals of that variety to undertake a certain form of labour.

No analysis, however subtle, of the physical conformation of the Jew could have suggested *a priori*, and still less could have proved, apart from ages of practical experience, that, running parallel with any physical characteristics which may distinguish him from his fellows, was an innate and unique intellectual gift in the direction of religion. The fact that, during three thousand years, from Moses to Isaiah, through Jesus and Paul, on to Spinoza,[4] the Jewish race has produced men who have given half the world its religious faith and impetus, proves that, somewhere and somehow, whether connected organically with that physical organization that marks the Jew, or as the result of his traditions and training, there does go this gift in the matter of religion. Yet, on the other hand, we find millions of Jews who are totally and markedly deficient in it, and to base any practical legislation for the individual even on this proven intellectual aptitude of the race as a whole would be manifestly as ridiculous as abortive. Yet more markedly, with the German – no consideration of his physical peculiarities, though it proceeded to the subtlest analysis of nerve, bone, and muscle, could in the present stage of our knowledge have proved to us what generations of experience appear to have proved, that, with that organization which constitutes the German, goes an unique aptitude for music. There is always the possibility of mistaking the result of training and external circumstance for inherent tendency, but when we consider the passion for music which the German has shown, and when we consider that the greatest musicians the world has seen, from Bach, Beethoven, and Mozart to Wagner,[5] have been of that race, it appears highly probable that such a correlation between the German organization and the intellectual gift of music does exist. Similar intellectual peculiarities seem to be connoted by the external differences which mark off other races from each other. Nevertheless, were persons of all of these nationalities gathered in one colony, any attempt to legislate for their restriction to certain forms of intellectual labour on the ground of their apparently proved national aptitudes or disabilities, would be regarded as insane. To insist that all Jews, and none but Jews, should lead and instruct in religious matters; that all Englishmen, and none but Englishmen, should engage in trade; that each German should make his living by music, and none but a German allowed to practise it, would drive to despair the unfortunate individual Englishman, whose most marked deficiency might be in the direction of finance and bartering trade power; the Jew, whose religious instincts might be entirely rudimentary; or the German, who could not distinguish one note from another; and the society as a whole would be an irremediable loser, in one of the heaviest of all forms of social loss – the loss of the full use of the highest capacities of all its members.

It may be that with sexes as with races, the subtlest physical differences between them may have their fine mental correlatives; but no abstract consideration of the human body in relation to its functions of sex can, in the present state of our knowledge, show us what intellectual capacities tend to vary with sexual structure, and nothing in the present or past condition of male and female give us more than the very faintest possible indication of the relation of their intellectual aptitudes and their sexual functions. And even were it proved by centuries of experiment that with the possession of the uterine function of sex tends to go exceptional intellectual capacity in the direction of mathematics rather than natural history, or an inclination for statecraft rather than for mechanical invention; were it proved that, generally speaking and as a whole, out of twenty thousand women devoting themselves to law and twenty thousand to medicine, they tended to achieve relatively more in the field of law than of medicine, there would yet be no possible healthy or rational ground for restricting the activities of the individual female to that line in which the average female appeared rather more frequently to excel.[6]

That even one individual in a society should be debarred from undertaking that form of social toil for which it is most fitted, makes an unnecessary deficit in the general social assets. That one male Froebel[7] should be prohibited or hampered in his labour as an educator of infancy, on the ground that infantile instruction was the field of the female; that one female with gifts in the direction of state administration, should be compelled to instruct an infants' school, perhaps without the slightest gift for so doing, is a running to waste of social life-blood.

Free trade in labour and equality of training, intellectual or physical, is essential if the organic aptitudes of a sex or class are to be determined. And our demand to-day is that natural conditions inexorably, but beneficently, may determine the labours of each individual, and not artificial restrictions.

As there is no need to legislate that Hindus, being generally supposed to have a natural incapacity for field sports, shall not betake themselves to them – for, if they have no capacity, they will fail; and, as in spite of the Hindus' supposed general incapacity for sport, it is possible for an individual Hindu to become the noted batsman of his age; so, also, there is no need to legislate that woman should be restricted in her choice of fields of labour; for the organic incapacity of the individual, if it exist, will legislate far more powerfully than any artificial, legal, or social obstruction can do; and it may be that the one individual in ten thousand who selects a field not generally sought by his fellows will enrich humanity by the result of an especial genius. Allowing all to start from the one point in the world of intellectual culture and labour, with our ancient Mother Nature sitting as umpire, distributing the prizes and scratching from the lists the incompetent, is all we demand, but we demand it determinedly. Throw the puppy into the water; if it swims, well; if it sinks, well; but do not tie a rope round its throat and weight it with a brick, and then assert its incapacity to keep afloat.

For the present our cry is, '*We take all labour for our province!*'

From the judge's seat to the legislator's chair; from the statesman's closet to the merchant's office; from the chemist's laboratory to the astronomer's tower, there is no post or form of toil for which it is not our intention to attempt to fit ourselves; and there is no closed door we do not intend to force open; and there is no fruit in the garden of knowledge it is not our determination to eat. Acting in us, and through us, nature we know will mercilessly expose to us our deficiencies in the field of human toil, and reveal to us our powers. *And, for to-day, we take all labour for our province!*

But, it may then be said: 'What of war, that struggle of the human creature to attain its ends by physical force and at the price of the life of others: will you take part in that also?' We reply: Yes; more particularly in that field we intend to play our part. We have always borne part of the weight of war, and the major part. It is not merely that in primitive times we suffered from the destruction of the fields we tilled and the houses we built; or that in later times as domestic labourers and producers, though unwaged, we, in taxes and material loss and additional labour, paid as much as our males towards the cost of war; nor is it that in a comparatively insignificant manner, as nurses of the wounded in modern times, or now and again as warrior chieftainesses and leaders in primitive and other societies, we have borne our part; nor is it even because the spirit of resolution in its women, and their willingness to endure, has in all ages again and again largely determined the fate of a race that goes to war, that we demand our controlling right where war is concerned. Our relation to war is far more intimate, personal, and indissoluble than this. Men have made boomerangs, bows, swords, or guns with which to destroy one another; we have made the men who destroyed and were destroyed! We have in all ages produced, at an enormous cost, the primal munition of war, without which no other would exist. There is no battlefield on earth, nor ever has been, howsoever covered with slain, which it has not cost the women of the race more in actual bloodshed and anguish to supply, than it has cost the men who lie there. *We pay the first cost on all human life.*

In supplying the men for the carnage of a battlefield, women have not merely lost actually more blood, and gone through a more acute anguish and weariness, in the long months of bearing and in the final agony of child-birth, than has been experienced by the men who cover it; but, in the long months and years of rearing that follow, the women of the race go through a long, patiently endured strain which no knapsacked soldier on his longest march has ever more than equalled; while, even in the matter of death, in all civilized societies, the probability that the average woman will die in child-birth is immeasurably greater than the probability that the average male will die in battle.

There is, perhaps, no woman, whether she have borne children, or be merely potentially a child-bearer, who could look down upon a battlefield covered with slain, but the thought would rise in her, 'So many mothers' sons! So many bodies brought into the world to lie there! So many months of weariness and pain while bones and muscles were shaped within; so many hours of anguish and struggle that breath might be; so many baby mouths drawing life at woman's breasts; – all this, that men might lay with glazed eyeballs, and swollen bodies, and fixed, blue, unclosed mouths, and great limbs tossed – this, that an acre of ground might be manured with human flesh, that next year's grass or poppies or karoo bushes may spring up greener and redder, where they have lain, or that the sand of a plain may have a glint of white bones!' And we cry, 'Without an inexorable cause, this should not be!' No woman who is a woman says of a human body, 'It is nothing!'

On that day, when the woman takes her place beside the man in the governance and arrangement of external affairs of her race will also be that day that heralds the death of war as a means of arranging human differences. No tinsel of trumpets and flags will ultimately seduce women into the insanity of recklessly destroying life, or gild the wilful taking of life with any other name than that of murder, whether it be the slaughter of the million or of one by one. And this will be, not because with the sexual function of maternity necessarily goes in the human creature a deeper moral insight, or a loftier type of social instinct than that which accompanies the paternal. Men have in all ages led as nobly as women in many paths of heroic virtue, and toward the higher social sympathies; in certain ages, being freer and more widely cultured, they have led further and better. The fact that woman has no inherent all-round moral superiority over her male companion, or naturally on all points any higher social instinct, is perhaps most clearly exemplified by one curious very small fact: the two terms signifying intimate human relationships which in almost all human languages bear the most sinister and antisocial significance are both terms which have as their root the term 'mother', and denote feminine relationships – the words 'mother-in-law' and 'step-mother.'

In general humanity, in the sense of social solidarity, and in magnanimity, the male has continually proved himself at least the equal of the female.

Nor will women shrink from war because they lack courage. Earth's women of every generation have faced suffering and death with an equanimity that no soldier on a battlefield has ever surpassed and few have equalled; and where war has been to preserve life, or land, or freedom, unparasitized and labouring women have in all ages known how to bear an active part, and die.

Nor will woman's influence militate against war because in the future woman will not be able physically to bear her part in it. The smaller size of her muscle, which would severely have disadvantaged her when war was conducted with a battle-axe or sword and hand to hand, would now little or at all affect her. If intent on training for war, she might acquire the skill for guiding a Maxim or shooting down a foe with a Lee-Metford[8] at four thousand yards as ably as any male; and undoubtedly, it has not been only the peasant girl of France, who has carried latent and hid within her person the gifts that make the supreme general. If our European nations should continue in their present semi-civilized condition, which makes war possible, for a few generations longer, it is highly probable that as financiers, as managers of the commissariat department, as inspectors of provisions and clothing for the army, women will play a very leading part; and that the nation which is the first to employ its women so may be placed at a vast advantage over its fellows in time of war. It is not because of woman's cowardice, incapacity, nor, above all, because of her general superior virtue, that she will end war when her voice is fully, finally, and clearly heard in the governance of states – it is because, on this one point, and on this point almost alone, the knowledge of woman, simply as woman, is superior to that of man; she knows the history of human flesh; she knows its cost; he does not.[9]

In a besieged city, it might well happen that men in the streets might seize upon statues and marble carvings from public buildings and galleries and hurl them in to stop the breaches made in their ramparts by the enemy, unconsideringly and merely because they came first to hand, not valuing them more than had they been paving-stones. But one man could not

208

do this – the sculptor! He, who, though there might be no work of his own chisel among them, yet knew what each of these works of art had cost, knew by experience the long years of struggle and study and the infinitude of toil which had gone to the shaping of even one limb, to the carving of even one perfected outline, *he* could never so use them without thought or care. Instinctively he would seek to throw in household goods, even gold and silver, all the city held, before he sacrificed its works of art!

Men's bodies are our woman's works of art. Given to us power of control, we will never carelessly throw them in to fill up the gaps in human relationships made by international ambitions and greeds. The thought would never come to us as woman, 'Cast in men's bodies; settle the thing so!' Arbitration and compensation would as naturally occur to her as cheaper and simpler methods of bridging the gaps in national relationships, as to the sculptor it would occur to throw in anything rather than statuary, though he might be driven to that at last!

This is one of those phases of human life, not very numerous, but very important, towards which the man as man, and the woman as woman, on the mere ground of their different sexual function with regard to reproduction, stand, and must stand, at a somewhat differing angle. The physical creation of human life, which, in as far as the male is concerned, consists in a few moments of physical pleasure; to the female must always signify months of pressure and physical endurance, crowned with danger to life. To the male, the giving of life is a laugh; to the female, blood, anguish, and sometimes death. Here we touch one of the few yet important differences between man and woman as such.

The twenty thousand men prematurely slain on a field of battle, mean, to the women of their race, twenty thousand human creatures to be borne within them for months, given birth to in anguish, fed from their breasts and reared with toil, if the numbers of the tribe and the strength of the nation are to be maintained. In nations continually at war, incessant and unbroken child-bearing is by war imposed on all women if the state is to survive; and whenever war occurs, if numbers are to be maintained, there must be an increased child-bearing and rearing. This throws upon woman as woman a war tax, compared with which all that the male expends in military preparations is comparatively light.

The relations of the female towards the production of human life influences undoubtedly even her relation towards animal and all life. 'It is a fine day, let us go out and kill something!' cries the typical male of certain races, instinctively. 'There is a living thing, it will die if it is not cared for,' says the average woman, almost equally instinctively. It is true, that the woman will sacrifice as mercilessly, as cruelly, the life of a hated rival or an enemy, as any male; *but she always knows what she is doing, and the value of the life she takes!* There is no lighthearted, careless enjoyment in the sacrifice of life to the normal woman; her instinct, instructed by practical experience, steps in to prevent it. She always knows what life costs; and that it is more easy to destroy than create it.

It is also true, that, from the loftiest standpoint, the condemnation of war which has arisen in the advancing human spirit, is in no sense related to any particular form of sex function. The man and the woman alike, who with Isaiah on the hills of Palestine, or the Indian Buddha under his bo-tree,[10] have seen the essential unity of all sentient life; and who therefore see in war but a symptom of that crude discoordination of life on earth, not yet at one with itself, which affects humanity in these early stages of its growth: and who are compelled to regard as the ultimate goal of the race, though yet perhaps far distant across the ridges of innumerable coming ages, that harmony between all forms of conscious life, metaphorically prefigured by the ancient Hebrew, when he cried, 'The wolf shall dwell with the lamb; and the leopard shall lie down with the kid; and the calf and the young lion and the fatling together and a little child shall lead them!'[11] – to that individual, whether man or woman, who has reached this standpoint, there is no need for enlightenment from the instincts of the child-bearers of society as such; their condemnation of war, rising not so much from the fact that it is a wasteful destruction of human flesh, as that it is an indication of the non-existence of that co-ordination, the harmony which is summed up in the cry, 'My little children, love one another.'

But for the vast bulk of humanity, probably for generations to come, the instinctive antagonism of the human child-bearer to reckless destruction of that which she has at so much cost produced, will be necessary to educate the race to any clear conception of the bestiality and insanity of war.

War will pass when intellectual culture and activity have made possible to the female an equal share in the control and governance of modern national life; it will probably not pass away much sooner; its extinction will not be delayed much longer.

It is especially in the domain of war that we, the bearers of men's bodies, who supply its most valuable munition, who, not amid the clamour and ardour of battle, but singly, and alone, with a three-in-the-morning courage, shed our blood and face death that the battlefield may have its food, a food more precious to us than our heart's blood; it is we especially, who in the domain of war, have our word to say, a word no man can say for us. It is our intention to enter into the domain of war and to labour there till in the course of generations we have extinguished it.

If to-day we claim all labour for our province, yet more especially do we claim those fields in which the difference in the reproductive function between man and woman may place male and female at a slightly different angle with regard to certain phases of human life.

The Dawn of Civilisation (1920)

When she died in 1920 Schreiner was working on a book about pacifism, the first politics she embraced without qualification. The following excerpt is from that book and was published originally in the *Nation and Atheneum* in 1921. Schreiner and her brother had been in contact with Gandhi's *satyagraha* movement and had begun to advocate peaceful civil disobedience as a means of protest. In 'The Dawn of Civilisation' Schreiner returns to her early memories of identity with the land and people of South Africa, this time correcting the tales of her childhood and describing how black people are used as 'beasts of labour' in South Africa. Schreiner's references to the Bible in this piece suggest links between her lifelong struggle against forms of both racial and sexual violence.

I Introduction

I have thrown these scattered thoughts, written at intervals during illness, into a somewhat personal form. I have done so intentionally, because I have felt that many persons, even those of high intellectual attainments, were not able to understand what the question of peace and war in its widest aspects meant to certain among us; that, for us, it stands for something far more intimate, personal, and of a far more organic nature than any mere intellectual conclusion – that, for some among us, as a man is compelled to feel the beating of his own heart and cannot shake himself from the consciousness of it, whether he will or no, so we are under a certain psychic compulsion to hold that view which we do hold with regard to war, and are organically unable to hold any other.

There are many ways in which a man at the present day may conscientiously object to war. His forebears may have been objectors and have handed down to him a tradition, which, from his earliest years, has impressed on him the view that war is an evil, not to be trafficked with. His ancestors may have been imprisoned and punished by the men of their own day, for holding what were then entirely new and objectionable views; but, where once a man can prove that he holds any opinions as a matter of inheritance and that they are shared by a certain number of his fellows under a recognised collective name, the bulk of human beings in his society may not agree with him, may even severely condemn him and desire to punish him; but, since the majority of human creatures accept their politics, their religion, their manners and their ideals purely as a matter of inheritance, the mass of men who differ from him are, at least, able to understand *how* he comes by his views. They do not regard him as a monstrosity and an impossibility, and are able to extend to him in some cases a certain limited tolerance; he comes by his views exactly as they come by theirs; and in so far they are able to understand him.

But a man may conscientiously object to war in quite another fashion. He may object to a definite and given war, for some definite, limited reason. He may believe that war to have been led up to by a false and mad diplomacy, to be based on a mistaken judgment of the national interests; to be even suicidal; and therefore he may feel compelled to oppose that particular war while the bulk of men and women in his society desire and approve of it. The unthinking herd, unable to understand or tolerate any opposition to the herd-will of the moment, may regard him as incomprehensibly wicked; but, at least, an appreciable number of intelligent persons, not sharing his view, will understand that a man may be sincerely compelled to oppose certain lines of public action which the majority of his fellows approve. They may hate him for opposing their will, they may attempt to ostracise and crush him; but, in their calmest and most reasonable moments, they do understand that they might themselves under certain circumstances be compelled to act in the same manner, and are willing, therefore, to allow him the virtue of possible sincerity, if nothing else.

But a man may object to war in another and far wider way.

His objection to it may not be based on any hereditary tradition, or on the teaching of any organised society, or of any of the great historic figures of the past; and, while he may indeed object to any definite war for certain limited and material reasons, these are subordinate to the real ground on which his objection rests. He may fully recognise the difference in type between one war and another; between a war for dominance, trade expansion, glory, or the maintenance of Empire, and a war in which a class or race struggles against a power seeking permanently to crush and subject it, or in which a man fights in the land of his birth for the soil on which he first saw light, against the strangers seeking to dispossess him; but, while recognising the immeasurable difference between these types (exactly as the man who objects to private murder must recognise the wide difference between the man who stabs one who has a knife at his throat and the man who slow-poisons another to obtain a great inheritance), he is yet an objector to all war. And he is bound to object, not only to the final expression of war in the slaying of men's bodies; he is bound to object, if possible, more strongly to those ideals and aims and those institutions and methods of action which make the existence of war possible and inevitable among men.

Also, while he may most fully allow that certain immediate and definite ends may be gained by the slaughter of man by man – not merely as where Jezebel gained possession of Naboth's vineyard,[1] for a time, by destroying him, or David acquired Uriah's wife by putting him in the forefront of battle,[2] but aims even otherwise excusable or even laudable – he is yet compelled to hold that no immediate gain conferred by war, however great, can compensate for the evils it ultimately entails on the human race. He is therefore unable to assist not merely in the actual carnage of war, but, as far as possible, in all that leads to its success.

This is the man, often not belonging to any organised religion, not basing his conviction on the teachings of authority external to himself, whom it appears so difficult, if not impossible, for many persons, sometimes even of keen and critical intellectual gifts, to understand.

214

We have, in South Africa, a version of a certain well-known story. According to this, an old Boer from the backveld goes for the first time to the Zoological Gardens at Pretoria and sees there some of the, to him, new and quite unknown beasts. He stands long and solemnly before one, and looks at it intently; and then, slowly shaking his head, he turns away. 'Daar *is* nie zoo'n dier nie!' ('There *is* not such a beast') he remarks calmly, as he walks away.

This story returns often to the mind at the present day, when watching the action of certain bodies of men called upon to pass judgment on the psychic conditions of their fellows, on the matter of slaughter and war. The good shopkeeper, the worthy farmer, the town councillor, the country gentleman, and dashing young military man may understand perfectly their own businesses of weighing and measuring goods, rearing cattle, levying rates, or polo playing, or the best way to cut and thrust in the slaughter of war; but, when suddenly called upon to adjudge on psychological phenomena of which they have no personal experience, they are almost compelled to come to the conclusion of the good old backveld Boer – 'Daar *is* nie zoo'n dier nie!' 'There *is* no such thing as a Conscientious Objector! He may stand before us; he may tell us what he feels; but we have no experience of such feelings. We know, therefore, that such a being *cannot* exist – and, therefore, it *does* not!'

In the few pages that follow I have allowed, as I said, a personal element to enter, and I have done so intentionally. As a rule, the more the personal element is eliminated in dealing with the large impersonal problems of human life, the wiser the treatment will be; and it is perhaps always painful in dealing with that to be viewed by those not in sympathy, to touch on those phases of life sacred to the individual as they never can be to any other. But I have felt that, perhaps only by a very simple statement of what one insignificant human creature has felt and does feel, it might perhaps be possible for me to make clear to some of my fellows that such a being as the universal conscientious objector to war does exist.

We are a reality! We do exist. We are as real as a bayonet with human blood and brains along its edge; we are as much a part of the Universe as coal or lead or iron; you have to count us in! You may think us fools, you may hate us, you may wish we were all dead; but it is at least something if you recognise that we are. 'To understand all is to forgive all,' it has been said; and it is sometimes even something more; it is to sympathise, and even to love, where we cannot yet fully agree. And therefore, perhaps, even the feeblest little attempt to make human beings understand how and why their fellows feel as they feel and are as they are, is not quite nothing.

II Somewhere, Some Time, Some Place

When a child, not yet nine years old, I walked out one morning along the mountain tops on which my home stood. The sun had not yet risen, and the mountain grass was heavy with dew; as I looked back I could see the marks my feet had made on the long, grassy slope behind me. I walked till I came to a place where a little stream ran, which farther on passed over the precipices into the deep valley below. Here it passed between soft, earthy banks; at one place a large slice of earth had fallen away from the bank on the other side, and it had made a little island a few feet wide with water flowing all round it. It was covered with wild mint and a weed with yellow flowers and long waving grasses. I sat down on the bank at the foot of a dwarfed olive tree, the only tree near. All the plants on the island were dark with the heavy night's dew, and the sun had not yet risen.

I had got up so early because I had been awake much in the night and could not sleep longer. My heart was heavy; my physical heart seemed to have a pain in it, as if small, sharp crystals were cutting into it. All the world seemed wrong to me. It was not only that sense of the small misunderstandings and tiny injustices of daily life, which perhaps all sensitive children feel at some time pressing down on them; but the whole Universe seemed to be weighing on me.

I had grown up in a land where wars were common. From my earliest years I had heard of bloodshed and battles and hairbreadth escapes; I had heard them told of by those who had seen and taken part in them. In my native country dark men were killed and their lands taken from them by white men armed with superior weapons; even near to me such things had happened. I knew also how white men fought white men; the stronger even hanging the weaker on gallows when they did not submit; and I had seen how white men used the dark as beasts of labour, often without any thought for their good or happiness. Three times I had seen an ox striving to pull a heavily loaded wagon up a hill, the blood and foam streaming from its mouth and nostrils as it struggled, and I had seen it fall dead, under the lash. In the bush in the kloof below I had seen bush-bucks and little long-tailed monkeys that I loved so shot dead, not from any necessity but for the pleasure of killing, and the cock-o-veets and the honey-suckers and the wood-doves that made the bush so beautiful to me. And sometimes I had seen bands of convicts going past to work on the roads, and had heard the chains clanking which went round their waists and passed between their legs to the irons on their feet; I had seen the terrible look in their eyes of a wild creature, when every man's hand is against it, and no one loves it, and it only hates and fears. I had got up early in the morning to drop small bits of tobacco at the roadside, hoping they would find them and pick them up. I had wanted to say to them, 'Someone loves you'; but the man with the gun was always there. Once I had seen a pack of dogs set on by men to attack a strange dog, which had come among them and had done no harm to anyone. I had watched it torn to pieces, though I had done all I could to save it. Why did everyone press on everyone and try to make them do what they wanted? Why did the strong always crush the weak? Why did we hate and kill and torture? Why was it all as it was? Why had the world ever been made? Why, oh why, had I ever been born?

The little sharp crystals seemed to cut deeper into my heart.

And then, as I sat looking at that little, damp, dark island, the sun began to rise. It shot its lights across the long, grassy slopes of the mountains and struck the little mound of earth in the water. All the leaves and flowers and grasses on it turned bright gold, and the dewdrops hanging from them were like diamonds; and the water in the stream glinted as it ran. And, as

I looked at that almost intolerable beauty, a curious feeling came over me. It was not what I *thought* put into exact words, but I seemed to *see* a world in which creatures no more hated and crushed, in which the strong helped the weak, and men understood each other, and forgave each other, and did not try to crush others, but to help. I did not think of it, as something to be in a distant picture; it was there, about me, and I was in it, and a part of it. And there came to me, as I sat there, a joy such as never besides have I experienced, except perhaps once, a joy without limit.

And then, as I sat on there, the sun rose higher and higher, and shone hot on my back, and the morning light was everywhere. And slowly and slowly the vision vanished, and I began to think and question myself.

How could that glory ever really be? In a world where creature preys on creature, and man, the strongest of all, preys more than all, how could this be? And my mind went back to the dark thoughts I had in the night. In a world where the little ant-lion digs his hole in the sand and lies hidden at the bottom for the small ant to fall in and be eaten, and the leopard's eyes gleam yellow through bushes as it watches the little bush-buck coming down to the fountain to drink, and millions and millions of human beings use all they know, and their wonderful hands, to kill and press down others, what hope could there ever be? The world was as it was! And what was I? A tiny, miserable worm, a speck within a speck, an imperceptible atom, a less than a nothing! What did it matter what *I* did, how *I* lifted my hands, and how *I* cried out? The great world would roll on, and on, just as it had! What if nowhere, at no time, in no place, was there anything else?

The band about my heart seemed to grow tighter and tighter. A helpless, tiny, miserable worm! Could I prevent one man from torturing an animal that was in his power; stop one armed man from going out to kill? In my own heart, was there not bitterness, the anger against those who injured me or others, till my heart was like a burning coal? If the world had been made so, so it was! But, why, oh why, had I ever been born? Why did the Universe exist?'

And then, as I sat on there, another thought came to me; and in some form or other it has remained with me ever since, all my life. It was like this: You cannot by willing it alter the vast world outside of you; you cannot, perhaps, cut the lash from one whip; you cannot stop the march of even one armed man going out to kill; you cannot, perhaps, strike the handcuff from one chained hand; you cannot even remake your own soul so that there shall be no tendency to evil in it; the great world rolls on, and *you* cannot reshape it; but this one thing only you can do – in that one, small, minute, almost infinitesimal spot in the Universe, where your will rules, there where alone you are as God, *strive* to make that you hunger for real! No man can prevent you there. In your own heart strive to kill out all hate, all desire to see evil come even to those who have injured you or another; what is weaker than yourself try to help; whatever is in pain or unjustly treated and cries out, say, 'I am here! I, little, weak, feeble, but I will do what I can for you.' This is all you can do; but do it; it is not nothing! And then this feeling came to me, a feeling it is not easy to put into words, but it was like this: You also are a part of the great Universe; what you strive for something strives for; *and nothing in the Universe is quite alone*; you are moving on towards something.

And as I walked back that morning over the grass slopes, I was not sorry I was going back to the old life. I did not wish I was dead and that the Universe had never existed. I, also, had something to live for – and even if I failed to reach it utterly – somewhere, some time, some place, it was! I was not alone.

More than a generation has passed since that day, but it remains to me the most important and unforgettable of my life. In the darkest hour its light has never quite died out.

In the long years which have passed, the adult has seen much of which the young child knew nothing.

In my native land I have seen the horror of a great war. Smoke has risen from burning homesteads; women and children by thousands have been thrown into great camps to perish there; men whom I have known have been tied in chairs and executed for fighting against strangers in the land of their own birth. In the world's great cities I have seen how everywhere the upper stone grinds hard on the nether, and men and women feed upon the toil of their fellow men without any increase of spiritual beauty or joy for themselves, only a heavy congestion; while those who are fed upon grow bitter and narrow from the loss of the life that is sucked from them. Within my own soul I have perceived elements militating against all I hungered for, of which the young child knew nothing; I have watched closely the great, terrible world of public life, of politics, diplomacy, and international relations, where, as under a terrible magnifying glass, the greed, the ambition, the cruelty and falsehood of the individual soul are seen, in so hideously enlarged and wholly unrestrained a form that it might be forgiven to one who cried out to the powers that lie behind life: 'Is it not possible to put out a sponge and wipe up humanity from the earth? It is stain!' I have realised that the struggle against the primitive, self-seeking instincts in human nature, whether in the individual or in the larger social organism, is a life-and-death struggle, to be renewed by the individual till death, by the race through the ages. I have tried to wear no blinkers. I have not held a veil before my eyes, that I might profess that cruelty, injustice, and mental and physical anguish were not. I have tried to look nakedly in the face those facts which make most against all hope – and yet, in the darkest hour, the consciousness which I carried back with me that morning has never wholly deserted me; even as a man who clings with one hand to a rock, though the waves pass over his head, yet knows what his hand touches.

But, in the course of the long years which have passed, something else has happened. That which was for the young child only a vision, a flash of almost blinding light, which it could hardly even to itself translate, has, in the course of a long life's experience, become a hope, which I think the cool reason can find grounds to justify, and which a growing knowledge of human nature and human life does endorse.

Somewhere, some time, some place – even on earth!

Afterword:
'The Prison-House
of Colonialism'

Review of Ruth First and Ann Scott's *Olive Schreiner*[1]

Nadine Gordimer

Who is qualified to write about whom? Subjects very often do not get the biographers their works and lives demand; they are transformed, after death, into what they were not. There must be a lot of fuming, beyond the grave.

Olive Schreiner has been one of the worst-served, from her spouse's version of her life, in accordance with what a husband would have liked his famous writer-wife to be, to the hagiographic selectivity of two or three other biographies which have appeared since her death in 1920. At last, the perfectly qualified candidates have presented themselves: two people who represent a combination of the dominant aspects of Schreiner's character, her feminism and her political sense: and each of whom corrects the preoccupational bias of the other.

Schreiner's feminism followed the tug of colonial ties with a European 'home'; it was conceived in relation to the position of women in late nineteenth-century Europe: through her tract, *Woman and Labour*, she is a Founding Mother of women's liberation in Britain, and one of her two new biographers, Ann Scott, is a young English feminist. Schreiner's political awareness was specific through her understanding of the relation of capitalist imperialism to racialism in South Africa; and Ruth First, her other biographer, is a South African radical activist thinker and fine writer who went into exile in Britain years ago but is now close to her – and Olive Schreiner's – real home again, teaching at the Eduardo Mondlane University in Mozambique.[2]

First and Scott make a superb combination and one is curious about how they overcame the tremendous differences between their two ideological approaches. Take the statement: 'We have tried to create a psychologically believable woman of the late nineteenth century largely on the basis of the psychoanalytic language of the twentieth'. Was Ruth First able to follow this basic approach because of the new attitude to psychoanalysis that has been penetrating Marxist thinking through the work of Jacques Lacan and others since the failure of the 1968 student uprising in Paris? The book is a model of disinterested collaboration and scholarship, and the reconciliation it achieves between the viewpoints of the authors and their subject brings great rewards for the reader.

This biography establishes a level of inquiry no previous biographer was perhaps in a position to attempt. So far ahead of her own times, Schreiner was obscured in succeeding ones by the kind of critical assessment then prevailing. Now First and Scott can write:

> We see Olive Schreiner's life and writing as a product of a
> specific social history. We are not only looking at what she
> experienced but at how she, and others, perceived that
> experience; at the concepts with which her contemporaries
> understood their world, and, again, at the consciousness that
> was possible for her time – after Darwin, before Freud, and
> during the period when Marx's *Capital* was written.

Olive Schreiner was born in South Africa of missionary parents and as a twenty-one-year-old governess in 1883 wrote *The Story of an African Farm*, a novel which brought her immediate world fame that has lasted ever since. In her work and life (she had the missionary sense of their oneness), it becomes clear from this study, she was hampered crucially by the necessity of fighting the ways of thought which imprisoned her and others, equipped only with the modes available within those concepts. Only once did she invent a form to carry her advanced perceptions: a literary one, for *The Story of an African*

Farm. Her short novel about the conquest of Rhodesia, *Trooper Peter Halket*, shows as true an interpretation of historical realities, re-read during the week of Zimbabwe's independence celebrations, as Schreiner claimed it did when she wrote it, during Rhodes's conquest of Mashonaland; but it has the preachy, nasal singsong of a sermon. When she wanted to find a way to express her political vision, she took up the form of allegory typical of the hypocritical Victorian high-mindedness she had rejected along with religious beliefs.

About sex, she lied to herself continually – protesting to her men friends that she wanted 'love and friendship without any sex element' in letters whose very syntax paces out yearning sexual desire. She recognized the sexual demands of women in a period when they were trained to believe that their role was merely to 'endure' male sexual demands, but she used Victorian subterfuges (on a par with the 'vapours'), disguised as feminism to hide a sense of shame at the idea of her own sexual appetite. The spectacle of the rebel dashing herself against the cold panes of convention is that of a creature doubly trapped: by a specific social history, and by the consciousness possible to her in her time.

First and Scott suggest further that Schreiner's reputation as an imaginative writer has suffered by the 'persistent view that her social comment is obtrusive and damaging to her work': the novel – *The Story of an African Farm* – on which that reputation rests has been acclaimed, sometimes by people who would not share even her liberal views, let alone the radical element in them, as having its genius in 'transcending politics', and by extension, Schreiner's political fervour. The present biographers will be interested to know that a reverse trend is now appearing in South African criticism; Schreiner is no longer praised for soaring above politics, but attacked for turning out to be nothing but the broken-winged albatross of white liberal thinking. C. I. Hofmeyr, a young white lecturer at an 'ethnic' university for South African Indians, said at a conference recently:

Although Schreiner was cognisant of the power of the
speculator and capitalist to triumph because of their access to

power, she nonetheless continued to harbour a tenuous optimism that justice, equality, and the rightness of the liberal democracy would come to triumph via the operation of the 'enlightened' liberal remnant of the English community. Of course, it did not, and the bourgeois democracy that Schreiner had hoped for soon developed into the repressive colonial state. This development is significant in so far as it shows the weaknesses in the thinking of Schreiner and her class.

If Schreiner was a 'genius', the lecturer continued, this was 'a critical category that obscures the extent to which she was rooted in nineteenth-century assumptions'.

Whether or not one can swallow this (old) view of genius as a class-determined concept rather than an innate, congenital attribute – and whether Schreiner had it or not – the tension in her relationship to these nineteenth-century assumptions, so brilliantly conveyed in this book, was the source of her achievements and her failures.

Olive Schreiner, like other South African writers (William Plomer, Roy Campbell, Laurens van der Post) up until after the Second World War, when writers both black and white became political exiles, looked to Europe and went to Europe. Some went permanently, after the initial success of work born specifically of their South African consciousness. Some went ostensibly because they had been reviled for exposing the 'traditional' South African way of life for what it is (Plomer, *Turbott Wolfe*). But the motive generally was a deep sense of deprivation, that living in South Africa they were cut off from the world of ideas; and underlying this incontestable fact (particularly for Schreiner, in her time) was another reason which some had a restless inkling was the *real* source of their alienation, although they could express it only negatively: that the act of taking the Union Castle mailship to what was the only cultural 'home' they could conceive of, much as they all repudiated jingoism, was itself part of the philistinism they wanted to put at an ocean's distance from them. Even Sol Plaatje, one of the first black writers, had this instinct, since he was using Western modes – journalism, the diary, the novel – to express black consciousness.

They went because the culture in which their writings could take root was not being created; a culture whose base would be the indigenous black culture interpenetrating with imported European cultural forms, of which literature was one: and, because the works they had written – or would have found it imperative to attempt, if they were to express the life around them – were solitary contradictions of the way in which that life was being conceptualized, politically, socially and morally.

Olive Schreiner felt stifled (the asthma she suffered from is a perfect metaphor) by the lack of any questioning exchange of ideas in the frontier society in which she lived. I suppose one must allow that she had a right to concern herself with a generic, universal predicament: that of the female sex. During her restless, self-searching years in England and Europe, and her association with Havelock Ellis, Eleanor Marx, Karl Pearson, women's suffrage and English socialism in the 1880s, she studied intensively theories on race and evolution and participated in progressive political and social movements; but feminism was her strongest motivation. Yet the fact is that in South Africa, now as then, feminism is regarded by people whose thinking on race, class and colour Schreiner anticipated, as a question of no relevance to the actual problem of the country – which is to free the black majority from white minority rule.

Her biographers point out that once living again in South Africa, she resigned from the Women's Enfranchisement League when its definition of the franchise qualification was changed so as to exclude black women. But in the South African context, where she always felt herself to belong, and to which she always returned, in the end to die there, the women issue withers in comparison with the issue of the voteless, powerless state of South African blacks, irrespective of sex. It was as bizarre then (when a few blacks in the Cape Colony had a heavily qualified vote) as now (when no black in the Republic of South Africa has a vote) to regard a campaign for women's rights – black or white – as relevant to the South African situation. Schreiner seems not to have seen that her wronged sense of self, as a woman, that her liberation, was a secondary matter within her historical situation. Ironically, here at least she shared the most persistent characteristic of her fellow colonials (discounting the priorities of the real entities around her) while believing she was protesting against racism.

First and Scott give a fascinating account of the neuroticism of this amazing woman, in whose tortured, heightened sense of being all the inherent contradictions of her sex and time existed. One enters into their biography as into a good discussion with people better informed on the subject than oneself.

For myself, I am led to take up the question of Olive Schreiner's achievement exclusively as an imaginative writer, in relation to the conceptual determinants within which she lived, even while warring against them. First and Scott quote the argument – and I think they see her wronged by it – that after *African Farm* her creativity 'disappeared into the sands of liberal pamphleteering'. The observation was originally mine. Their book confirms for me, that whatever else she may have achieved, Schreiner dissipated her creativity in writing tracts and pamphlets rather than fiction. This is not to discount her social and political mission; neither is it to attempt to nail her to the apartheid *Tendenzroman*. It is to assert that by abandoning the search for a form of fiction adequate to contain the South African experience, after her abortive experiments with a 'distancing' allegory, she was unable in the end to put the best she had – the power of her creative imagination – to the service of her fierce and profound convictions, and her political and human insight. It is true that, as First and Scott claim, 'almost alone, she perceived the race conflicts during South Africa's industrial revolution in terms of a world-wide struggle between capital and labour'. But she wrote about these insights instead of transforming them through the creation of living characters into an expression of the lives they shaped and distorted. This could have achieved the only real synthesis of life and work, of ideology and praxis, for Olive Schreiner, raising the conscious-ness of the oppressed from out of the colonial nightmare, and that of the oppressor from out of the colonial dream, and telling the world what she, uniquely, knew about the quality of human life deformed by those experiences.

Chronology

(Compiled from Clayton [1983], First and Scott [1981], and Thompson [1985].)

1806	England takes Cape Colony from Dutch for second time; for over a century Dutch (Boers) have been importing slaves to develop farming and trade.
1815	Uprising of Boer vigilantes on frontier, later known as 'Slagternek Rebellion'.
1828	Cape Colony frees 'Hottentots and other free persons of Colour' from legal restrictions.
1834–38	British Parliament emancipates slaves.
1836–40	Approximately 5,000 Boers (Afrikaner 'voortrekkers') leave Cape Colony with their Coloured servants; later known as 'Great Trek'.
1837	Gottlob Schreiner marries Rebecca Lyndall, daughter of dissenting London preacher; arrive at their first mission station on Eastern frontier in 1838; daughter Kate born soon afterward.
Dec. 1838	Afrikaners defeat Zulu ('Battle of Blood River').
1842	London Missionary Society investigates Gottlob's shady financial dealings and land speculation; he founds Basel mission in Basutoland.
1843	England annexes Natal.
1852–54	England recognises South African Republic (Transvaal) and Orange Free State as independent Afrikaner states; Gottlob works in Bloemfontein, then Wittenbergen; Rebecca very ill.
1855	24 March, Olive Emilie Albertina Schreiner born, ninth of 12 children, named after 3 dead brothers.
1857	William Philip (W. P.) Schreiner born.
1864	Ellie Schreiner, little sister to whom *From Man to Man* dedicated, born; dies following year.
1866	Gottlob declared insolvent; family breaks up due to poverty.
1867	Diamond mining begins in Griqualand West; struggle for territory intensifies.

1870	Schreiner begins work intermittently as governess; also writing first short stories.
1871	Reads Spencer's *First Principles*; meets Julius Gau, her first love, while nursing his sister; asthma begins when she returns to poor, sick and dependent parents; announces that she is to be called 'Olive' not 'Emilie'.
1872	Announces then breaks off engagement to Gau; writing story about diamond fields, her first allegory ('The Lost Joy'), and *Undine*.
1873	Reads works by J. S. Mill and Darwin; begins another novel, called *Other Men's Sins*.
1874	Emotionally exhausting, mindless work as governess; five posts in seven years; buys and reads Emerson's *Essays*.
1876	Finishes but decides not to publish *Undine*; begins 'Thorn Kloof' (*Story of an African Farm*?) and combines other short stories into *Saints and Sinners* (early version of *From Man to Man*).
1877	England annexes Transvaal; Afrikaner Bond formed under Jan Hofmeyr.
1879	Olive completes early draft of *African Farm* (not yet with that title).
1880–81	Transvaal Afrikaners regain independence in the First Boer War; Olive sends *Saints and Sinners* to England; ms. returned for revision; still writing *African Farm*.
1881	Olive sails to England; becomes ill during first days of nurse's training at Royal Infirmary, Edinburgh.
1882	*African Farm* accepted by Chapman and Hall; as 'Palinsky Smith' Olive publishes short stories for children.
1883	*The Story of an African Farm* (2 vols) by 'Ralph Iron'.
1884	Olive begins lifelong correspondence with Havelock Ellis; they have unsuccessful love affair; she meets Eleanor Marx.
1885	Meets Karl Pearson, Edward Carpenter, and George Moore, who proposes; joins Men and Women's Club; W. T. Stead's exposé of child prostitution in *Pall Mall Gazette*.
1886–87	Olive breaks off relationship with Pearson; leaves England in distress; travels on Continent, writing allegories and introduction to Mary Wollstonecraft's *A Vindication of the Rights of Woman*; gold mining begins on Witwatersrand.
1889	British acquisition of Rhodesia underway; Olive meets Cecil Rhodes in England; has 'nervous feeling' she will marry him; she sails back to Africa in October.
1890	Pearson marries Maria Sharpe; Olive meets Rhodes in Cape Town and invites him to visit her; she moves to

Matjesfontein and begins articles about Africa for *Fortnightly Review* (these become *Thoughts on South Africa*).

1891	Ellis marries Edith Lees; *Dreams* published; also 'Woman and the Family' in Carpenter's *Sheffield Anarchist*; Olive writes satiric skit on Parliamentary debate on Flogging Bill.
1892	Writing short stories; breaks with Rhodes; meets Samuel Cron Cronwright.
1893	*Dream Life and Real Life* published; brother W. P. becomes attorney-general to Rhodes.
1894	Olive marries Cron; they settle briefly at his farm, then move to Kimberley because of her asthma.
1895	Daughter born, dies during night; Cronwright reads 'The Political Situation' in Kimberley Town Hall.
1895–96	Jameson's unsuccessful 'raid' into Transvaal forces Rhodes's resignation; Olive writes *Trooper Peter Halket of Mashonaland*.
1897	Olive and Cron sail to England; *Trooper Peter* published.
1898	Transvaal forces conquer the Venda, completing white conquest of African population of South Africa; W. P. Prime Minister of Cape until 1900; Olive and Cron return to Johannesburg ('Hell'); marriage a disaster.
1899–1902	Anglo-Boer War, or (Second) Boer War; England defeats Afrikaner republics; Olive's house looted; publishes *English South-African's View*, an anti-war pamphlet; makes speech as leader of women's protest movement.
1902	Olive working on *Woman and Labour*, also *From Man to Man* and additional allegories, including 'Eighteen Ninety-Nine'.
1905	'Letter on "Taal"' in *Cape Times*.
1906	*Letter on the Jew* published.
1908	Movement toward unification begins, conflict between federalists and unionists; Olive and W. P. oppose 'union' proposed by Merriman and Smuts; 'Letter on Women's Suffrage' in *Cape Times*.
1909	*Closer Union* published; W. P. Schreiner and Gandhi lead protest delegation to London against Colour Bar in South Africa Bill.
1910	Cape Colony, Natal, Transvaal and Orange Free State form Union of South Africa; white-controlled, self-governing British dominion under Louis Botha.
1911	*Woman and Labour* published.
1912	Founding of African National Congress (ANC).
1913	Native Land Act limits African landownership to 'reserves'; Olive resigns vice-presidency of Cape Women's Enfranchisement League when they come out only in

favour of white women's suffrage; very ill and marriage under additional stress.

1914 J. B. M. Hertzog forms the first Afrikaner National Party; England declares war on Germany; Olive and W. P. travelling in Germany; worker strikes on Rand quelled by Smuts.

1915 Olive in England; writes 'Who Knocks at the Door?'.

1916 Publishes message on conscientious objectors in *Labour Leader*; begins longer work on pacifism ('The Dawn of Civilisation').

1920 Returns to Cape, dies at Wynberg on 11 December.

1921 Cron reinters Olive at Buffelskop, above his old farm.

1923 *Thoughts on South Africa* and *Stories, Dreams and Allegories* published.

1924 Cronwright-Schreiner's *Life* and *Letters of Olive Schreiner* published.

1926 *From Man to Man* published.

1929 *Undine* published.

1948 D. F. Malan's National Party wins general election and begins to apply *apartheid* policy.

1952 ANC and allies launch passive resistance campaign against unjust laws.

1960 Police kill 67 African anti-pass demonstrators at Sharpeville; government bans African political organisations; *Closer Union* reissued by Constitutional Reform Association.

1961 South Africa becomes republic, leaves Commonwealth.

1966–68 Lesotho, Botswana, and Swaziland become independent states and members of the UN; *The Story of an African Farm* republished.

1974 *Trooper Peter Halket* published in Johannesburg.

1975–76 Angola and Mozambique become independent states; *Story of an African Farm* produced on stage in South Africa.

1976–77 At least 575 die in disturbances in Soweto and other black townships.

1977 UN Security Council imposes arms embargo on South Africa.

1980 Zimbabwe (formerly Rhodesia) gains independence.

1983 *Olive Schreiner: A One-Woman Play*, by Stephen Gray produced.

1984 New constitution gives Asians and Coloured people but not Africans limited participation in South African government; prolonged and widespread resistance in townships; Bishop Desmond Tutu awarded Nobel Peace Prize and elected Anglican Bishop of Johannesburg.

1986– Continued resistance in black townships; occasional guerrilla attacks on white country clubs and shopping malls; South African government imposes 'state of emergency', giving police added authority and denying journalists access to townships; Tutu, Winnie Mandela and others call for economic sanctions against South Africa; governments of United States and England consider economic ties and 'influence' in the area more important than movement toward majority rule.

At year end, over 300 people have been killed since the 'state of emergency' began in June. Rent strikes and work boycotts increase in the townships, as Black and white activists organise 'Christmas Against the Emergency'. Major United States and British companies – including International Business Machines, General Motors, and Barclays Bank – sell their South African subsidiaries to white business-people in South Africa. In a new set of 'emergency measures', the South African government imposes strict censorship and, essentially, outlaws protest; Black police deployed to quell unrest in Port Elizabeth and elsewhere. Amnesty International and other groups protest against police brutality, rape, and the widespread incarceration of young children.

Notes

In the notes to the texts by Olive Schreiner, original notes written by either the author or Cronwright-Schreiner are found in quotation marks and identified (OS) or (CS). In cases where their notes require further clarification, I have added information in square brackets [thus] or afterwards.

Introduction

1 In Cory Library, Rhodes University, Grahamstown; quoted in Clayton, ed. (1983), p. 123.

2 See Bennett (1928), p. 309; Brittain (1933, rpt 1978), p. 41; and Vicinus (1985), p. 273, for various contemporary accounts of Schreiner's influence; Clayton, ed. (1983) for reviews of her writings; Lawrence Lerner, 'Olive Schreiner and the Feminists', and Alan Bishop, '"With Suffering and Through Time"', both in Smith and Maclennan, eds (1983), for importance to feminist movement.

3 Fradkin (1979), p. 76, notes the dramatisations; Clayton, ed. (1983), p. 225, lists Stephen Gray, *Olive Schreiner: A One-Woman Play* (Cape Town: Philip, 1983).

4 'Colonial Man' is (in this case) the phrase of Stephen Gray, as is the publishing history of *Trooper Peter*; see 'The Trooper at the Hanging Tree', in Clayton, ed. (1983), pp. 198–208.

5 See L. Thompson (1985) for Afrikaners' rewriting of history in the formation of a racist 'political mythology'.

6 Review of Ruth First and Ann Scott, *Olive Schreiner: A Biography*, *Times Literary Supplement*, 15 August 1980; reprinted here as an *Afterword*.

7 For discussions of ideology and language that have influenced mine see Cameron (1984), Fields (1982), Foucault (1977), J. Thompson (1984), and Volosinov (1973); for gender and language in the context of racial and cultural difference see Gates, ed. (1985), especially articles by Derrida, Pratt, and Spivak.

8 Cronwright-Schreiner, ed. (1924b), and First and Scott (1980) are my main sources for biographical information. I have also followed Fradkin's (1979) suggestion that we read Schreiner *against* rather than simply as the product or the proponent of the various political and formal struggles with which she was involved. See bibliography

for additional and related works.

9 Wilhelm (1979), pp. 65–7; First and Scott, chap. 2; also see Beer (1983), Ellis (1940), Gibbons (1973), Rowbotham and Weeks (1977), and Webb (1926, rpt 1980).

10 I discuss Schreiner's narrative reworkings of evolutionary theory in Barash (1986); also see Beer (1983).

11 See Fradkin (1977) and Walkowitz (1986) for discussions of the Men and Women's Club.

12 Kaplan (1979) discusses Wollstonecraft's attempt to rationalise and downplay women's sexuality as part of Wollstonecraft's response to Rousseau.

13 See Kevles (1984) for centrality of eugenics in late nineteenth-century; Weeks (1981) and Jeffreys (1985) for relationship between discourses of eugenics and sexuality; Davin (1978) for eugenics and imperialism; and Rose, Lewontin and Kamin (1984) for how sociobiology picks up where eugenics leaves off, continuing to operate as a conservative political force.

14 Vicinus (1985).

15 Liddington and Norris (1978), esp. pp. 143–211; in contrast Davis (1982), pp. 30–69, shows how the women's movement in the United States grew out of women's work with the Abolition campaign.

16 Walkowitz (1980), esp. chaps. 9 and 12.

17 Judith Walkowitz, 'Male Vice and Feminist Virtue', in Snitow *et al.*, eds. (1983), pp. 43–61, for discourse of victimisation; and Walkowitz (1986) for sexual politics of the Club.

18 Compare Beatrice Webb's 'scientific' relationship to women in London's East End when she disguised herself as a worker among them in order to do 'social investigation'; Nord (1985), pp. 165–77.

19 Showalter (1986) discusses this Victorian phenomenon at length; see also First and Scott, pp. 129–44.

20 Ellis's 'case history' of Schreiner is found in *Studies in the Psychology of Sex*, Vol. 3 (1928), Appendix B, History 9; Jeffreys (1985), chap. 7, argues that Ellis's belief in eugenics made him especially fearful of women's communities and potential lesbianism.

21 First and Scott (1980), p. 162; Walkowitz (1986), pp. 51–3; also see Schreiner, 'Professor Pearson on the Woman Question', *Pall Mall Gazette*, 29 January 1889.

22 *Letters*, p. 209.

23 Wilhelm (1979), pp. 63–4; Clayton (1985), pp. 32–3; and Clifford (1974), pp. 3–30.

24 My argument here owes much to Gray, 'The Trooper at the Hanging Tree', in Clayton, ed. (1983), esp. pp. 204–6.

25 Ibid., p. 207.

26 Ellen Kuzwayo, *New Internationalist*, 159 (1986), p. 13, argues that feminists in the West consistently fail to understand the importance

of women standing 'side by side with our men' in liberation
struggles. Also see Patterson (1982), pp. 38 et seq., for how 'natal
alienation' is central to the symbolism and practice of slavery cross-
culturally; Bernstein (1985) and Kuzwayo (1985) for women's
centrality in holding together the Black community in South Africa.

27 See Barash (1986) for a longer discussion of evolutionary theory and
racism in *Woman and Labour*.

28 Virginia Woolf, review of *The Letters of Olive Schreiner*, *New Republic*
42 (18 March 1925), p. 103.

29 Jacques Derrida, 'Racism's Last Word' (trans. Peggy Kamuf), in
Gates, ed. (1985), pp. 296–7, makes the case for South Africa; see
Davis (1982), chap. 11, and Jacquelyn Dowd Hall, 'The Mind that
Burns in Each Body: Women, Rape and Racial Violence' in Snitow
et al., eds. (1983), pp. 339–60, for other discussions of how white
men's enforcement of laws about rape and marriage combine racist
and sexist restraints; and Patterson (1982), esp. chaps. 2 and 11, for
how slavery as a system destroys natal kinship and sexual choice
and manipulates the social order through symbols of sexual
authority and hierarchy.

30 I have found it helpful to think of 'racism' both as a discourse that
cuts across time creating and enforcing oppression, and as
specific – historical and material – articulations of that discourse.
See Davis (1982), Fields (1982), and Patterson (1982) for discussions
of the relationship between historical changes and continuities in
ideological forms.

31 Gordimer enacts these conflicts in fiction in *July's People* (1981).

The Child's Day

1 *Hottentot*: colonial name given to pale-skinned, indigenous Khoikhoi
people of western South Africa; often stock farmers.

2 'Oh yes, God! What shall we now say?' (OS).

3 *Swedenborg*: Emanuel Swedenborg (1688–1772), Swedish natural
scientist, theologian, and mystic; author of *Principia Rerum Naturalium*
(1734) and *Oeconomia Regni Animalis* (1740–1) and founder of
Swedenborg societies, which became the Church of New Jerusalem.

4 *kappie*: large sun-bonnet, often with elaborate embroidery, worn by
Dutch women in South Africa.

5 *Kaffir*: Arabic word meaning 'infidel' or 'devil'; derogatory colonial
name given to range of Bantu-speaking peoples of South Africa,
roughly equivalent to 'Negro' or 'Nigger' in the United States.

6 *kraals*: sheepfolds.

7 *Bushman stone*: San ('Bushmen') in area of Cape Colony were known
for elaborate rock-painting; part of their religious and cultural life

for thousands of years, San rock-paintings also reflected historical changes and thus came to depict Boer settlers as they moved into the area.

8 *Cape Dutch*: Boer settlers' language; derived from Dutch of the Netherlands and sometimes called 'the Taal', or language, and later Afrikaans; vehicle of Afrikaner nationalism and solidarity. See Schreiner's 'Letter on "the Taal"' (excerpted in *Letters*: 388–91).

9 *. . . and Katje found hers behind the kraal*: Schreiner is here making a distinction between the domestic ease of the Boer mother's child-bearing and the complete lack of material comforts experienced by her African servants in similar situations; that the babies are 'found' may also refer to their being the offspring of white men's denied but ongoing sexual relationships with their African servants, as happens later in *From Man to Man*.

10 Rebekah's mind is filled with bits and pieces of eighteenth-century poetry and Dissenting hymns; these and the Bible are her major sources of (mis)information about the world. Schreiner's father was a German missionary, her mother the daughter of an English Dissenting minister. Church-going, Bible-reading, and strict rules about everything from clothing to conduct pervaded her youth (First and Scott: 31–50).

11 *Cock-o-veet*: 'The Bush-shrike, a very handsome bird with resonant call notes of great beauty – a prime favourite of Olive's.' (CS).

12 *Kaffir plums*: South African ornamental tree with edible fruit.

13 *puff-adder*: thick, venomous South African snake that distends its body when irritated.

14 *What Hester Durham Lived For*: like the allegorical tales, such as Adams (1855), which Schreiner read as a child and which influenced her own 'dreams'. *Sepoys* are natives of India employed as soldiers under colonial rule.

15 *The Assyrian came down –* : Cf. *Isaiah* 19:23 and Byron, 'The Destruction of Sennacherib', one of his 'Hebrew Melodies' (c. 1815).

16 *Romans came and they took away her country . . .* : Rebekah's (slightly misquoted) source is William Cowper, 'Boadicea: An Ode' (1780), esp. ll. 13–14 and 17–20; however, Rebekah takes words like 'progeny' and 'pregnant' later in the poem to mean Boadicea is a mother rather than a warrior. Gibbon's *History of the Decline and Fall of the Roman Empire* (1777–98) was one of Schreiner's favourite books and is another source for the stories about Roman cruelty to women and children. Finally, similarities are suggested between the ruthlessness of the Roman and British empires.

17 *Jane Taylor's Hymns for Infant Minds*: Jane Taylor (b. 1795) and her sister, Ann Taylor Gilbert (b. 1782) were separately and together the authors of numerous hymns, poems and moral tales for children. *Hymns for Infant Minds* (1809) was Jane Taylor's second hymnal,

published when she was fourteen years old.

18 *Elijah*: Jewish prophet, traditionally the harbinger of apocalypse; see *I Kings* 17–18 and *II Kings* 1, 2 and 4.

19 *thorn . . . myrtle-tree*: Cf. *Isaiah* 55:13.

20 *Miss Plumtree's Bible stories*: either Annabella Plumptre, *Stories for Children* (1804); or Anne and Annabella Plumptre, *Tales of Wonder* (3 vols., 1818). In a 1903 letter to Havelock Ellis, Schreiner still recalls such childhood stories vividly (*Letters*: 240).

21 *stramonium*: thorn-apple, seeds and leaves of which have narcotic effects.

22 *stoep*: verandah.

23 *mier-kat*: small mammal, occasionally tamed; feared to carry rabies.

24 "'My fatherland's force!" – so Olive wrote it. But the expression is Afrikaans . . . and should be *My Vaderland se vos* (pronounced almost "May vahderlahnd ser fos"), probably a corruption of an old Nederlands expression, meaning "My fatherland's God."' (CS). In his zealousness to point out his wife's errors, Cronwright misses the point: the whole of 'The Child's Day' has been told through a child's eyes and through the hodge-podge of ideas she has received from a variety of speakers and texts.

The Woman Question

1 *Achilles . . . Maxim gun*: Achilles, usually represented as fierce and implacable, was the chief Greek hero of the Trojan War; Richard I (1157–99) spent the bulk of his reign as king of England involved in foreign combat; the Maxim gun was an automatic machine gun invented by Hiram Maxim (1840–1916).

2 'The problem of the unemployed male is, of course, not nearly so modern as that of the unemployed female. It may be said in England to have taken its rise in almost its present form as early as the fifteenth century, when economic changes began to sever the agricultural labourer from the land, and rob him of his ancient forms of social toil. Still, in its most acute form, it may be called a modern problem.' (OS). Cf. Karl Pearson, 'Woman and Labour' (1894a).

3 *penny-a-liner*: hack writer.

4 *Krupp*: famous German family of gun manufacturers; supplied munitions to over 40 countries in the nineteenth century; later, as supporters of Hitler, used slave labour from concentration camps in their factories.

5 *Worth*: in *Woman and Labour* Schreiner changes 'Worth' to 'the male dress-designer'.

6 'There is, indeed, something pathetic in the attitude of many a good old mother of the race, who having survived, here and there, into

the heart of our modern civilisation, is sorely puzzled by the change in woman's duties and obligations. She may be found looking into the eyes of some ancient crone, who, like herself, has survived from a previous state of civilisation, seeking there a confirmation of a view of life of which a troublous doubt has crept even into her own soul. "I," she cries, "always cured my own hams, and knitted my own socks, and made up all the linen by hand. We always did it when we were girls – but now my daughters object!" And her old crone answers her: "Yes, *we* did it; it's the right thing; but it's so expensive. It's so much cheaper to buy things ready made!" And they shake their heads and go their ways, feeling that the world is strangely out of joint when duty seems no more duty. Such women are, in truth, like a good old mother duck, who, having for years led her ducklings to the same pond, when that pond has been drained and nothing is left but baked mud, will still persist in bringing her younglings down to it, and walks about with flapping wings and anxious quacks, trying to induce them to enter it. But the ducklings, with fresh young instincts, hear far off the delicious drippings from the new dam which has been built higher up to catch the water, and they smell the chickweed and the long grass that is growing up beside it; and absolutely refuse to disport themselves on the baked mud or to pretend to seek for worms where no worms are. And they leave the ancient mother quacking beside her pond and set out to seek for new pastures – perhaps to lose themselves upon the way? – perhaps to find them? To the old mother one is inclined to say, "Ah, good old mother duck, can you not see the world has changed? You cannot bring the water back into the dried-up pond! Mayhap it was better and pleasanter when it was there, but it has gone for ever; and, would you and yours swim again, it must be in other waters. New machinery, new duties."' (OS).

7 *'May thy wife's womb never cease from bearing . . . '*: perhaps a version of a real African greeting, but in this context part of Schreiner's mystification of Black African women's relationship to child-bearing.

8 *reign of Justinian*: 527–65 A.D.

9 *Black Death of 1349*: bubonic plague; produced black spots on skin and swept through Asia and Europe in the mid-fourteenth century.

10 *zymotic disease*: infectious disease.

11 *If a woman becomes weary . . .* : Martin Luther (1483–1546), prolific theological writer, translator of the Bible into German vernacular, and leader of the Protestant Reformation, was not known for his egalitarian views toward women.

12 *Though shalt bear . . .* : see *Genesis* 1:22 and 3:16.

13 'The difference between the primitive and the modern view on this matter is aptly and quaintly illustrated by two incidents. Seeing a

certain Bantu [i.e. native African] woman who appeared better cared for, less worked, and happier than the mass of her companions, we made inquiry, and found that she had two impotent brothers; because of this she herself had not married, but had borne by different men fourteen children, all of whom when grown she had given to her brothers. "They are fond of me because I have given them so many children, therefore I have not to work like the other women; and my brothers give me plenty of mealies [maize or corn] and milk," she replied, complacently, when questioned, "and our family will not die out." And this person, whose conduct was so emphatically anti-social on all sides when viewed from the modern standpoint, was evidently regarded as pre-eminently of value to her family and to society because of her mere fecundity. On the other hand, a few weeks back appeared an account in the London papers of an individual who, taken up at the East End for some brutal offence, blubbered out in court that she was the mother of twenty children." "You should be ashamed of yourself!" responded the magistrate; "a woman capable of such conduct would be capable of doing anything!" and the fine was remorselessly inflicted. Undoubtedly, if somewhat brutally, the magistrate yet gave true voice to the modern view on the subject of excessive child-bearing.' (OS).

14 'As regards modern civilised nations, we find that those whose birth-rate is the highest per woman are by no means the happiest, most enlightened, or powerful; *nor do we even find that the population always increases in proportion to the births*. France, which in many respects leads in the van of civilisation, has one of the lowest birth-rates per woman in Europe; and among the free and enlightened population of Switzerland and Scandinavia the birth-rate is often exceedingly low; while Ireland, one of the most unhappy and weak of European nations, had long one of the highest birth-rates, *without any proportional increase in population or power*. With regard to the different classes in one community, the same effect is observable. The birth-rate per woman is higher among the lowest and most ignorant classes in the back slums of our great cities, than among the women of upper and cultured classes, mainly because the age at which marriages are contracted always tends to become higher as the culture and intelligence of individuals rises, but also because of the regulation of the number of births after marriage. Yet the number of children reared to adult years among the more intelligent classes probably equals or exceeds those of the lowest, owing to the high rate of infant mortality where births are excessive.' (OS).

15 'It is recorded that Balaam's ass saw the angel with flaming sword, but Balaam saw it not!' (OS). See *Numbers* 22:23.

16 *drones*: male honeybees, or people who live off the labour of others.

17 'The nearest approach to complete parasitism on the part of the vast

body of males occurred perhaps in ancient Rome at the time of the decay and downfall of the empire, when the bulk of the population, male as well as female, was fed on imported corn, wine and oil, and supplied even with entertainment, almost entirely without exertion or labour of any kind; but this condition was of short duration, and speedily contributed to the downfall of the diseased empire itself. Among the wealthy and so-called upper classes, the males of various aristocracies have frequently tended to become completely parasitic after a lapse of time, but such a condition has always been met by a short and sharp remedy; and the class has fallen, or become extinct. The condition of the males of the upper classes in France before the Revolution affords an interesting illustration of the point.' (OS). Cf. Wollstonecraft (1792, rpt 1975).

18 'It is not without profound interest to note the varying phenomena of sex-parasitism as they present themselves in the animal world, both in the male and in the female forms. Though among the greater number of species in the animal world the female form is larger and more powerful rather than the male (i.e. among birds of prey, such as eagles, vultures, falcons, etc. and among fishes, insects, etc.), yet sex-parasitism appears among both sex forms. In certain shell-fish, for example, the female carries about in the folds of her shell three or four minute and quite inactive males, who are entirely passive and dependent upon her. Among bees and ants, on the other hand, the female has so far degenerated that she has entirely lost the power of locomotion; she can no longer provide herself or her offspring with nourishment, or defend or even clean herself; she has become a mere passive distended bag of eggs, without intelligence or activity, she and her offspring existing through the exertions of the slaves and workers of the community. Among other insects, such for example as the common field-bug, another form of female parasitism prevails; and while the male remains a complex, highly active, and winged creature, the female, fastening herself by the head into the flesh of some living animal and sucking its blood, has lost wings and all activity, and power of locomotion; having become a mere distended bladder, which when filled with eggs bursts and ends a parasitic existence which has hardly been life. It is not impossible, and it appears indeed highly probable, that it has been this degeneration and parasitism on the part of the female which has set its limitation to the evolution of bees and ants, creatures which, having reached a point of mental development in some respects almost as high as that of man, have yet become curiously and immovably arrested. The whole question of sex-parasitism among the lower animals is one throwing suggestive and instructive side-lights on human social problems, but is too extensive to be here entered on.' (OS).

19 'The relation of female parasitism generally, to the peculiar
   phenomenon of prostitution, is fundamental. Prostitution can never
   be adequately dealt with, either from the moral or the scientific
   standpoint, unless its relation to the general phenomenon of female
   parasitism be fully recognised. It is the failure to do this, which
   leaves so painful a sense of abortion on the mind, after listening to
   most modern utterances on the question, whether made from the
   emotional platform of the moral reformer, or the intellectual
   platform of the would-be scientist. We are left with a feeling that the
   matter has been handled but not dealt with; that the knife has not
   reached the core.' (OS).

20 'See Jowett's translation of Plato's "Banquet" [*Symposium*]; but for
   full light on this important question the entire literature of Greece in
   the fifth and fourth centuries BC should be studied.' (OS). *Xanthippe*
   was Socrates' wife, the *Agora* the cultural center of the ancient Greek
   city-state, and *Alcibiades* a beautiful man of a noble Athenian family
   who was thought to be Socrates's lover and who is a character in the
   Symposium.

21 *Aspasia . . . Sappho*: Aspasia of Miletus, a courtesan, was the lifelong
   companion and advisor of Pericles; Sappho, a much-praised lyric
   poet of the 7th century BC, wrote love poems to her women friends
   and probably led a school for girls on the island of Lesbos.

22 'Like almost all men remarkable for either good or evil, Alexander
   [Alexander III of Macedon, or Alexander the Great, 356–23 BC]
   inherited from his mother [Olympias; Philip II of Macedon was his
   father] his most notable qualities – his courage, his intellectual
   activity, and an ambition indifferent to any means that made for his
   own end. Fearless in her life, she fearlessly met death "with a
   courage worthy of her rank and domineering character, when her
   hour of retribution came"; and Alexander is incomprehensible till
   we recognise him as rising from the womb of Olympia.' (OS).

23 *Pericles . . . Teutonic folk*: Pericles (c. 500–429 BC) dominated Athenian
   politics with his rhetoric and his policies from 460 BC to his death;
   Leonidas, king of Sparta, was Greek commander at Thermopylae
   (480 BC); by 'Teutonic' Schreiner means Germanic, or of northern
   European descent.

24 *Lucretia . . . mother of the Gracchi*: Lucretia was believed to have killed
   herself after confessing to her husband that she had been raped;
   Cornelia, mother of two Roman rulers known for their compassion
   in battle and conquest (2nd century BC), once said of her sons
   'these are my jewels'.

25 'Indeed must not the protest and the remedy in all such cases, if
   they are to be of any avail, take their rise within the diseased class
   itself?' (OS).

26 *Suetonius . . . .*: imperial secretary under Trajan in the first and

second centuries AD; wrote *De Vita Caesarum* (*Lives of the Caesars*) and books on rhetoric and grammar; 'Augustus' was the title given to Julius Caesar, as first Roman emperor, in 27 BC.

27 *Strabo*: Greek Stoic and traveler (c. 64 BC–19 AD), wrote seventeen-volume *Geography* and (now lost) *Historical Memoirs*.

28 *Florus*: the name or pseudonym of one who wrote the *Epitome*, a history of Rome based on Livy's.

29 'The South African Boer woman after two thousand years appears not wholly to have forgotten the ancestral tactics.' (OS) See 'The Boer Woman and the Modern Woman Question' in *Thoughts on South Africa*.

30 *Valerius Maximus . . . Tacitus . . .* : Valerius Maximus wrote *Facta et Dicta Memorabilia*, a book for orators organised by subject; Tacitus (c. 55–117AD), military officer under Vespasian, wrote major *Histories* and *Annals* of the period prior to and including his own life.

31 'This picture of the labouring as opposed to the parasitic ideal of womanhood appears under the heading *The Words of King Lemuel: the oracle which his mother taught him*. At risk of presenting to the reader that with which he is already painfully familiar, we here transcribe the passage; which, allowing for differences in material and intellectual surroundings, paints also the ideal of the labouring womanhood of the present and of the future:

> Her price is far above rubies.
> The heart of her husband trusteth in her. . . .
> *Give her the fruit of her hands;*
> *And let her works praise her in the gates*.' (OS).

Schreiner here includes the whole of *Proverbs* 31.

32 'Of the other deleterious effects of unearned wealth on the individual or class possessing it, such as its power of lessening human sympathy, etc., we do not now speak, as, while ultimately and indirectly, undoubtedly, tending to disintegrate a society, they do not necessarily and immediately enervate it, which enervation is the point we are here considering.' (OS).

33 *Marcus Aurelius*: Roman emperor (161–80AD), wrote twelve books of devotional *Meditations*.

34 'It is not uncommon in modern societies to find women of a class relatively very moderately wealthy, the wives and daughters of shopkeepers or professional men, who, if their male relations will supply them with a very limited amount of money without exertion on their part, will become as completely parasitic and useless as women with untold wealth at their command.' (OS).

35 'There is indeed an interesting analogous tendency on the part of the parasitic male, wherever found, to shield his true condition from his own eyes and those of the world by playing at the ancient

ancestral forms of male labour. He is almost always found talking loudly of the protection he affords to helpless females and to society, though he is in truth himself protected through the exertion of soldiers, policemen, magistrates, and society generally; and he is almost invariably fond of dangling a sword or other weapon, and wearing a uniform, for the assumption of militarism without severe toil delights him. But it is in a degenerate travesty of the ancient labour of hunting (whereby at terrible risk to himself, and with endless fatigue, his ancestors supplied the race with meat and defended it from destruction by wild beasts) that he finds his greatest satisfaction; it serves to render the degradation and uselessness of his existence less obvious to himself and to others than if he passed his life reclining in an arm-chair.

'On Yorkshire moors today, may be seen walls of sod behind which hide certain human males, while hard-labouring men are employed from early dawn in driving birds toward them. As the birds are driven up to him, the hero behind his wall raises his deadly weapon, and the bird, which it had taken so much human labour to rear and provide, falls dead at his feet; thereby greatly to the increase of the hunter's glory, when, the toils of the chase over, he returns to his city haunts to record his bag. One might almost fancy one saw arise from the heathery turf the shade of some ancient Teutonic ancestor, whose dust has long reposed there, pointing a finger of scorn at his degenerate descendant, as he leers out from behind the sod wall. During the later Roman empire, Commodus, in the degenerate days of Rome, at great expense had wild beasts brought from distant lands that he might have the glory of slaying them in the Roman circus; and medals representing himself as Hercules slaying the Nemean lion were struck at his order. We are not aware that any representation has yet been made in the region of plastic art of the hero of the sod wall; but history repeats itself – that also may come in time. It is to be noted that these hunters are not youths, but often ripely adult men, before whom all the lofty enjoyments and employments possible to the male in modern life, lie open.' (OS).

Three Dreams in a Desert

1 'The banks of an African river are sometimes a hundred feet high, and consist of deep shifting sands, through which in the course of ages the river has worn its gigantic bed.' (OS).

The Buddhist Priest's Wife

1 *vis inertiae*: force of inertia.
2 *frumps*: dowdy or ill-dressed, usually older women.

Dream Life and Real Life: A Little African Story

1 *Karroo* (or *karoo*): high pastoral tableland of South Africa; a place Schreiner revered and where she wished to be buried.
2 *Boer*: South African of Dutch descent, especially those who became farmers; now called Afrikaners. See Thompson (1985; esp. chapter 2) for the Boers' political and religious mythology of their privileged relationship to the land of South Africa.
3 *sluits* (or *sloots*): 'The deep fissures, generally dry, in which the superfluous torrents of water are carried from the Karroo plains after thunderstorms.' (OS).
4 *Bushman*: colonial name given to the San, a nearly extinct group of South African hunters of the area that became the Cape Colony.
5 *English navvy*: labourer; originally one who built canals or other navigation ways.
6 *kopjes* (or *koppies*): 'Kopjes, in the karroo, are hillocks of stones, that rise up singly or in clusters, here and there; presenting sometimes the fantastic appearance of old ruined castles or giant graves, the work of human hands.' (OS).
7 *coney* (or *cony*): rabbit; also a dupe.
8 *krantz*: 'precipice.' (OS).

Five pieces from *Dreams*

A Dream of Wild Bees

1 Olive Schreiner was her parents' ninth child.

Eighteen Ninety-Nine

1 *'Thou fool . . . '*: *I Corinthians* 15:36.
2 *Northern Transvaal*: Afrikaner Republic annexed by Great Britain in 1877.
3 *daub-and-wattle house*: house patched together quickly from indigenous building materials; Boer settlers' house.
4 *Cape Colony*: southwestern South Africa; area British took from

Notes

Dutch in early nineteenth century.

5 *long trek northward*: the Afrikaner 'Great Trek' of the 1830s; central to Afrikaner political mythology is the vortrekkers' departure from areas occupied by the British in this period. The Afrikaners' story is most often told as one of exodus (the North being a sort of New Jerusalem) and legitimate claims to lands which were already inhabited and worked by native Africans (L. Thompson).

6 *Free State*: Orange Free State; an Afrikaner Republic.

7 *outspanned*: stopped temporarily; at night during the 'Great Trek' oxen were unharnessed from the wagons and the wagons linked together as a 'laager' or line of defence.

8 *terrible day when, at Weenan . . . old men fell before the Zulus, and the assegais of Dingaan's braves drank blood*: Schreiner's protagonist remembers only when one side of a complex series of events in 1838 which were referred to later as 'Dingaan's Day' and the 'Battle of Blood River', or more generally the 'Kaffir Wars'. Weenan, literally 'place of weeping', is the Boer name for the place where Zulu soldiers led by Dingaan surprised and killed a group of invading vortrekkers led by Piet Retief. In retaliation, on 15 December 1838, a small number of Boers led by Andries Pretorius formed a laager and, armed with guns and cannons, killed about 3,000 Zulus who had been carrying only assegais and spears. This last event came to be called the 'Battle of Blood River' because of the numerous Zulu casualties (L. Thompson). The old woman's patchy memory conflates these two events, ignoring the violence and racism of her own ancestors.

9 *trekked away from Natal*: like Cape Colony, Natal was ruled by British colonial government.

10 *Laings Nek . . . and Spion Kop*: series of battles between British and Dutch in the Transvaal in 1880s, in which outnumbered Boer farmers defeated British soldiers (Lehmann).

11 *Witwaters Rand*: '"white water's ridge," now known as the Rand, where Johannesburg and the great mines are situated.' (OS).

12 *wildebeest*: gnu; large mammal, with characteristics of ox and antelope.

13 *veld*: unforested, grassy areas of South Africa.

14 *mealie field*: maize or corn field.

15 *victories of Ingogo and Amajuba*: see note 10; Amajuba (or Majuba Hill) was the most famous Boer victory, in which the British commander was killed.

16 *velschoens*: homemade, raw-hide shoes worn by Boer settlers.

17 *'Slachters Nek . . . '*: 'Butchers Neck'; place at eastern border of Cape Colony where English from Cape Town purchased cattle from Dutch farmers. In 1815–16 Hans Bezuidenhout led a group of what might now be called 'vigilantes' against the enforcement of British

rule in the area near Cradock (where Schreiner grew up). Because Bezuidenhout was feared and betrayed by other Boers, the 'rebellion' failed. Bezuidenhout was killed when found; five people were to be hanged and several others punished for high treason. However, the executions failed the first time due to the use of rotten ropes, so the convicts had to be hanged a second time. These events have been reshaped subsequently to make Bezuidenhout a hero, a tragic leader of Afrikaner nationalism (L. Thompson).

18 *Boer women . . . Drakens Berg Mountains . . .* : spectacular Dragon Mountains between Lesotho and Natal; in places over 11,000 feet high, separate the coast from the 'High Veld'. Like 'Weenan' (note 8), a case in which Schreiner's old woman thinks in terms of resisting British rule in this area but ignores Boers' stealing lands from indigenous Africans. Here, however, she reshapes the usual Afrikaner myth, putting women's words and women's work, rather than their innocence and victimisation, at the center of a people's struggle for freedom. Kuzwayo (1985) argues similarly that African women's emotional and physical labour is at the center of the present liberation struggle in South Africa.

19 *koekies and sasarties*: 'little cakes and meat prepared in a certain way.' (OS).

20 *Krugersdorp, and Johannesburg, and Pretoria*: major centres of mining industry, investment of foreign capital, and exploitation of South African labourers in British colony and later. See *Trooper Peter Halket of Mashonaland* (1897) and *An English South-African's View of the Situation* (1899) for Schreiner's criticism of this form of capitalism and its abuses.

21 *Dr Jameson made his raid*: 1895 attack planned by Cecil Rhodes to create havoc in the Transvaal and to bring the railroads under English control; the 'raid' failed miserably (thus 'white flag' of surrender below) and Rhodes considered it the demise of his political career.

22 *kaross of jackals' skins*: blanket.

23 *Field-Cornet*: local Boer official; 'burgher' is another name for a Boer settler.

24 *Mauser*: German rifle, especially magazine rifle, c. 1897.

25 *Delagoa Bay*: or Bay of Lourenço Marques, in southern Mozambique; symbol of Dutch colonists' economic independence, access to trade with Continent free from British intervention.

26 *biltong*: sun-dried meat.

27 *vierkleur ribbon*: ribbon made from flag of the Transvaal Republic.

28 *khakies*: 'soldiers.' (OS).

29 *pugaree* (or *pagri*): light scarf or turban worn to protect from sun and heat.

30 *unsifted*: 'unstrained.' (OS).

31 *unknown . . . unnamed . . . forgotten dead . . .* : Romantic epitaph to the struggles of heroic but otherwise unacknowledged common people. See Thomas Gray, *Elegy Written in a Country Churchyard* (c. 1750) for a similar sentiment.

32 *syndicate of Jews in Johannesburg and London*: here and elsewhere Schreiner blames capitalism on Jewish bankers and businessmen. She later modified her desire to keep Jewish people out of South Africa, coming out in favor of both local toleration and a Jewish homeland in her *Letter on the Jew* (1906). Jewish immigration to South Africa was limited in the early twentieth century, and curtailed in 1937 at the height of Nazi atrocities against Jewish people in Eastern Europe; until 1951 South Africa's Racial Laws included anti-Jewish clauses (Derrida, in Gates, ed. [1985]: 297).

The Native Question

1 *Teutonic*: Germanic, i.e. English, German, Dutch, or Scandinavian; Schreiner tends to generalise about these diverse peoples as a single 'race', especially in *Woman and Labour*.

2 *Taal*: Afrikaans; dialect spoken and written by Dutch or Boer settlers in South Africa; symbol of Boer nationalism and independence.

3 *wealth of five Rands*: i.e. wealth of five gold mines.

4 *Nemesis*: Greek goddess of retribution; retributive justice.

5 *Cavour . . . Robert Bruce*: powerful, nationalist leaders and thinkers: Count Cavour (1810–61), Italian politician largely responsible for uniting Italy under House of Savoy; Charles-Maurice de Talleyrand-Périgord (1754–1838), deputy to National Assembly during last years of French Revolution, influential foreign minister under Napoleon I and several later governments; William Wallace (1844–97), Scottish philosopher, works include *The Logic of Hegel* (1873) and *Epicureanism* (1880); Robert Bruce, family of medieval Scottish kings.

Woman and War

1 'The division of labour between the sexes in ancient Egypt and other exceptional countries, is a matter of much interest, which cannot here be entered on.' (OS).

2 'The young captured animals would probably be tamed and reared by the women.' (OS).

3 'In thinking of physical sex differences, the civilised man of modern times has always to guard himself against being unconsciously

misled by the very exaggerated external sex differences which our unnatural method of sex clothing and dressing the hair produces. The unclothed and natural human male and female bodies are not more divided from each other than those of the lion and lioness. Our remote Saxon ancestors, with their great, almost naked, white bodies and flowing hair worn long by both sexes, were but little distinguished from each other; while among their modern descendants the short hair, darkly clothed, manifestly two-legged male differs absolutely from the usually long-haired, colour bedizened, much beskirted female. Were the structural differences between male and female really one-half as marked as the artificial visual differences, they would be greater than those dividing, not merely any species of man from another, but as great as those which divide orders in the animal world. Only a mind exceedingly alert and analytical can fail ultimately to be misled by habitual visual misrepresentation. There is not, probably, one man or woman in twenty thousand who is not powerfully influenced in modern life in their conception of the differences, physical and intellectual, dividing the human male and female, by the grotesque exaggerations of modern attire and artificial manners.' (OS).

4 *Spinoza*: Benedict de Spinoza (1632–77), Jewish Rationalist philosopher; elaborated theory of 'monism', or all being reducible to a single category, such as, in Spinoza's case, 'pantheism' (everything is part of god).

5 *Bach . . . Wagner*: famous European composers: Johann Sebastian Bach (1685–1750); Ludwig van Beethoven (1770–1827); Wolfgang Amadeus Mozart (1756–91); Richard Wagner (1813–83).

6 'Minds not keenly analytical are always apt to mistake mere correlation of appearance with causative sequence. We have heard it gravely asserted that between potatoes, pigs, mud cabins and Irishmen there was an organic connection: but we who have lived in Colonies, know that within two generations the pure-bred descendant of the mud cabiner becomes often the successful politician, wealthy financier or great judge; and shows no more predilection for potatoes, pigs, and mud cabins than men of any other race.' (OS).

7 *Froebel*: Friedrich Froebel (1782–1852), German educator who developed 'kindergarten'; also developed spiritual philosophy of the unity of all things.

8 *Lee-Metford*: sleek, accurate, nineteenth-century rifle with .45-calibre bullets.

9 'It is noteworthy that even Catherine of Russia, a ruler and statesman of a virile and uncompromising type, and not usually troubled with moral scruples, yet refused with indignation the offer of Frederick of Prussia to pay her heavily for a small number of Russian recruits in an age when the hiring out of soldiers was

common among the sovereigns of Europe.' (OS).

10 *with Isaiah . . . or the Indian Buddha . . .* : Schreiner here conflates 'prophets' of two very different religious traditions; points up her tendency to generalise around these religious symbols and figures rather than reflecting real similarities or differences between them.

11 *'The wolf shall dwell with the lamb . . . '*: *Isaiah* 11:6.

The Dawn of Civilisation

1 *Jezebel . . . Naboth's vineyard*: Jezebel figures for a belief in absolute monarchy; Naboth's vineyard was taken by outsiders' murdering him; part of the larger story of the fall of Ahab (Jezebel's husband) in *I Kings* 21 and 22:34 et seq. and *II Kings* 9:24, 33 and 10:1–11.

2 *David acquired Uriah's wife . . .* : Bathsheba; David raped her while Uriah was away in battle, then had Uriah killed; see *II Samuel* 11: 1–4 and 6–21.

Afterword by Nadine Gordimer

1 Ruth First and Ann Scott, *Olive Schreiner*, André Deutsch, 1980. This review originally published in *The Times Literary Supplement*, 15 August 1980.

2 Ruth First, exiled South African historian and wife of Joe Slovo, a leader of the African National Congress, was killed by a letter bomb in Maputo, Mozambique, in 1981. Many believe the South African government is responsible for her death.

Select Bibliography

Manuscript collections (from Clayton [1983])

Albany Library, 1820 Settlers Memorial Division, Grahamstown.
Bodleian Library, Oxford University, Milner Papers.
Brenthurst Library, Oppenheimer Collection, Johannesburg.
Cory Library, Rhodes University, Grahamstown.
Cradock Library, Municipality of Cradock (includes Schreiner's books).
Durham University Library, William Plomer Collection.
Fryde Collection, privately owned, Johannesburg.
Humanities Research Center, University of Texas, Austin (Havelock Ellis correspondence).
J. W. Jagger Library, Africana and Special Collections, University of Cape Town.
National English Literary Museum and Documentation Centre, Grahamstown.
Rhodes House Library, Oxford.
Sheffield City Library, Edward Carpenter Collection.
South African Library, Special Collections, Cape Town.
Strange Collection, Johannesburg Public Library.
University College Library, London, Karl Pearson Collection.

Bibliographies

Davis, Roslyn (1972), *Olive Schreiner 1920–1971*, Johannesburg, University of Witwatersrand Department of Bibliography.
Verster, E. (1946), *Olive Emilie Albertina Schreiner*, University of Cape Town School of Librarianship.
Note: many of Schreiner's shorter and journalistic writings are included in neither of these bibliographies.

Schreiner's works

The Story of an African Farm (1883, rpt 1968), New York, Schocken (preface by Doris Lessing); there are several other modern editions, including one with an introduction by Dan Jacobson (Harmondsworth, Penguin, 1971).

Dreams (1890), London, Unwin.

Dream Life and Real Life (1893), London, Unwin.

The Political Situation (1896), London, Unwin (paper written with and read at public meeting by S. C. Cronwright-Schreiner).

Trooper Peter Halket of Mashonaland (1897, rpt 1974), Johannesburg, A. Donker.

An English South-African's View of the Situation. Words in Season (1899), London, Hodder & Stoughton.

A Letter on the Jew (1906), Cape Town, H. Liberman.

Closer Union (1909), London, Fifield.

Woman and Labour (1911, rpt 1978), London, Virago.

Thoughts on South Africa (1923), London, Unwin.

Stories, Dreams and Allegories (1923), London, Unwin.

Cronwright-Schreiner, S. C., ed. (1924a), *The Letters of Olive Schreiner*, London, Unwin.

From Man to Man; or, Perhaps Only . . . (1926, rpt 1982), London, Virago.

Undine (1929), London, Benn.

Note: I have not included works which are reprints or excerpts of the works listed above. In all cases I have listed the date of first edition and, where possible, an easily available modern edition.

Biographical studies and sources

Beeton, Ridley (1974a), 'In Search of Olive Schreiner in Texas', *Texas Quarterly*, 17.3, pp. 105–54.

Beeton, Ridley (1983), *Portraits of Olive Schreiner: A Manuscript Sourcebook*, Johannesburg, Donker.

Buchanan-Gould, Vera (1948), *Not Without Honour: The Life and Writings of Olive Schreiner*, London, Hutchinson.

Cronwright-Schreiner, S. C. (1924b), *The Life of Olive Schreiner*, London, Unwin.

Findlay, Joan, ed. (1954), *The Findlay Letters (1806–1870)*, Pretoria, Van Schaik.

First, Ruth and Scott, Ann (1980), *Olive Schreiner, A Biography*, London, Andre Deutsch.

Friedmann, Marion (1955), *Olive Schreiner: A Study in Latent Meanings*, Johannesburg, University of Witwatersrand.

Gregg, Lyndall (1957), *Memories of Olive Schreiner*, London, Chambers.

Hobman, D. L. (1955), *Olive Schreiner: Her Friends and Times*, London, Watts.

Meintjes, Johannes (1965), *Olive Schreiner: Portrait of a South African Woman*, Johannesburg, Keartland.

Walker, Eric (1937), *W. P. Schreiner, A South African*, Oxford University Press.

Social and intellectual context

Adams, William (1855), *Sacred Allegories*, London, Rivingtons.

Appleman, Philip, ed. (1979), *Darwin*, New York, Norton.

Bachofen, J. J. (1861, rpt 1967), *Myth, Religion, and Mother Right, Selected Writings of J. J. Bachofen*, trans. Ralph Mannheim, Princeton University Press.

Bennett, Arnold (1928), *The Savour of Life*, Garden City, Doubleday.

Brittain, Vera (1933, rpt 1978), *Testament of Youth*, London, Virago.

Burrow, J. W. (1970), *Evolution and Society*, Cambridge University Press.

Carpenter, Edward (1918), *My Days and Dreams*, London, Allen & Unwin.

Clayton, Cherry, ed. (1983), *Olive Schreiner*, Johannesburg, McGraw-Hill (includes extensive bibliography, excerpts from unpublished journals and letters, reviews of Schreiner's works, and essays by South African writers).

Davin, Anna (1978), 'Imperialism and Motherhood', *History Workshop Journal*, 5, pp. 9–65.

Ellis, Havelock (1928), *Studies in the Psychology of Sex*, Vol. 3, Philadelphia, Davis.

Ellis, Havelock (1940), *My Life*, London, William Heinemann.

Emerson, Ralph Waldo (1906), *Emerson's Essays*, London, Dent.

Engels, Friedrich (1884, rpt 1972), *The Origin of the Family, Private Property, and the State*, New York, International Publications Co.

Fradkin, Betty (1977), 'Olive Schreiner and Karl Pearson', *Quarterly Bulletin of South African Library*, 31.4, pp. 83–93.

Fradkin, Betty (1978), 'Havelock Ellis and Olive Schreiner's "Gregory Rose"', *Texas Quarterly*, 21.3, pp. 145–53.

Gibbons, Tom (1973), *Rooms in the Darwin Hotel*, Nedlands, University of Western Australia.

Gilman, Charlotte Perkins (1911), *The Man-Made World*, London, Unwin.

Jeffreys, Sheila (1985), *The Spinster and her Enemies: Feminism and Sexuality, 1880–1930*, London, Pandora.

Kapp, Yvonne (1979), *Eleanor Marx*, Vol. 2: *The Crowded Years (1884–1898)*, London, Virago.

Kevles, Daniel (1985), *In the Name of Eugenics: Genetics and the Uses of Human Heredity*, New York, Knopf.

Lane, Ann, ed. (1981), *Charlotte Perkins Gilman Reader*, London, Women's Press.

Liddington, Jill, and Norris, Jill (1978), *One Hand Tied Behind Us: The*

Rise of the Women's Suffrage Movement, London, Virago.

Mill, J. S. (1869, rpt 1983), *The Subjection of Women*, London, Virago.

Nord, Deborah (1985), *The Apprenticeship of Beatrice Webb*, Basingstoke, Macmillan.

Pearson, Karl (1894a), 'Women and Labour', *Fortnightly Review*, 61, p. 561–77.

Pearson, Karl (1894b), 'Socialism and Natural Selection', *Fortnightly Review*, 62, pp. 1–21.

Rose, Steven, Kamin, Leon, and Lewontin, R. C. (1984), *Not in Our Genes: Biology, Ideology, and Human Nature*, Harmondsworth, Penguin.

Rowbotham, Sheila and Weeks, Jeffrey (1977), *Socialism and the New Life: The Personal and Sexual Politics of Edward Carpenter and Havelock Ellis*, London, Pluto.

Semmel, Bernard (1960), *Imperialism and Social Reform, English Social-Imperialist Thought, 1895–1914*, London, Allen & Unwin.

Showalter, Elaine (1986), *The Female Malady: Women, Madness and English Culture, 1830–1980*, New York and London, Pantheon and Virago.

Spencer, Herbert (1855), *Principles of Psychology*, London, Longman.

Spencer, Herbert (1862), *First Principles*, London, Williams & Norgate.

Spender, Dale, ed. (1984), *Feminist Theorists*, New York, Pantheon.

Stanley, Liz (1985), 'Feminism and Friendship: two essays on Olive Schreiner', *Studies in Sexual Politics*, 8 (University of Manchester Department of Sociology).

Vicinus, Martha, ed. (1972), *Suffer and Be Still: Women in the Victorian Age*, Bloomington, University of Indiana Press.

Vicinus, Martha (1985), *Independent Women: Work and Community for Single Women, 1850–1920*, London, Virago.

Walkowitz, Judith (1980), *Prostitution and Victorian Society: Women, Class and the State*, Cambridge University Press.

Walkowitz, Judith (1986), 'Science, Feminism and Romance: The Men and Women's Club, 1885–89', *History Workshop Journal*, 21, pp. 36–59.

Webb, Beatrice (1926, rpt 1980), *My Apprenticeship*, Cambridge University Press.

Weeks, Jeffrey (1981), *Sex, Politics, and Society: The Regulation of Sexuality since 1800*, London, Longman.

Winkler, Barbara Scott (n.d.), 'Victorian Daughters: The Lives and Feminism of Charlotte Perkins Gilman and Olive Schreiner', University of Michigan Occasional Papers in Women's Studies, 13.

Wollstonecraft, Mary (1792, rpt 1975), *A Vindication of the Rights of Woman*, New York, Norton.

Literary history, criticism and theory

Barash, Carol (1986), 'Virile Womanhood: Olive Schreiner's Narratives of a Master Race', *Women's Studies International Forum*, 9.4.

Barrell, John (1980), *The Dark Side of the Landscape: the Rural Poor in English Painting, 1730–1840*, Cambridge University Press.

Barrett, Michèle (1980), *Women's Oppression Today: Problems in Marxist Feminist Analysis*, London, Verso.

Beer, Gillian (1983), *Darwin's Plots: Evolutionary Narrative in Darwin, George Eliot and Nineteenth-Century Fiction*, London, Routledge & Kegan Paul.

Beeton, Ridley (1972), 'Two Notes on Olive Schreiner's Letters', *Research in African Literatures* (Austin), 3, pp. 180–9.

Beeton, Ridley (1974b), *Olive Schreiner, A Short Guide to her Writings*, Cape Town, Timmins.

Beeton, Ridley (1980), 'The Signals of Great Art?: A Manuscript of Olive Schreiner's Unfinished Novel', *Standpunte* (Cape Town), 145, pp. 4–13.

Berkman, Joyce (1977), 'The Nurturant Fantasies of Olive Schreiner', *Frontiers* (Boulder), 2.3, pp. 8–17.

Calder, Jenni (1976), *Women and Marriage in Victorian Fiction*, London, Thames & Hudson.

Cameron, Deborah (1984), *Feminism and Linguistic Theory*, London, Macmillan.

Clayton, Cherry (1985), 'Life into Fiction', *English in Africa*, 12.1, pp. 29–39.

Clifford, Gay (1974), *The Transformations of Allegory*, London, Routledge & Kegan Paul.

Colby, Vineta (1970), *The Singular Anomaly: Women Novelists of the Nineteenth Century*, New York University Press.

Cunningham, A. R. (1973), 'The New Woman Fiction of the 1890s', *Victorian Studies*, 17.4, pp. 177–86.

Eagleton, Terry (1975), *Myths of Power: A Marxist Study of the Brontës*, London, Macmillan.

Foucault, Michel (1977), *Language, Counter-Memory, Practice*, Oxford, Blackwell.

Gates, Henry Louis, Jr., ed. (1985), *'Race', Writing, and Difference*, special issue of *Critical Inquiry*, 12.1.

Gilbert, Sandra and Gubar, Susan (1979), *The Mad Woman in the Attic: The Woman Writer and the Nineteenth-century Literary Imagination*, Yale University Press.

Gordimer, Nadine (1961), 'The Novel and the Nation in South Africa', in G. D. Killam, ed. (1973), *African Writers on African Writing*, London, Heinemann Educational, pp. 33–52.

Gordimer, Nadine (1968), 'English-language Literature and Politics in South Africa', *Journal of Southern African Studies*, 2.2, pp. 205–29; also rpt in Heywood, ed. (1976), pp. 99–120.

Heywood, Christopher, ed. (1976) *Aspects of South African Literature*, London, Heinemann Educational.

Kaplan, Cora (1983), 'Wild Nights, Pleasure/Sexuality/Feminism', in Stephen Bennett, ed. (1983), *Formations: Of Desire*, London, Routledge & Kegan Paul, pp. 15–35.

Margarey, Kevin (1963), 'The South African Novel and Race', *Southern Review* (Adelaide), 1, pp. 27–45.

Marquard, Jean (1979), 'Olive Schreiner's "Prelude": The Child as Artist', *English Studies in Africa* (Johannesburg), 22.1, pp. 1–11.

Meyers, Jeffrey (1973), *Fiction and the Colonial Experience*, Ipswich, Boydell Press.

Moi, Toril (1985), *Sexual/Textual Politics: Feminist Literary Theory*, London, Methuen.

Olsen, Tillie (1978, rpt 1980), *Silences*, London, Virago.

Parker, Kenneth, ed. (1978), *The South African Novel in English: Essays in Criticism and Society*, London, Macmillan.

Ravilious, C. P. (1977), '"Saints and Sinners": An Unidentified Olive Schreiner Manuscript', *Journal of Commonwealth Literature* (Leeds), 12.1, pp. 1–11.

Rive, Richard (1972), 'Olive Schreiner: A Critical Study and Checklist', *Studies in the Novel*, 4, pp. 231–51.

Rive, Richard (1973), 'New Light on Olive Schreiner', *Contrast* (Cape Town), 8.4, pp. 40–7.

Rive, Richard (1974), 'Introduction to "Diamond Fields" and an edited version of the MS.', *English in Africa* (Grahamstown), 1.1, pp. 1–29.

Samkange, Stanlake (1966), *On Trial for My Country*, London, Heinemann.

Sarvan, C. P. (1984), 'Olive Schreiner's "Trooper Peter" – an Altered Awareness', *International Fiction Review*, 11.1, pp. 45–7.

Showalter, Elaine (1978), *A Literature of their Own*, London, Virago.

Smith, M., van Wyk and Maclennan, Don, eds. (1983), *Olive Schreiner and After: Essays in Honour of Guy Butler*, Cape Town, Philip.

Sprange, Claire (1976), 'Olive Schreiner: Touchstone for Lessing', *Doris Lessing Newsletter*, 1, pp. 4–5 and 9–10.

Thompson, John (1984), *Studies in the Theory of Ideology*, Cambridge, Polity.

Volosinov, V. N. (1973), *Marxism and the Philosophy of Language*, New York and London, Seminar.

Walsh, William (1970), *A Manifold Voice: Studies in Commonwealth Literature*, London, Chatto & Windus.

Wilhelm, Cherry (1979), 'Olive Schreiner: Child of Queen Victoria, Stories, Dreams and Allegories', *English in Africa*, 6.2, pp. 63–9.

Williams, Raymond (1977), *Marxism and Literature*, Oxford University Press.

Gender, race, and South Africa

Benjamin, Anne, ed. (1985), *Part of My Soul, Winnie Mandela*, Harmondsworth, Penguin.

Bernstein, Hilda (1985), *For their Triumphs and for their Tears: Women in South Africa*, London, International Defense and Aid Fund.

Bryan, B., Dadzie, S., and Scafe, S. (1985), *The Heart of the Race: Black Women's Lives in Britain*, London, Virago.

Commonwealth Group of Eminent Persons (1986), *Mission to South Africa, The Commonwealth Report*, Harmondsworth, Penguin.

Davis, Angela (1982), *Women, Race and Class*, London, Women's Press.

de Kiewiet, C. W. (1941, rpt 1966), *A History of South Africa: Social and Economic*, Oxford University Press.

Dyer, Marie (1970), 'Olive Schreiner's Liberalism', *Reality* (Pietermaritzburg), 2, pp. 18–22.

Fields, Barbara J. (1982), 'Ideology and Race in American History', J. Morgan Kousser and James M. McPherson, eds, *Region, Race, and Reconstruction*, Oxford University Press, pp. 143–77.

Fradkin, Betty (1979), 'Olive Schreiner – an opposite picture', *Contrast* (Cape Town), 12.3, pp. 75–88.

Fryer, Peter (1984), *Staying Power, The History of Black People in Britain*, London, Pluto.

Gordimer, Nadine (1981), *July's People*, New York, Viking.

Gray, Stephen (1983), *Olive Schreiner: A One-Woman Play*, Cape Town, Philip.

Hay, Margaret and Stichter, Sharon, eds. (1984), *African Women South of the Sahara*, New York and London, Longman.

Kuzwayo, Ellen (1985), *Call Me Woman*, London, Women's Press.

Lehmann, Joseph (1985), *The First Boer War*, London, Cape.

Lelyveld, Joseph (1985), *Move Your Shadow: South Africa, Black and White*, New York Times Books.

Lipman, Beata (1984), *We Make Freedom: Women in South Africa*, London, Pandora.

Marks, Shula and Rathbone, Richard (1982), *Industrialisation and Social Change in South Africa*, London, Longman.

Ortner, Sherry and Whitehead, Harriet, eds (1981), *Sexual Meanings: The Cultural Construction of Gender and Sexuality*, Cambridge University Press.

Patterson, Orlando (1982), *Slavery and Social Death*, Harvard University Press.

Peterson, K. H. and Rutherford, A., eds. (1986), *A Double Colonisation:*

Colonial and Post-Colonial Women's Writing, Mundelstrup and Oxford, Dangeroo.

Snitow, Ann, Stansell, Christine, and Thompson, Sharon, eds (1983), *Powers of Desire*, New York, Monthly Review Press; *Desire: The Politics of Sexuality*, London, Routledge & Kegan Paul.

Spivak, Gayatri Chakravorty (1981), 'French Feminism in an International Frame', *Yale French Studies*, 61, pp. 154–84.

Thompson, Leonard (1985), *The Political Mythology of Apartheid*, Yale University Press.

Troup, Freda (1972), *South Africa, An Historical Introduction*, London, Eyre Methuen.

Ungar, Sanford J. (1985), *Africa: The People and Politics of an Emerging Continent*, New York, Simon & Schuster.

Index

Index

Pandora Press is a feminist press, an imprint of Routledge &
Kegan Paul. Our list is varied – we publish new fiction,
reprint fiction, history, biography and autobiography, social
issues, humour – written by women and celebrating the lives
and achievements of women the world over. For further
information about Pandora Press books, please write to the
Mailing List Dept at Pandora Press, 11 New Fetter Lane,
London EC4P 4EE or in the USA at 29 West 35th Street,
New York, NY 10001–2291.
Some Pandora titles you will enjoy:

WE MAKE FREEDOM
Women in South Africa
Beata Lipman

Beata Lipman, a white journalist, was active in the liberation
movement in South Africa and worked on the banned
Congress paper *New Age*. She left South Africa for exile in
Britain in 1963. Many years later she was sent back on a film
assignment and, discovering that she could enter the country
without attracting attention, she made up her mind to return,
this time in order to record the voices of the women who
struggle and endure there. Most of those to whom she spoke
are black, a few are white. In this book, their words come
through with a power and immediacy which shockingly
conveys the texture of daily life in a country organised
entirely on the proposition that the majority of its people
simply do not count as full human beings.

'Anyone who claims still to doubt the practical daily pain of
apartheid – never mind the true justice issues – should be

childhood and confrontation and survival in the burning
cities, courage and humour amidst rural poverty, and the
heroic struggle against a system which began more than 300
years ago when white colonists claimed sovereignty over 'the
fairest Cape in all the World'. Beautifully illustrated with
woodcuts by Bongiwe Dhlomo, the collection includes stories
by Fatima Beer, Sheila Fugard, Nadine Gordimer, Bessie
Head, Ellen Kuzwayo, Liseka Mda, Goina Mhlope, Bernadette
Mosala, Maud Motanyane, Menan du Plessis, Elsa Steytler,
Miriam Tlali and Gladys Thomas.

A STATE OF FEAR
Menan du Plessis

The setting is Cape Town in the stormy winter of 1980, a
time of open unrest – the bus boycott, the meat boycott, the
boycotting of classes at black and so-called 'Coloured'
schools. The novel consists of the deliberately subjective
narrative of Anna Rossouw, a young white teacher at a
Coloured high school, who shelters two of her pupils when
they arrive on her doorstep. They are engaged in some kind
of political resistance, though Anna never quite knows what:
from one night-mission Wilson does not return; Felicia moves
out soon afterwards.

Anna's concern for them is central to her attempts to
understand herself within the disturbed society of which she
is a part, and yet not part, as is her reconstruction of her own
childhood and family relationships. People and places are
vividly portrayed in this probing, dramatic story.

Winner of the 1985 Olive Schreiner Prize

obliged to read these strong, courageous, dogged voices.'

Sara Maitland, New Statesman

'It is wonderfully true and also cool enough to give the picture to people who are not at all involved.'

Naomi Mitchison

' . . . women do not sit down bemoaning their position. They continue to fight for the freedom of all the people of Azania, and if you want to know just how determined they are, read Lipman's book.'

Sithembile Zulu, Spare Rib

'compelling and unforgettable'

Anti-Apartheid News

'The book could not have a better title.'

Civil Liberty

'Beata Lipman's book allows black women to speak for themselves.'

West Africa

SOMETIMES WHEN IT RAINS
Stories by South African Women
edited by Ann Oosthuizen

> Sometimes when it rains
> I think of times
> When we had to undress
> Carry the small bundles of uniforms and books
> On our heads
> And cross the river after school

This first ever collection of contemporary South African women writers bears witness to an enduring culture with a dazzling variety of stories from intimate glimpses into